Political Philosophy and Public Purpose

Series Editor
Michael J. Thompson, William Paterson University, New York, NY,
USA

This series offers books that seek to explore new perspectives in social and political criticism. Seeing contemporary academic political theory and philosophy as largely dominated by hyper-academic and overly-technical debates, the books in this series seek to connect the politically engaged traditions of philosophical thought with contemporary social and political life. The idea of philosophy emphasized here is not as an aloof enterprise, but rather a publicly-oriented activity that emphasizes rational reflection as well as informed praxis.

Rob Hunter · Rafael Khachaturian ·
Eva Nanopoulos
Editors

Marxism and the Capitalist State

Towards a New Debate

palgrave
macmillan

Editors
Rob Hunter
Washington, DC, USA

Rafael Khachaturian
University of Pennsylvania
Philadelphia, PA, USA

Eva Nanopoulos
Queen Mary University of London
London, UK

ISSN 2524-714X   ISSN 2524-7158   (electronic)
Political Philosophy and Public Purpose
ISBN 978-3-031-36166-1   ISBN 978-3-031-36167-8   (eBook)
https://doi.org/10.1007/978-3-031-36167-8

This Palgrave Macmillan imprint is published by the registered company Springer Nature Switzerland AG
The registered company address is: Gewerbestrasse 11, 6330 Cham, Switzerland

ACKNOWLEDGEMENTS

This volume has been long in the making. It began with the questions raised in the Introduction, amidst the revival of interest in Marx and Marxism in the wake of the global financial crisis of 2008. As the global turbulence of the past decade gave rise to new social movements and struggles that challenged the capitalist consensus of the past fifty years, it soon became clear that they were raising political, strategic, and theoretical questions about the state. The question of the capitalist state—its form, role, and future vis-a-vis the emancipatory struggles of the twenty-first century—increasingly drew the attention of a new generation of critical theorists. These running conversations spanned traditional venues like journals, conferences, workshops, reading groups, and the left publishing ecosystem (including a number of chapters here that first began as contributions to the *Legal Form* blog), but were also generated by less formal discussions on social media. The present volume draws and builds upon these conversations, advancing what we hope will be an ongoing debate that can help illuminate the conflicts and struggles of the present.

As with any book, especially an edited volume, this collection's intellectual contributors far exceed the editors and authors. Umut Özsu played an invaluable role as an interlocutor over the course of this project, while Honor Brabazon, Stuart Schrader, Igor Shoikhedbrod, and Camila Vergara provided constructive input at an internal workshop during its initial stages. We wish to thank Thea Riofrancos and Cemal Burak Tansel for their engagement with the ideas and themes raised in this book. We also wish to pay tribute to the late Leo Panitch, whose influence on many of the themes developed in the volume and Marxism more broadly, alongside his sustained devotion to the promotion of emerging voices, has been invaluable to the present volume and to critical scholarship more broadly.

We are grateful to Michael J. Thompson for initially proposing the idea of an edited volume on contemporary discussions of the state for Palgrave Macmillan's Political Philosophy and Public Purpose series, and to him and Michelle Chen for guiding the volume through its initial stages. We also wish to thank Supraja Yegnaraman, Madison Allums, and Rebecca Roberts for providing valuable editorial support from Palgrave Macmillan at all stages of the project.

Ed Rooksby unexpectedly passed away while this volume was in preparation. A brilliant young scholar at the forefront of the critical discussions featured in this volume, Ed was slated to contribute a chapter on structural reforms, the capitalist state, and socialist strategy. We hope that this volume can serve as a small testament to the groundwork that he helped lay for others.

Much has happened since this project was first initiated, both in the world and in our personal lives. As ever, we are grateful to those close to us for their patience, love, and support.

PRAISE FOR *MARXISM AND THE CAPITALIST STATE*

"A Marxist rethinking and critique of the state is urgent in a period when the capitalist state is in crisis, yet also becoming even more aggressively neoliberal and authoritarian, intensifying inequalities, accentuating the crisis of social reproduction, and enhancing the dynamics of climate disaster. This collection from a younger generation of scholars, coming from different traditions of historical materialism, brings forward not only the theoretical and analytical richness of the Marxist tradition but also its indispensability for any project of radical social transformation."
—Panagiotis Sotiris, *Hellenic Open University, Greece and author of* A Philosophy for Communism: Rethinking Althusser *(2020)*

"From the Covid pandemic to global warming to vulnerable supply chains, it has become commonplace to observe the 'return of the state.' This volume adds much-needed rigor to such discussions. There is no better moment to revisit and advance Marxist state theory."
—Thea Riofrancos, *Associate Professor of Political Science, Providence College, USA*

"In a time where the illusions of a fully globalised world or of an 'empire' have evaporated, this volume provides an enlightening series of Marxian analyses for understanding the renewed centrality of the state in its relationship with the contemporary political economy. The volume contains a masterfully orchestrated set of arguments and insights for a materialist theory of the state and will undoubtedly serve as a reference point for future debate."

—Marco Goldoni, *Senior Lecturer in Legal Theory, Glasgow University, UK*

CONTENTS

Notes on Contributors

Scott M. Aquanno is Assistant Professor of Political Science at Ontario Tech University and Visiting Associate at the Global Labour Research Centre at York University. He is the author of *Crisis of Risk: Subprime Debt and US Financial Power from 1944 to Present* (Edward Elgar, 2021) and co-author (with Stephen Maher) of *The Fall and Rise of American Finance: From J.P. Morgan to BlackRock* (Verso, 2024).

Alyssa Battistoni is Assistant Professor of Political Science at Barnard College, where she works and teaches on climate and environmental politics, capitalism, Marxism, feminism, and other topics in social and political theory. She received her Ph.D. in Political Science from Yale University in 2019 and has held fellowships at the Harvard University Center for the Environment and the Institute for Advanced Study. Her academic work has been published in *Political Theory, Perspectives on Politics*, and *Contemporary Political Theory*, and she writes frequently for publications including *New Left Review, The Nation, Dissent, n+1, Boston Review*, and *Jacobin*. Alyssa is the co-author of *A Planet to Win: Why We Need a Green New Deal* (Verso, 2019), with Kate Aronoff, Daniel Aldana Cohen, and Thea Riofrancos, and is currently working on a book manuscript titled *Free Gifts: Capitalism and the Politics of Nature*.

Jasmine Chorley-Schulz is a Ph.D. candidate in Political Science at the University of Toronto. Her research focuses on labour, class, and the international. She is part of the editorial collective of the *Legal Form* blog and teaches political theory and international relations.

Nate Holdren holds a Ph.D. in History from the University of Minnesota and is the author of *Injury Impoverished: Workplace Accidents, Capitalism, and Law in the Progressive Era*. He is employed as an Associate Professor in the Program in Law, Politics, and Society at Drake University.

Rob Hunter holds a Ph.D. in Politics from Princeton University. His research interests lie at the intersection of the critique of political economy, state theory, and public law. He is a member of the *Legal Form* editorial collective.

Rafael Khachaturian is a Lecturer in Critical Writing at the University of Pennsylvania. His research spans Marxism and critical social theory, theories of the state, the history of the social sciences, and post-Soviet and post-communist politics. He has published in journals such as *Polity, Contemporary Political Theory, Political Research Quarterly, Historical Materialism, and Science & Society,* and his public writing has appeared in *Jacobin, Dissent,* and *The Nation.* He holds a Ph.D. in Political Science from Indiana University Bloomington. He is also Associate Faculty with the Brooklyn Institute for Social Research.

Dimitrios Kivotidis is a Lecturer in Constitutional Law at Goldsmiths, University of London. His research focuses on legal and political theory, constitutional law and human rights, as well as the relationship between law and political economy. He is a member of the editorial collective of *Legal Form,* a forum for Marxist analysis and critique.

Stephen Maher is Assistant Professor of Economics at SUNY Cortland, and Associate Editor of the *Socialist Register.* His research examines the role of the state in the political and economic development of corporate capitalism. He is the author of *Corporate Capitalism and the Integral State: General Electric and a Century of American Power* (Palgrave, 2022), as well as (with Scott M. Aquanno) *The Fall and Rise of American Finance: From J.P. Morgan to BlackRock* (Verso, 2024).

Michael A. McCarthy is an Associate Professor of Sociology at Marquette University. He is the author of *Dismantling Solidarity: Capitalist Politics and American Pensions since the New Deal* (Cornell University Press, 2017) and helps edit the journal *Critical Sociology.* He is currently undertaking several projects, including a book on power, democracy, and finance, tentatively titled *The Master's Tools: A Theory of Democratic Rupture*, which is under contract with Verso Books.

Kirstin Munro is an Assistant Professor of Economics at The New School for Social Research. The major theme of her research is the overlapping relationships between people, the economy, and the environment. She serves on the Editorial Board of *The Review of Radical Political Economics*, and has published in that journal as well as *Critical Sociology*, *Capital & Class*, *Environment and Planning: E*, *Science & Society*, *Energy Policy*, and *Energy Research and Social Science*. Her book, *The Production of Everyday Life in Eco-Conscious Households: Compromise, Conflict, Complicity*, was published by Bristol University Press in 2023.

Eva Nanopoulos is Senior Lecturer in Law at Queen Mary, University of London. She is the author of the *Juridification of Individual Sanctions and the Politics of EU Law* (Hart, 2020), the co-editor of *The Crisis Behind the Euro-Crisis* (Cambridge University Press, 2019) and is currently working on a new project funded by the Leverhulme Trust entitled 'A Decolonial Legal History of Sanctions'. She also co-edits the blog *Legal Form* and she is co-director of series of the Queen Mary Centre of Law and Society in a Global Context and co-founded its 'Law and Marxism' series.

Chris O'Kane teaches political economy at St. John's University. He works on critical theory. His work has appeared in a number of interdisciplinary journals. Along with Werner Bonefeld, he is co-editor of *Adorno and Marx: Negative Dialectics and the Critique of Political Economy* (London: Bloomsbury Academic Press, 2022).

Introduction: Reopening the State Debate

Rob Hunter, Rafael Khachaturian, and Eva Nanopoulos

1 Why Theorize the Capitalist State Today?

If the 'short twentieth century' marked an 'age of extremes' (Hobsbawm 1994), the long twenty-first century that began in 1991 is set to become an age of disaster. Far from marking the end of history characterized by a triumph of liberal capitalism, the post-Cold War period witnessed the exacerbation of crisis tendencies that threaten not only political, legal and social institutions as we know them, but also social reproduction as such and the survival of the ecosphere. Among the many salient expressions of these tendencies are inter-state violence, war, and the bloody hardening of borders for persons (but not capital); global economic turmoil

---

R. Hunter
Washington, DC, USA
e-mail: jrh@rhunter.org

R. Khachaturian (✉)
University of Pennsylvania, Philadelphia, PA, USA
e-mail: rafkhach@sas.upenn.edu

E. Nanopoulos
Queen Mary University of London, London, UK
e-mail: e.nanopoulos@qmul.ac.uk

and cascading financial shocks; and globally-but-unevenly distributed environmental devastation and ecological breakdown.

This age of crises has been accompanied by what has been described as a 'revival' of interest in Marx and Marxism, broadly understood (e.g. Musto 2020). Signs of this new intellectual direction include the growing number of academic journals and book series dedicated to promoting Marxist theory and analyses, popular publications bringing Marxist insights to bear on contemporary events, as well as more wide-ranging and distinctively interdisciplinary monographs or research handbooks responding directly to this trend, whether by taking stock of the development of Marxism, by revisiting and expanding key Marxist concepts, ideas and methods, or by applying them to new problems and challenges.

Missing from this revival, however, has been a sustained re-examination of the capitalist state. Numerous monographs, edited volumes, and journal articles have adumbrated Marxist analyses of the capitalist state—particularly the profoundly influential debates in Marxist thinking about law, rights, and the state in the 1960s and 1970s. Recent scholarship has also contributed to the development of Marxist state theory and generated new insights on the capitalist state, including in the present stage of capitalist development. More generally, 'it is now acknowledged that capitalism's development cannot be understood without comprehending the intrinsic importance of the state' (Heller 2011, 7). But renewed attention to historical debates about the specificity of the capitalist state is not sufficient. The current moment demands renewed commitment to the systematic critique and understanding of the state as an essential feature of capitalist society.

Marx did not offer a fully developed theory of the state, and the subsequent tradition of Marxist engagements with the capitalist state displays a range of sometimes radically different views. Nevertheless—and contrary to claims about alleged downplaying of the importance of politics and the political—there is widespread agreement in the Marxist tradition(s) on the state's significance for any serious analysis of the constitution, reproduction, and overcoming of capitalist social relations. If, after decades of theoretical and political crisis, Marxism is once again demonstrating its importance for the task of developing a deep understanding of social structures in contemporary capitalist societies, this cannot possibly sideline the problem of the capitalist state, which is critical to both our understanding and potential solutions to the crisis of global capitalism.

What is more, the question of the state cannot be avoided in any discussion of the causes and contours of the present moment—one of mounting ecological catastrophe; sustained imperialist violence; the immiseration, marginalization, and extermination of ever-growing populations of those who have been expelled or excluded from the circuits of capital; and the ongoing exploitation and subordination of the vast majority of people worldwide who own little or nothing other than their own labour power. States discipline the working class and enforce the exchange of that labour power, acting as necessary moments in a transnational regime of capital circulation. In their demarcation of borders, they regulate, contain, and exclude populations from defined national and international spaces. And they help to restrain emancipatory social movements, channelling their disruptive potential into palatable social reforms. In today's age, sobered from the turn of the millennium highs of 'globalisation' and 'empire', it is clear that the state remains the basis of the institutional power of the capitalist class.

It is with the awareness of these challenges that the contributors to this volume aim to spark a reappraisal of both the capitalist state and the theoretical resources that may be brought to bear upon it. Rather than a comprehensive survey of the capitalist state in all of its determinations and contradictions, this volume is both a provocation and an invitation—to debate, to re-examinations, and to the production and refinement of Marxist state theory and social theory more broadly.

Part 2 of this introduction provides a brief overview of the place of the state in Marxist thought. In addition to the works of Marx and Engels, we draw attention to two particular developments in Marxist state theory that are especially germane to the present volume. One is the notion of the relative autonomy of the political from the economic, capturing the idea that the activity of the state and the resulting class antagonisms are not mere superstructural reflections of a base of economic relations, but structurally determined by the capitalist mode of production, such that the state cannot be treated as either an instrument or a subject that can freely implement (or be made to implement) particular policies without respect to the society-pervading imperative that capital be valorized. Elaborations on this approach often describe the capitalist state as a particular terrain that both conditions class struggle and also serves as its object. The other is the concept of the state as a historically specific social form. Associated with, and developed within, a variety of traditions—such as Frankfurt School critical theory, the *Neue Marx-Lektüre* ('new reading of Marx'), and Open Marxism—this position sees the capitalist state not as a distinct social reality but as the specifically *political* appearance of the determinate social relations that constitute capitalist society. These two developments are by no means symmetrical or neatly complementary.[1] Yet they give form to commonly shared intuitions about the relationship between the capitalist state and the capitalist economy.

Part 3 introduces the reader to the essays comprising the volume. In addition to individual summaries of each chapter, we draw out the thematic and conceptual linkages across them—as well as the tensions and disagreements between them. Like the Marxist tradition as a whole (and the object of its critique—the capitalist mode of production), this collection is less a harmonious unity than a dynamic constellation of debates, perspectives, and positions.

Part 4 points beyond this volume to the broader scope of state theorizing that should take place within the Marxism of tomorrow. The particular cases examined by the authors in this volume do not exhaust the scope of the work that needs to be undertaken to adequately map out the capitalist state's relations to the many aspects of domination and unfreedom under capitalism. These include, but are not limited to, racialization and hierarchies constructed on the basis of fetishisms of race, ethnicity, and nationality; the specifically juridical and institutional dimensions of subordination and domination on the basis of sexuality and gender; the dynamics of the inter-state system and the position of migrants, refugees, and the stateless; the fate of constitutional democracy as a specific political form of capitalist social relations, and its alternatives; and the violence and conflict that permeate and constitute the inter-state order.

2   Theorizing the Capitalist State: A Brief History

Marx himself never propounded a fully developed critique of the state in any form—capitalist or otherwise. Scattered remarks found throughout writings from all stages of his life reveal a mind that was attentive to organized political authority and its contradictory relationship with relations

---

[1] For an attempt at establishing a complementarity between these two clusters of views, see Gallas (2011).

of production and exchange. However, it is primarily in his earlier writings that Marx focused directly on juridical and political relations as they appear in bourgeois society. Here we encounter some of the themes that would continue to animate Marx's thinking about the state as he began to focus more of his efforts on the critique of political economy.

In his critique of Hegel's *Philosophy of Right*, Marx discerned the 'institutionalized illusion' of society's separation into civil society and the state, such that the latter appears to be separately constituted, independent from relations of production and exchange (Murray 1988, 32). In actuality, the 'antinomy of the political state and civil society' is 'the contradiction of the abstract political state' with itself (Marx and Engels 1975, 3:91). The self-contradiction of the 'political' state derives from its abstraction from the social relations that condition its own possible existence. The bourgeois state appears as neutral, even natural, and standing above and beyond the sectional and sectoral conflicts that are characteristic of bourgeois society; and yet it is the political appearance of that particular society, and not of any kind of society-in-general. Political relations are no less historically specific than economic relations; nor can these be comprehended as fully distinct from one another, no matter their apparent independence. Marx famously summarized this claim with recourse to the base/superstructure metaphor in the Preface to *A Contribution to the Critique of Political Economy*, and reiterated it in the first volume of *Capital*:

> My view is that each particular mode of production, and the relations of production corresponding to it at each given moment, in short 'the economic structure of society', is 'the real foundation, on which arises a legal and political superstructure and to which correspond definite forms of social consciousness', and that 'the mode of production of material life conditions the general process of social, political and intellectual life' (Marx 1990, I:175).

This claim for the mutual implication of state and economy as historically determinate forms of social relations is not a denial of the specificity of the state as a definite pattern of social relations. Marx was familiar with the bourgeois state's appearance as the 'concentration of bourgeois society' or the 'concentrated and organized force of society' (Marx 1973, 108; 1990, I:915). (Indeed, he developed this insight in an earlier form in *The Eighteenth Brumaire of Louis Bonaparte*, narrating how the prior history of class struggles in French society culminated in a new form of state power that only appeared to be independent of society.) This concentrated force may be self-contradictory in its concept, yet its capacities are by no means imaginary. These capacities are themselves contradictory; in the concluding section of the first volume of *Capital*, Marx surveyed the central, and violent, role of the bourgeois state in the consolidation and generalization of a society whose most elementary form and foundational mediating category is value: 'so-called primitive accumulation' was not the innocent outcome of *doux commerce* but a history of private *and* public violence written in 'letters of blood and fire' (Marx 1990, I:875). And yet the organized force of bourgeois society could be exercised so as to improve the lot of industrial workers, as Marx famously discussed in Chapter 10 of *Capital*; the machinery of the bourgeois state was not simply subservient to the will of individual capitalists or to a notional common interest of the capitalist class as a whole (Steinberg 2010).

Of course, the Factory Acts were not the first steps on a parliamentary road to socialism. Engels would later refer to the bourgeois state as the 'ideal personification' of capital *in toto* (Marx and Engels 1987, 25:266). This ideal capitalist—precisely because of its constitution as the general, 'organised force' of society, in contrast to the competition between and among particular capitals—was capable of, and indeed the only means for, the articulation of a 'general interest' in bourgeois society. In this sense the Factory Acts may be seen as auguring the later reforms that stabilized, rather than inhibited, the expansion of capital, by imposing a kind of rationality and foresight that could not be pursued by individual capitalists, who are otherwise compelled by the law of value to compete with one another by reducing the cost of variable capital.

This conception of the state, however underdeveloped, is unlike the (rather instrumentalist) conception of the state on offer in the *Communist Manifesto*. Rather than a mere illusion or shroud drawn over class rule, or an instrumentality through which 'the individuals of a ruling class assert their common interests' (Marx and Engels 1976, 5:90) against society as a whole, the bourgeois state is instead seen, on this view, as the politico-institutional expression of a society that can reproduce itself only through the continued and expanded accumulation of capital. Previous thinkers—including not a few in the tradition of liberal political economy—had recognised the possibility of the wealthy controlling or using state institutions for their own benefit. Marx and Engels did not simply insist on complicating the notional separation of public power and private privilege. What was distinctive about their conception of the state was their apprehension of it as the necessarily political counterpart to the economic relations of the production and exchange of commodities. Neither the state nor the economy are self-sustaining or self-subsistent; both are historically specific, determinate, and given shape by definite social relations. The bourgeois state's very existence may only be possible in bourgeois society—that is, a society whose 'laws of motion' can be identified only with those of capital—and yet it retains its own distinctive specificity.

This specificity has been explored in a variety of ways. For many Marxists of the Second International, it was to be understood in terms of the relationship between the means and the relations of production. The state *qua* superstructure necessarily reflected and corresponded to capitalist property relations: specifically, private control of the means of production coupled with proletarians' double freedom as owners of their own labour power and little else. For more reform-minded Marxists, this meant that the state was or could be a neutral apparatus of social cohesion that was accessible to the working class through parliamentary means; for their critics this meant that the bourgeois state was and only could be an 'organ for the oppression of one class by another' (Lenin 2014, 43). Both poles of this debate were to attract considerable attention in relation to political developments in the rest of the twentieth century—from decolonial and anti-imperial struggles in the global South to the rise and fall of North Atlantic social democracy, and from struggles against state-sanctioned domination with respect to gender and race to attempts to embed material gains for workers within the institutional fabric of the constitutional state (Eley 2002; Albo et al. 2018).

In the latter half of the twentieth century, Marxist political analysis began to move beyond the limits of this dichotomy. Beyond the ossification of the base/superstructure metaphor into Stalinist orthodoxy, and the rejection of Marx's conception of the state along with his critique of political economy as deterministic or mechanistic (a familiar conceit in liberal dismissals of Marxism), twentieth-century Marxist state theory evinced considerable diversity and depth. In particular, interwar contributions—from those of the Austro-Marxists to the theorisation of nationalism and constitutionalism; to members of the Frankfurt School such as Franz Neumann and Otto Kirchheimer to the theorization of fascism, parliamentary democracy, and constitutional theory; to Antonio

Gramsci's elaboration of the concepts of hegemony, civil society, and the revolutionary party—may be mentioned but not adequately summarized here.

However, two twentieth-century developments in Marxist state theory, both formulated as critiques of Communist orthodoxy and adjacent to the Western European left, are of particular relevance to the present volume, due to their prominence in the recent revival of Marxism more broadly: the theorization of the capitalist state's relative autonomy and materiality as a social relation, and the conception of the capitalist state as a historically specific social form peculiar to capitalist society. Both of these trends came into their own in the second half of the twentieth century, amid a more general reappraisal of the received categories of classical Marxism—especially technicist or reductionist accounts of the primacy of an economic 'base' vis-a-vis a juridico-political 'superstructure'. Such a model easily lent itself to instrumentalist accounts of the state that saw society's political and legal determination as arising out of a dialectic between the means and relations of production. In the 1950s and 1960s, that view achieved prominence in both the USSR and among Western Communist parties as the theory of state monopoly capitalism, which saw the state as fusing with corporate capital into a unified system of economic exploitation and political domination (Jessop 1982, 32).

Following widespread disillusionment with Stalinism, Marxist state theory in the 1960s and 1970s notably moved away from economic determinism and reductionism. Informed by Althusser's influential reading in *Reading Capital* (Althusser and Balibar 1969) and *For Marx* (Althusser 1970), Nicos Poulantzas' *Political Power and Social Classes* (1973) established what soon became known as a 'structuralist' theory of the capitalist state. At the centre of Poulantzas' theory was the argument that the capitalist mode of production was constituted by separate and relatively autonomous levels or regional instances. The separation between the economic and political instances, which mirrored the separation between economic and political power in the capitalist mode of production, lent a particular role to the capitalist state: that of the factor of unity and cohesion within the capitalist mode of production, and to varying degrees, in more specific capitalist social formations. Spanning the political, economic, and ideological levels, the state was an ensemble of structures and a point of condensation unifying both structures and class practices/struggles in all their heterogeneity, displacements, and contradictions. The relative autonomy of the state, as a function of its place and role within the capitalist mode of production, allowed it to act as the field where the long-term political interests of the capitalist classes could be forged from out of competing class fractions, even as their short-term economic interests drove them apart. At the same time, the state also disorganized the working class through the ideological and repressive means at its disposal.

The famous debate between Poulantzas and Ralph Miliband that unfolded in the *New Left Review* in the late 1960s and early 1970s catalysed a new wave of state theorization in the Anglosphere (Poulantzas 1969; Miliband 1970; Miliband 1973; Poulantzas 1976). Miliband's *The State in Capitalist Society* (1969) had provided a compelling indictment of pluralist theories about the relative diffusion of power and influence in liberal-democratic, capitalist societies, arguing that the state did in fact represent the interests of the capitalist classes. However, Poulantzas' critical assessment of Miliband's thesis as allegedly operating within an instrumentalist framework concerning the relationship between the economically dominant classes and state institutions did much to popularize the notion of the relative autonomy of the state. In the latter formulation, the capitalist state did not enact the preferences of the capitalist class due to the bourgeois background of its personnel, nor due to a mere alignment of interests between the capitalist class and state managers. Instead, the relative autonomy of the state was a structural feature of the capitalist mode of production, such that both the capitalist classes and state managers were merely the bearers of the objective structures of the state's role within the reproduction of the capitalist mode of production.

The Miliband-Poulantzas debate became akin to a prerequisite touchstone for most subsequent discussions of the state in political sociology over the following decade (Gold et al. 1975; Block 1977; Holloway and Picciotto 1978; Therborn 1978; Skocpol 1980; Evans , Rueschemeyer, and Skocpol 1985; Clarke 1991). Indeed, its unsatisfactory resolution remained the final verdict on the theoretical project of developing a Marxist approach to the state well into the new millennium (Aronowitz and Bratsis 2002; Jessop 2008; Barrow 2016). Arguably, the reification of the debate as one of instrumentalism vs. structuralism contributed to the perception that Marxist discussions of the state had reached a dead end, even as more recent scholarship has questioned that dichotomy (Barrow 2008); it is also worth noting that Miliband and Poulantzas themselves converged on matters of political practice, if not theory, by the end of the 1970s, including in their critical assessments of Eurocommunism and gradualist theories of the road to socialism (Miliband 1978; Poulantzas 1979).

Poulantzas' shift from a more structural-functionalist to a social relational approach to the state culminated with his final work, *State, Power, Socialism* (Poulantzas 1978). Now theorizing the capitalist state more as a 'condensation' of the balance of forces in the class struggle, he emphasized the manner in which class struggles were embedded within the materiality of the state, thereby introducing contradictions into its various apparatuses. While Poulantzas' earlier theory could perhaps have fallen under the rubric of a 'politicist' analysis that rebutted the economic determinism of the base/superstructure model only by ignoring the specificity of capitalist production (Holloway and Picciotto 1978, 4), his later work may perhaps be seen as bridging the relative autonomy and social form approaches (Gallas 2011; Bonefeld 2014, 185–86 n4).

In turn, social form theories of the state can be traced variously to the work of Evgeny Pashukanis, the state derivation debate, early Frankfurt School critical theory, and the renewed appreciation of Marx's critical encounter with Hegel in his mature thought. Social form theories proceed from the premise that capitalist society is a totality of historically specific social forms necessarily appearing as determinate social relations. On this account, the apparent separation of the political and the economic is an objective illusion—one that is constitutive of bourgeois sociality as such—that may be apprehended as a surface appearance of a contradictory totality of social relations (rather than a brute fact that must be explained on its own terms). As such, social form theories of the state are also premised on transcending the purported dichotomy between economic relations and juridical or political institutions. Against both the economism of viewing the state as subservient to, or arising from, production relations, as well as the politicism of viewing the economy as constituted without remainder by law-making, social form theories apprehend the state as an essential determination of a historically specific society, one that is characterized by the generalized production and exchange of commodities. As such an essential determination of society— that is, as a social form—the state can neither be seen as anterior to economic relations nor merely subordinated to them. Beyond this rejection of the fetishization of the distinction between bourgeois state and civil society, the similarities end; there is no articulated wholeness to social form theories of the state, the tensions between which mirror the expanding multiplicity of Marxian thought. The conclusions and implications drawn from such theories cannot be adequately summarized here; however, perhaps the most important implication drawn from many accounts of the capitalist state as social form is the claim that the capitalist state is form-determined such that it may not negate, subvert, or dismantle the unfreedom and misery through which capitalism is reproduced. The state's form constrains and delimits the range of possible policies that it may adopt or enforce; this is attributable not to the power of the capitalist class or the state of play in a contest among classes, but to the historically specific social form of capital itself.

The challenge of the non-identity of the class state—neatly encapsulated in Pashukanis' rhetorical question as to 'why does class rule not remain what it is?'—was a major motivation behind the 'state derivation' debate among West German Marxists (Holloway and Picciotto 1978; Sumida 2018). Attending to the form-determination of law and the state permits an appreciation of their specificity as 'impersonal' and 'separate from society'—a central concern of those interpretations of Marx's critique that emphasize the historical specificity of the forms or essential determinations of definite social relations in their entirety (Williams 1988; Smith 2017). The apparent separation of law and the state from civil society—apparent, and yet not merely illusory, as we shall see below—presents a challenge to reductive understandings of the state as an institutional servitor of the capitalist class. Class rule is non-identical with itself; it cannot 'remain what it is'. The bourgeois state cannot be identified with the capitalist class (or fractions of the capitalist class) in either its composition or its activity. Nor, for that matter, can the bourgeois state and the capitalist class be said to have identical, unmediated interests (Heinrich 2012, 208–13). This would appear to be an argument in favour of the position described in the previous section—to wit, that the state and the relations of production are (relatively) autonomous from one another. However, social form theorists insist that both state and economy must be understood as the forms of appearance of one and the same social reality (Bonefeld 2014, 165–85). The 'anonymous rule of money and the law' is the bifurcated appearance of a contradictory and antagonistic totality (Clarke 1988, 127).

It is both the case and not the case that the juridical and the political are 'impersonal' as well as 'separate' from civil society (including relations of production and exchange). It is the case insofar as this distinction is, indeed, a surface appearance of capitalist society. For that very reason, it is a socially objective category mediating and constraining the behaviour of social individuals. But such objectivity is at the same time false—or, more precisely, fetishized. The separation of the political and the economic is not a natural kind or a universal feature of human societies; it is a historically conditioned form of appearance of a particular society, one that is specified by the production of commodities for the sake of exchange in the pursuit of surplus value. Economism and politicism are the two faces of a single coin; they are both expressions of the misapprehension of capitalist society's essential determinations as separate and self-subsistent. It is not sufficient, on this account, to describe the state and the economy as autonomous—no matter how relatively or in how mediated a fashion—from one another. To do so would be to affirm their fetishized appearance as self-subsistent natural kinds, rather than as socially constituted (and hence historically specific) categories. In short: for the social form approach, the capitalist state is not separable or autonomous (not even relatively) from the valorization of capital. An adequate critique of either can only be an adequate critique of capital as such; and while the state may loom large in considerations about the emancipatory transformation of social relations, it does not do so as a beacon of hope.

3   THEORIZING THE CAPITALIST STATE: TOWARDS A RENEWED DEBATE

3.1   Attending to Pressing Challenges

The volume self-consciously continues in this lineage of Marxist debates on the capitalist state. Reflecting the richness, variety and even disagreements of earlier phases, the contributors draw from a range of different tendencies, approaches, and bodies of literature, from within the Marxist tradition of the critique of political economy and also beyond it. Despite their diversity, however, the contributors share a commitment to a core claim that the specificity of the modern state must be understood in relation to capitalist social relations of production and reproduction. They also share a common methodological standpoint: to look beyond the dichotomy between a rigidly deterministic or instrumentalist conception of the capitalist state, on the one hand; and the notion that the state—and political relations in general—are autonomous or separate from the material production and reproduction of social life, on the other hand. Rather than simply affirming either pole of this dichotomy, the chapters explore different aspects of the ways in which specific aspects of the capitalist state are interrelated with the relations of production, exchange, exploitation, and immiseration that are characteristic of the capitalist mode of production.

The first four chapters focus on contemporary concerns. Alyssa Battistoni opens the volume with an exploration of the urgent question of whether a 'substantial break with capitalism is necessary in order to address climate change, and whether the "capitalist state" can really be expected to act in ways that challenge the interest of fossil capital'. Rather than taking a position on these questions, Battistoni maps differing sets of claims about the relationship between capital and nature and the relationship between capital and the state. Such 'stylised ideal-types' are not blueprints for action; they are aids to grappling with the contradictions that emerge from any serious attempt to understand the possibilities for the use of public power in the pursuit of mitigating catastrophic climate change and ecological degradation. In particular, they assist in investigating the kinds of social movements and collective actors that can be articulated with existing and future climate struggles.

Dimitrios Kivotidis casts doubt on techno-optimist interpretations of the increasing digitalization of social life and the prospects for the automation of socialist management of production. The increasing mediation of social and political life by social media and digital 'platforms' has no inherent emancipatory potential; such technologies do not constitute a neutral, autonomous historical force but rather a social relation arising out of—and conditioned by—'the capitalist framework within which they operate'. Arguing against both 'techno-pessimism' and 'techno-optimism', Kivotidis makes the case that digitalization can contribute to 'democratic forms of decision-making'—only in conjunction with struggles for the democratic control of production itself. Digital mediation of existing social relations is not a royal road to socialism.

Rafael Khachaturian examines the social crisis caused by the Covid-19 pandemic through the lens of the role and capacities of the capitalist state, and more specifically, of its 'authoritarian neoliberal' form in today's United States. Contextualizing the pandemic within the broader transformation of the state in recent decades, especially since the 2008 financial crisis, Khachaturian suggests that the coronavirus exacerbated a crisis of social reproduction that the state has been incapable of meeting. Considering contemporary calls for public power to play a greater role in terms of care and social protection, he questions whether the state, understood as a condensation of class forces and a reproducer of capitalist class power, is capable of meeting these demands. Instead of a revolutionary window of opportunity, what we are faced with is a prolonged interregnum, in which the state continues to facilitate capitalist accumulation even while its reproductive and ideological roles come under further strain.

Stephen Maher and Scott M. Aquanno document the development and consolidation of central banking's insulation from (nominally democratic) parliamentary oversight, which underwent an unexpected proof of concept in the United States during the presidency of Donald Trump. Concomitant with the increasing salience of financialization in the postwar period, Maher and Aquanno describe the rising importance of the American state to global capital accumulation, and the expansion of the roles and capacities of the institutions comprising that state's 'financial branch' (the Federal Reserve, the Department of the Treasury, and related institutions). Maher and Aquanno do not simply emphasize the political construction of the independence of this financial branch from direct public control; indeed, such insulation from democratic contestation has often been touted as one of the chief advantages of central banking. Instead, they explore the increasing dependence of global capital accumulation—on a worldwide scale—on its functioning, whose centrality may be attributed not only to its political independence, but also its role as a node for 'the structural integration of state power with the capitalist economy'. The incoherence—and ultimate failure—of the Trump administration's attempt to radically restructure institutions like the Fed can only be explained by taking a broad view of the history of global finance in the twentieth century, and the articulation of the 'financial branch' with global processes of accumulation.

3.2 Reconsidering Enduring Questions

The themes of war, violence, and death are prominent in the next section of the volume, which focuses more closely on discrete features or activities of the capitalist state. Jasmine Chorley-Schulz focuses on soldiers as workers employed by capitalist states. The role of the armed combatant and the military/civilian distinction are often fetishized as transhistorical features of all societies of a certain complexity. By contrast, Chorley-Schulz argues that it is impossible to make sense of the role of the military except 'within the context of historical class antagonism and struggle'.

Soldiers and officers must be understood as 'people situated within histor-ical social relations, and not merely abstract agents of the state'. Taking this approach allows for a more fine-grained understanding of the rela-tionship between industrial production and the military activities of the capitalist state, as well as the state's interest in the cultivation of what Engels referred to as 'human material' in the pursuit of military supe-riority over rival states: 'The class struggle shapes military institutions in class societies…we should be interested in these institutions not just when they are deployed, but also as they are reproduced and particularly in who is reproducing them'.

Eva Nanopoulos expands on this theme by looking at what she calls the 'war-emergency paradigm'—the deployment of the language of war, security and threats coupled with access to an 'exceptional' legal arsenal—as a prevalent mode of governing of the contemporary capitalist state. Linking this back to the question raised by Alyssia Battistoni in the opening chapter, she uses Marxist theories of war and emergency to chart a way of approaching the question of whether we should reject or embrace the war-emergency paradigm. She considers some of the dilemmas raised when it comes to responding to crises such as pandemics or climate change, which require both urgent action and radical rupture with the ordinary institutions and processes that define the capitalist state. Using pacification theory, she highlights the connections between the war-emergency paradigm as a modality of state power and capital accumu-lation, and hence the dangers of either a politics of embrace or rejection. Returning to the writings of Marx and Engels, she argues that the war-emergency paradigm also expresses the contradictions of our present age of crises and catastrophe and that the question should best be approached as a theoretically informed but also political decision of which tactic is more likely to advance the class struggle and create conditions for emancipatory change.

Kirstin Munro offers an immanent critique of social reproduction theory (SRT), arguing that socially reproductive labour is not separable from the 'exploitation and domination [that] are inherent to the orga-nization of production and reproduction in capitalism'. In contrast to the view of many proponents of SRT, who conceive of the reproduction of labour power as a kind of 'life-making' activity anterior to capitalist social relations, for Munro, social reproduction in capitalism is always the reproduction of a specifically capitalist society. Even unproductive workers—that is, those engaged in work that does not directly valorize capital—are 'complicit in the reproduction of capitalist society as a whole'. Munro illustrates this argument with an examination of the work of unproductive workers in the 'public sector', such as nurses, teachers, social workers, and professional state employees. Insofar as they are directly engaged in the reproduction of commodity labour power—the only commodity that most patients, students, clients, and citizens possess, which they must sell in order to reproduce themselves—these workers are not engaged in a pre-political or non-economic endeavour. They are making and re-making subjects of capitalism who will be adequate to the society-pervading imperative that capital be continuously valorized. This points not only to a contradiction at the heart of SRT, but also to the unviability of the claim that the capitalist state is or can be a neutral instrument for the oversight of production and the provision of surplus.

Nate Holdren examines the capitalist state as an abettor of what Engels termed 'social murder', specifically through its mediation of the immiseration, exclusion, and the very production of surplus populations. Holdren draws upon a diverse literature that documents how 'capitalism kills, continually, in its normal operations'—death and dismemberment are not accidental but essential to the generalized production of commodities. The capitalist state is directly implicated in capitalism's 'necessary lethality' not simply through its use of violence to defend property and maintain the mass dispossession of the working class, but also through its management and mediation of contestation over and against the maiming and killing that are integral to capitalist production. The concept of depoliticization plays a central role in this analysis; not only does the capitalist state depoliticize capitalism's 'necessary lethality', but its own 'personnel themselves face pressures to render the state's disciplinary actions as specifically depoliticised'. The capitalist state's contradictions are such that it can sometimes furnish an institutional space for successful efforts to mitigate social murder to hold specific actors to account; however, in general, 'the capitalist state tends to redistribute rather than to end mass killing'.

3.3   Developing New Approaches

The final three chapters turn to methodological interventions. For Michael McCarthy, it is essential that, in Marxist state theory, the concrete must be made to ground the abstract. McCarthy calls for charting a middle course 'between contingency and functional necessity' in the analysis of capitalist states. The plural is important; for McCarthy, a focus on the diversity of concretions—both across time, and across the multiplicity of states in the world—is crucial; otherwise 'understanding actually-existing capitalist states' will not be possible. Positioning his argument against the structuralism of the early Poulantzas, McCarthy contends that the capitalist state 'can—and indeed has—become a force against capital itself'. However, the working class's capacity to turn the capitalist state against capital is mediated and constrained by its own atomization and decomposition, just as capitalists face a collective action problem as a class and state personnel must juggle the competing imperatives of securing both the conditions for accumulation and legitimation. For McCarthy, only a 'conjunctural' approach can make sense of—and guide analysis of—such a situation, in which the state is both the object and terrain of class struggle.

Chris O'Kane's chapter, by contrast, presents a critique of accounts of the capitalist state that present it as the terrain of class struggle—as well as of 'revolutionary' theories that stress the capitalist state's incapacity to moderate or mitigate the effects of capitalism's crisis tendencies. He considers the implications of the negative-dialectical approach of Frankfurt School critical theory for conceptualizing the capitalist state, contrasting it with theories of the state that tend to treat it as an instrument or as a reflection of economic determinations. Drawing upon Horkheimer and Adorno and related currents in critical theory, O'Kane depicts the capitalist state as a moment in the 'negative totality' of capitalist society. Such a 'negative-dialectical critique of the state critiques the form and capacities of the capitalist state', a state whose 'reliance on and reinforcement of' the accumulation of capital is fundamental. Such a state is the state of a society that reproduces through 'permanent catastrophe'. On such a view, 'redistributive state policies do not then build either public power or the political will for class struggle; instead, they create bureaucratic agencies that undermine workers' autonomy and depoliticise class struggle'.

Finally, Rob Hunter presents the case for understanding the capitalist state as a historically specific form of social relations, one which can be apprehended only in relation to the contradictory totality of capitalist society. Like O'Kane, he understands the capitalist state as a moment in the contradictory totality of capitalist social relations; specifically, it is the essential political determination of a society dominated by, and reproduced through, the accumulation of capital *qua* self-valorizing value. Hunter emphasizes the historical specificity of such a state, warning against succumbing to the fetishism of treating it as a self-subsistent or natural category. Apprehending the capitalist state as a historically specific social form allows us to understand that state violence and coercion are appearances of the impersonal domination that characterizes capitalist society itself. The capitalist state is neither a tool to be wielded against the capitalist class, nor is it dominated by the capitalist class; rather, it is the political form of appearance of a society in which all individuals are dominated by capital.

3.4   Common Themes and Concerns

Despite their varied content, the chapters traverse a number of shared themes and concerns. Methodologically, the inadequacy of instrumentalist conceptions of the state is a unifying theme. In one way or another, all of the chapters in this volume draw upon and extend the insight that the capitalist state is sensitive to and conditioned by capital accumulation, and yet also meaningfully distinct from it and does not merely operate at the behest of the capitalist class.

Common to a number of the chapters is an emphasis on returning to the work of Marx and Engels. Chorley-Schulz's and Nanopoulos' contributions both engage with the themes of war, the military and soldiers in their writings, which remain under-investigated. Holdren also returns to the work of Engels, whose notion of 'social murder' has gained increased popularity for understanding a variety of contemporary phenomena, from the necropolitics of the coronavirus to increased levels of social and economic inequalities. Prominent too is the value of bringing Marxist state theory into conversation with Marxist analysis in other fields, from ecological Marxism in Battistoni's chapter, to theories of imperialism in Kivotidis' chapter, and of security and policing in Nanopoulos' chapter. This draws out the importance of the capitalist state as the mediator between these seemingly independent spheres—as well as the distinctively interdisciplinary approach of the Marxist tradition in seeking to grasp phenomena from the standpoint of the social totality.

Beyond these methodological concerns a number of key themes emerge, some of which feature perpetual questions concerning the operation of the capitalist state, while others relate to new areas in which the capitalist state has acquired central significance, through the continuing expansion of capitalist social relations.

Among the perennial questions that the chapters address is the question of violence, alongside other non-violent forms of repression and coercion. Organized state violence and the centralization of force have been central to every stage of capitalist development, from the historical emergence and development of capitalism, to the convulsions of the twentieth century, to the contemporary moment. Such violence is organized against states' own citizens, through policing, systems of apartheid, organized abandonment, and ascription to hierarchies of race, gender, and sexuality; it is also organized against other states through war, which Marxists have frequently recognised even when liberal theorists have not. Chorley-Schulz's chapter highlights a lacuna in Marxist theorizing of state capacities and power: the workers who perform the violent work of the state, meting out death and destruction in the pursuit of state aims in warfare. Violence is also never far from considerations on the origins of catastrophic climate change in the consolidation of capitalist society at a planetary scale. As Battistoni argues, the abstraction that attends so much state theory (Marxist and otherwise) can obscure, rather than illuminate, 'concretely existing nature' and the state's mediation of capital's relation to it. Similarly, Holdren's exploration of social murder exposes the inescapable—yet often hidden—violence inherent in the capitalist state's attempts to respond to death, dismemberment, and disruption in all aspects of the lives of social individuals and their society, in a variety of ways—in their natural and social environments, their work, and their health.

Holdren, Khachaturian, Munro, and Nanopoulos' chapters all emphasize the uneasy dialectic between state intervention and the coercive maintenance of the conditions necessary for continued capital accumulation. Among the issues collectively raised by these chapters is the manner in which capitalist states deploy prerogative powers—especially in moments of emergency, war, and crisis—to decide on matters of life and death, whether by attention or by neglect. At the same time, the state's dual role as both sovereign and caretaker also raises the question of its relationship to social reproduction, as the paradoxical relationship between the provision of care and the exercise of repression is explored in several chapters. Munro, for example, not only intervenes in long-standing debates over social reproduction theory but recovers and extends a critique of the state as the central point of provision of essential goods such as housing and medical care, pointing to the ways in which the workers delivering such care can become agents of state repression. Meanwhile, Khachaturian argues that the pandemic has exacerbated a wider crisis of social reproduction that introduces further contradictions into the already-strained capitalist state.

This question of the capacities, contradictions, and weaknesses of the state points to the broader distinctiveness of Marxist theory of the capitalist state, but also to the critical thrust of Marxism as a revolutionary project. Marx did not only pursue a critique of political economy, but a *'ruthless criticism of all that exists'* (Marx and Engels 1975, 3:142, emphasis in original). The critique of the state is a natural extension of that project, since the state—whether understood as a 'special machine' of class rule, the political form of capitalist society, a condensation of class struggles in the capitalist mode of production, or something else—remains the externalized representation of that society to itself. A critical theory of the state, then, is also always an interrogation of a given social order and its own self-expression in political terms. A critique of that order is also an expression of the ultimate goal of Marxist theory: social revolution and the overcoming of capitalist relations.

But if we cannot theorize the state without also connecting it to political practice, we face the crucial question: What will be the role of the state in the transition from capitalism, and the struggles leading up to and constituting that transition? Even if one insists that 'the *real* movement which abolishes the present state of things' (Marx and Engels 1976, 5:49, emphasis in original) cannot be prefigured or predicted, such that we must look to social practice rather than theory to learn the answers to such questions, it is nevertheless unavoidable to ask those questions rigorously and with analytic clarity. If the replacement of the capitalist mode of production consists in the prior planning of production through collective deliberation rather than the posterior validation of commodity production through the mediation of monetary exchange, then what would or could be the role of a state (or even anything like a state) in such a shift?

Several chapters directly or indirectly address this question, with varying conclusions. Battistoni, for example, focuses on the unavoidable question of the role of the state in the transition away from a mode of production whose carbon-intensive, planet-heating, ocean-acidifying, and species-destroying tendencies have already caused damage that only highly organized and carefully coordinated effort on a large scale can begin to mitigate. Meanwhile, Kivotidis' chapter casts doubt on techno-optimistic

outlooks on the prospects for achieving socialism through the entrench-
ment of capitalist technologies, which have developed through (and in
order to control) struggles over production, surveillance, and repression.
Emancipation will occur through the intensification of the class struggle
at the heart of contemporary society, and not through the intervention
of enlightened technocrats or a simple change in ownership of means of
production that are organized for the extraction of surplus value.

Ultimately, emancipation through class struggle is, as the short twentieth century illustrated, no straightforward or easy prospect. Beyond
the barriers to emancipation that are commonly adduced in the present
moment—the atomization and decomposition of class, and the concomitant decline in solidarity and weakening of networks and communities of
struggle—many of the chapters collected here illuminate the specific role
of the state in the determination of those barriers. Maher and Aquanno's
chapter vividly illustrates the capacity of powerful state institutions—such
as the 'financial branch' of the government of the United States—to
engage in concerted attempts to secure, stabilize, and preserve conditions for sustained capital accumulation. Meanwhile, both O'Kane and
Hunter argue that a struggle to seize the capitalist state cannot be a
struggle against capitalism; the emancipatory transformation of capitalist
social relations necessarily involves the abolition of the political form of
appearance of that society. McCarthy, by contrast, contends that the capitalist state may be a resource in the class struggle—but even this is never
guaranteed, given the disparity in the balance of forces between capital
and labour.

Finally, no discussion of the capitalist state is complete without a
contemplation of the institutional structure of an emancipated society.
In *The Civil War in France*, Marx argued that 'the working class cannot
simply lay hold of the ready-made state machinery and wield it for their
own purpose'—a position far-removed from the call in the *Manifesto*
for the proletariat to seize the bourgeois state (Marx and Engels 1986,
22:533; cf. Hudis 2012, 183–87). What, if anything, will replace such a
state in a postcapitalist society? Marx insisted that he was not concerned
with 'writing recipes...for the cook-shops of the future' (Marx 1990,
I:99). But if the socialist polity is not 'a *state of affairs* which is to be
established, an *ideal* to which reality [will] have to adapt itself' (Marx
and Engels 1976, 5:49, emphasis in original)—in other words, if it is
not possible to draw up a blueprint of the political form of emancipated
society prior to its realization in history—it is nevertheless difficult to

avoid imagining what shape it might take. Moreover, the critique of the capitalist state reveals what aspects, roles, or capacities that the institutions of an emancipated society will *not* have—a point made in both O'Kane and Hunter's chapters. In any event, the institutional mediation of postcapitalist society will no doubt look very different from the capitalist state. As Kivotidis argues in his chapter, a socialist state will be concerned not with the maintenance of capitalist social relations and the protection of private property, but with the enablement of collective deliberation over the planning and implementation of social production. Such a state would not concern itself with depoliticizing social murder (cf. Holdren's chapter), with the abandonment of the vulnerable (cf. Khachaturian's chapter), or with the organization, cultivation, and deployment of violence (cf. Chorley-Schulz and Nanopoulos' chapters), but instead concern itself with human needs and human flourishing.

4   THEORIZING THE CAPITALIST STATE: FUTURE DIRECTIONS

The volume aims to illustrate the value of returning to Marxist theories of the capitalist state in the hope of once again opening up debate on the capitalist state. As such, it is far from exhaustive—whether in terms of the scholarship it engages with, the methods that it uses, or the themes that it explores. Many old questions, such as the role of the state in the transition to socialism and the 'dictatorship of the proletariat', would merit re-examination in the light of modern conditions. But looking forward, at least three issues require urgent attention if a revival of the state debate, as part of the broader revival of Marx and Marxism, is to speak to the many 'morbid symptoms' of our age of crises and catastrophe, and the lived experiences of those most directly affected by it.

The first is the role of the state in the production, reproduction and exploitation of difference along racial, gender, sexual, religious, national and other lines alongside class, drawing from the multiple traditions that have considered the relationship between capitalism and other forms of oppression, including Marxist feminism, Black Marxism, queer Marxism, and decolonial Marxism, to name only a few.

The initial flourishing of Marxist feminism in the 1970s and 1980s had included debates about the capitalist state (Barrett 1980; Sargent 1981; Vogel 1983; MacKinnon 1989; for an overview, see Jessop 2001, 157–161). After its desuetude at the end of that period, the current moment is witnessing a renewed attention to gender, sexuality, care work, and the household as specifically capitalist social relations (Arruzza 2016; Giménez 2018; Gonzalez 2011; Munro 2019; Wendling 2013). The role of the state—and of state violence in particular—has been foregrounded in many of these debates. State violence has likewise featured in Marxist engagements with race and racism (e.g. Hall et al. 1978; Davis 1983; Roediger 1991; Fields and Fields 2014). Early Marxist analyses of race in the works of scholars such as Robert Miles (1982) or Stuart Hall (2021) are now being supplemented by a growing interest in the relationship between capitalism and racism (e.g. Singh 2016; Bhattacharyya 2018). Scholars are returning to Marxism to move beyond intersectional spatial models of discrimination that conceive of different forms of oppression as interconnected but ultimately separate social forms. Social reproduction theorists like David McNally, for example, have tried to integrate gender, class, and race as dynamic social relations within a unitary capitalist totality in which 'the organic whole is constituted in and through its parts ... but it is not reducible to its parts', building on Patricia Hill Collins' insight that 'interlocking systems of oppression ought to be understood as "part of a single, historically created system"' (McNally 2017, 106).

But there remains a need for dialogue between these traditions and Marxist theories of the state, along the lines undertaken by Battistoni in reading together ecological Marxism and Marxist state theory. The resurgence of racism and misogyny that have accompanied the rise of various 'populist' far-right movements and deepened authoritarian forms of neoliberal states make it urgent for Marxist theories of the state to attend to the inter-relationships between the specifically capitalist state and domination, subordination, and marginalization on the basis of gender and sexuality. More generally, because Marxist state theorizing is predicated on an understanding of capitalist society as consisting of more than purely 'economic' determinations, its scope must encompass the antagonisms and contradictions inherent in that society's relations. This is not to say that, to succeed, a Marxist theory of the state must adequately explain or account for all of the determinations of capitalist society; however, it must be able to at least accommodate and account for them when advancing its own explanations. Contrary to Marxist analyses that conceive of class and class struggle as autonomous from, and having some kind of priority over, other forms of domination and contestation, we insist that further development of the Marxist critique of the capitalist state must attend to the mutual constitution of and presupposition between, all of capitalist society's determinations.

Second, there is the question of imperialism. Part of the Marxist revival has already included a call for Marxist theories of imperialism to reach out to theories of the capitalist state (Mohandesi 2022), and the same is true for theories of the state, which should be informed by the histories and theories of colonialism, imperialism, and the expansion and consolidation of the world market. Certainly we should continue to 'be wary of the idealist correlation between economic integration and international peace' (Nanopoulos 2021, 395). The state played a key role in processes of primitive accumulation both within territorial borders and 'abroad' in the inter-state system, and through the violent subsumption of increasing numbers of people and places to the imperatives of generalized commodity production and exchange. The state's role in the constitution of world market relations is no less central today (Copley and Moraitis 2021). And while it may be the case that 'the existence of the state as many states is at a more concrete level than the determination of the state itself on the basis of the value-form' (Reuten and Williams 1989, 299), this hardly means that the multiplicity of states and the dynamics of the inter-state system are irrelevant to the task of comprehending capitalism as a society with a global scope. There remains a wide variety of contradictions even within the unity of the set of capitalist states. For example, it is hardly possible to speak of capitalist states in the established metropolitan core as being similar in all respects to states in the periphery of global capitalist society—even if, in their essential determinations, both kinds remain specifically capitalist. Moreover, what distinguishes economic policies pursued by capitalist states today from the developmentalist regimes of the past (Alami et al. 2022)? These and other questions also require pushing beyond the traditional Eurocentrism of state theorizing, both in its historical forms and contemporary concerns, bringing the analytical tools of Marxian social theory to bear on semi-peripheral and peripheral societies and modifying those concepts in the process.

In a similar vein, greater attention must also be paid to the transformations of the capitalist state resulting from the transnationalisation of capitalism and the changing forms of capitalist accumulation and imperialism, including under the dominance of finance capital. The Mandel–Poulanztas debate in the 1960s had already considered some of these themes, with Mandel arguing that the (European) capitalist state would develop into a European super-state, and Poulantzas arguing that we had entered a new stage of imperialism dominated by the United States, in which the capitalist state would be transformed to serve the interests of transnational capital, but not superseded as such (Auvrey and Durand 2019). In turn, many contemporary Marxists have delved further into the inter-relationship between the state and global capitalism (Rosenberg 1994; Bonefeld and Holloway 1996; Aronowitz and Bratsis 2002; Panitch and Gindin 2013; Anievas and Nişancıoğlu 2015). And again, at this level too, Marxist state theory will have to be attuned to the interconnections between the various forms of oppression and imperialism in further engaging the role of the capitalist state in their (mutual) constitution and reproduction, which many scholars have painstakingly explored, such as Silvia Federici's inquiries into the mutual constitution of women's status, oppression, and colonization; Eric Williams' reconstruction of the connections between capitalism, racism and slavery, and W.E.B. Du Bois' work on global colour lines.

Finally, it is as important as ever to continue in Marx's footsteps with a commitment to unmasking the secret of bourgeois society, in striving for theories that do not merely interpret social phenomena and form, but do so with a view to transforming them. To achieve this, Marxist state theory must attend to concrete developments, while at the same time avoiding becoming a mere transcription of the topical. Is it appropriate to speak of a crisis of constitutional democracy, such that an authoritarianism distinct from liberal modes of governance is truly on the rise (Brown 2015; Fraser 2022)? Or are the same core contradictions of the bourgeois state assuming seemingly different (and superficially unfamiliar) appearances (Landa 2012; Hunter 2021, 204–7)? If so, what are the concrete implications for our theory of the state and its role in transition to socialism? More generally, what is the capitalist state's role in the contexts of imperialism, (de)colonization and the post-colonial order, and the maintenance of border regimes of exclusion and expulsion through the violence of the law and of increasingly militarized state personnel? Our goal is that, in this age of crises, catastrophe, and sharpening contradictions, this collection will build on both 'intellectual pessimism' but also on the optimism that the revival of Marxist theory may provide us with a path to move in a more hopeful direction.

REFERENCES

Alami, Ilias, Milan Babic, Adam D. Dixon, and Imogen T. Liu. 2022. 'Special Issue Introduction: What Is the New State Capitalism?' *Contemporary Politics* 28 (3): 245–63.

Albo, Greg, Leo Panitch, and Alan Zuege, eds. 2018. *Class, Party, Revolution: A Socialist Register Reader*. Chicago: Haymarket.

Althusser, Louis. [1965] 1969. *For Marx*. London: Verso.

Althusser, Louis and Etienne Balibar. 1965 [1970]. *Reading Capital*. London: Verso.

Anievas, Alex, and Kerem Nişancıoğlu. 2015. *How the West Came to Rule: The Geopolitical Origins of Capitalism*. London: Pluto Press.

Aronowitz, Stanley, and Peter Bratsis, eds. 2002. *Paradigm Lost: State Theory Reconsidered*. Minneapolis: University of Minnesota Press.

Arruzza, Cinzia. 2016. 'Functionalist, Determinist, Reductionist: Social Reproduction Feminism and Its Critics'. *Science & Society* 80 (1): 9–30.

Auvrey, Tristan, and Cédric Durand. 2019. 'A European Capitalism? Revisiting the Mandel-Poulantzas Debate'. In *The End of the Democratic State: Nicos Poulantzas, a Marxism for the 21st Century*, edited by Jean-Numa. Ducange and Razmig Keucheyan, 145–65. Cham: Palgrave Macmillan.

Barrett, Michèle. 1980. *Women's Oppression Today: Problems in Marxist Feminist Analysis*. London: Verso.

Barrow, Clyde W. 2008. 'Ralph Miliband the Instrumentalist Theory of the State: The (Mis)Construction of an Analytic Concept'. In *Class, Power, and the State in Capitalist Society: Essays on Ralph Miliband*, edited by Paul Wetherly, Clyde W. Barrow, and Peter Burnham, 84–108. Basingstoke: Palgrave Macmillan.

Barrow, Clyde W. 2016. *Toward a Critical Theory of States: The Poulantzas-Miliband Debate After Globalization*. Albany: SUNY Press.

Bhattacharyya, Gargi. 2018. *Rethinking Racial Capitalism: Questions of Reproduction and Survival*. Lanham, MD: Rowman and Littlefield.

Block, Fred. 1977. 'The Ruling Class Does Not Rule: Notes on the Marxist Theory of the State'. *Socialist Revolution* 33 (May–June): 6–28.

Bonefeld, Werner. 2014. *Critical Theory and the Critique of Political Economy: On Subversion and Negative Reason*. New York: Bloomsbury.

Bonefeld, Werner, and John Holloway, eds. 1996. *Global Capital, National State and the Politics of Money*. Basingstoke: Macmillan.

Brown, Wendy. 2015. *Undoing the Demos: Neoliberalism's Stealth Revolution*. New York: Zone Books.

Clarke, Simon. 1988. *Keynesianism, Monetarism and the Crisis of the State*. Cheltenham: Edward Elgar.

Clarke, Simon, ed. 1991. *The State Debate*. Basingstoke: Macmillan.

Copley, Jack, and Alexis Moraitis. 2021. 'Beyond the Mutual Constitution of States and Markets: On the Governance of Alienation'. *New Political Economy* 26 (3): 490–508.

Davis, Angela Y. 1983. *Women, Race & Class*. New York: Vintage.

Dimick, Matthew. 2021. 'Pashukanis' Commodity-Form Theory of Law'. In *Research Handbook on Law and Marxism*, edited by Paul O'Connell and Umut Özsu, 115–38. Cheltenham: Edward Elgar.

Eley, Geoff. 2002. *Forging Democracy: The History of the Left in Europe, 1850–2000*. New York: Oxford University Press.

Evans, Peter B., Dietrich Rueschemeyer, and Theda Skocpol. 1985. *Bringing the State Back In*. Cambridge: Cambridge University Press.

Fields, Karen E., and Barbara J. Fields. 2014. *Racecraft: The Soul of Inequality in American Life*. London: Verso.

Fraser, Nancy. 2022. *Cannibal Capitalism: How Our System Is Devouring Democracy, Care, and the Planet and What We Can Do About It*. London: Verso.

Gallas, Alexander. 2011. 'Reading "Capital" with Poulantzas: "Form" and "Struggle" in the Critique of Political Economy'. In *Reading Poulantzas*, edited by Alexander Gallas, Lars Bretthauer, John Kannankulam, and Ingo Stutzle, 89–106. London: Merlin Press.

Giménez, Martha E. 2018. *Marx, Women, and Capitalist Social Reproduction: Marxist-Feminist Essays*. Leiden: Brill.

Gold, David A., Clarence Y. H. Lo, and Erik Olin Wright. 1975. 'Recent Developments in Marxist Theories of the Capitalist State'. Parts I & II. *Monthly Review* (October and November): 29–41, 36–51.

Gonzalez, Maya Andrea. 2011. 'Communization and the Abolition of Gender'. In *Communization and Its Discontents: Contestation, Critique, and Contemporary Struggles*, edited by Benjamin Noys, 219–34. Wivenhoe: Minor Compositions.

Hall, Stuart. 2021. *Selected Writings on Race and Difference*. edited by Paul Gilroy and Ruth Wilson Gilmore. Durham: Duke University Press.

Hall, Stuart, et al. 1978. *Policing the Crisis: Mugging, the State, and Law and Order*. Basingstoke: Macmillan.

Heinrich, Michael. 2012. *An Introduction to the Three Volumes of Karl Marx's Capital*. Translated by Alexander Locascio. New York: Monthly Review Press.

Heller, Henry. 2011. *The Birth of Capitalism: A 21st Century Perspective*. London: Pluto Press.

Hobsbawm, Eric. 1994. *The Age of Extremes: A History of the World, 1914–1991*. New York: Vintage.

Holloway, John, and Sol Picciotto. 1978. 'Introduction: Towards a Materialist Theory of the State'. In *State and Capital: A Marxist Debate*, edited by John Holloway and Sol Picciotto, 1–31. London: Edward Arnold.

Hudis, Peter. 2012. *Marx's Concept of the Alternative to Capitalism*. Leiden: Brill.

Hunter, Rob. 2021. 'Marx's Critique and the Constitution of the Capitalist State'. In *Research Handbook on Law and Marxism*, edited by Paul O'Connell and Umut Özsu, 190–208. Cheltenham: Edward Elgar.

Jessop, Bob. 1982. *The Capitalist State: Marxist Theories and Methods*. Oxford: Martin Robertson.

———. 2008. 'Dialogue of the Deaf: Some Reflections on the Poulantzas-Miliband Debate'. In *Class, Power, and the State in Capitalist Society: Essays on Ralph Miliband*, edited by Paul Wetherly, Clyde W. Barrow, and Peter Burnham, 132–57. Basingstoke: Palgrave Macmillan.

———. 2001. 'Bringing the State Back In (Yet Again): Reviews, Revisions, Rejections, and Redirections.' *International Review of Sociology*. 11 (2): 149–173.

Landa, Ishay. 2012. *The Apprentice's Sorcerer: Liberal Tradition and Fascism*. Chicago, Illinois: Haymarket Books.

Lenin, V. I. 2014. *State and Revolution: Fully Annotated Edition*. Edited by Todd Chretien. Haymarket Books.

MacKinnon, Catharine A. 1989. *Toward a Feminist Theory of the State*. Cambridge: Harvard University Press.

McNally, David. 2017. 'Intersections and Dialectics: Critical Reconstructions in Social Reproduction Theory'. In *Social Reproduction Theory: Remapping Class, Recentering Oppression*, edited by Tithi Bhattacharya, 94–111. London: Pluto Press.

Marx, Karl. 1973. *Grundrisse: Foundations of the Critique of Political Economy*. Translated by Martin Nicolaus. London: Penguin Books.

———. 1990. *Capital: A Critique of Political Economy*. Translated by Ben Fowkes. Vol. I. London: Penguin Books.

Marx, Karl, and Friedrich Engels. 1975. *Marx and Engels Collected Works*, vol. 3. London: Lawrence & Wishart.

———. 1976. *Marx and Engels Collected Works*, vol. 5. London: Lawrence & Wishart.

———. 1986. *Marx and Engels Collected Works*, vol. 22. London: Lawrence & Wishart.

———. 1987. *Marx and Engels Collected Works*, vol. 25. London: Lawrence & Wishart.

Miliband, Ralph. 1969. *The State in Capitalist Society*. New York: Basic Books.

———. 1970. 'The Capitalist State: Reply to Nicos Poulantzas'. *New Left Review* I/59 (Jan–Feb.): 53–60.

———. 1973. 'Poulantzas and the Capitalist State'. *New Left Review* I/82 (Nov–Dec): 83–92.

———. 1978. 'Constitutionalism and Revolution: Notes on Eurocommunism'. *Socialist Register* 15: 158–171.

Miles, Robert. 1982. *Racism and Migrant Labour: A Critical Text*. London: Routledge.

Mohandesi, Salar. 2022. 'Imperialism'. In *The Sage Handbook of Marxism*, Vol. 1, edited by Alberto Toscano, Sara R. Farris, and Svenja Bromberg, 430–47. London: Sage.

Munro, Kirstin. 2019. '"Social Reproduction Theory", Social Reproduction, and Household Production'. *Science & Society* 83 (4): 451–68.

Murray, Patrick. 1988. *Marx's Theory of Scientific Knowledge*. Atlantic Highlands, NJ: Humanities Press.

Musto, Marcello, ed. 2020. *The Marx Revival: Key Concepts and New Interpretations*. Cambridge: Cambridge University Press.

Nanopoulos, Eva. 2021. 'From Class-Based Project to Imperial Formation: European Union Law and the Reconstruction of Europe'. In *Research Handbook on Law and Marxism*, edited by Paul O'Connell and Umut Özsu, 375–98. Cheltenham: Edward Elgar.

Pashukanis, Evgeny B. 1989. *Law and Marxism: A General Theory*. Translated by Barbara Einhorn. London: Pluto Press.

Panitch, Leo, and Sam Gindin. 2013. *The Making of Global Capitalism: The Political Economy of American Empire*. London: Verso.

Poulantzas, Nicos. 1973 [1968]. *Political Power and Social Classes*. London: New Left Books.

———. 1976. 'The Capitalist State: A Reply to Miliband and Laclau'. *New Left Review* I/95 (Jan–Feb.): 63–83.

———. 1978. *State, Power, Socialism*. London: Verso.

———. 1979. 'Interview with Nicos Poulantzas'. *Marxism Today*. July 1979: 194–201.

Reuten, Geert, and Michael Williams. 1989. *Value-Form and the State: The Tendencies of Accumulation and the Determination of Economic Policy in Capitalist Society*. London: Routledge.

Roediger, David R. 1991. *The Wages of Whiteness: Race and the Making of the American Working Class*. London: Verso.

Rosenberg, Justin. 1994. *The Empire of Civil Society: A Critique of the Realist Theory of International Relations*. London: Verso.

Sargent, Lydia, ed. 1981. *The Unhappy Marriage of Marxism and Feminism: A Debate on Class and Patriarchy*. London: Pluto Press.

Singh, Nikhil Pal. 2016. 'On Race, Violence, and So-Called Primitive Accumulation'. *Social Text* 34 (3): 27–50.

Skocpol, Theda. 1980. 'Political Responses to Capitalist Crisis: Neo-Marxist Theories of the State and the New Deal'. *Politics & Society* 10 (2): 155–201.

Smith, Tony. 2017. *Beyond Liberal Egalitarianism: Marx and Normative Social Theory in the Twenty-First Century*. Leiden: Brill.

Steinberg, Marc W. 2010. 'Marx, Formal Subsumption and the Law'. *Theory and Society* 39 (2): 173–202.

Sumida, Soichiro. 2018. 'Die Zusammenfassung der bürgerlichen Gesellschaft in der Staatsform: Zu Marx'. *Theorie Des Staats.' Marx-Engels Jahrbuch* 2017 (1): 41–60.

Therborn, Göran. 1978. *What Does the Ruling Class Do When it Rules?* London: Verso.

Vogel, Lise. 1983. *Marxism and the Oppression of Women: Toward a Unitary Theory*. New Brunswick: Rutgers University Press.

Wendling, Amy E. 2013. 'Second Nature: Gender in Marx's Grundrisse'. In *In Marx's Laboratory: Critical Interpretations of the Grundrisse*, edited by Riccardo Bellofiore, Guido Starosta, and Peter D. Thomas, 347–69. Leiden: Brill.

Williams, Michael, ed. 1988. *Value, Social Form and the State*. Houndmills: Macmillan.

State, Capital, Nature: State Theory for the Capitalocene

Alyssa Battistoni

Although 'environmental issues' have long been treated as marginal in both mainstream politics and Marxist thought, climate change has brought ecological concerns to the forefront of twenty-first-century politics. Until recently, market mechanisms like carbon taxes and cap-and-trade systems have been the dominant policy approach to reducing carbon emissions. In recent years, however, states have begun to play a more direct role in decarbonization via "green industrial policy" aimed at spurring private investment, while proponents of a Green New Deal demand the likes of large-scale public investment and bans on fossil fuel extraction (Aronoff et al. 2019; Gabor 2023; Klein 2019; Meaney 2022; Riofrancos 2019). These developments have also sparked new debates on the left over whether a more substantial break with capitalism is necessary in order to address climate change, and whether the 'capitalist state' can really be expected to act in ways that challenge the interests of fossil capital (Arboleda 2020; Bernes 2019; Clover 2019; Hunter 2021; Mann and Wainwright 2018).

A. Battistoni (✉)
Barnard College, New York, New York, USA
e-mail: abattist@barnard.edu

R. Hunter et al. (eds.), *Marxism and the Capitalist State*,
Political Philosophy and Public Purpose,
https://doi.org/10.1007/978-3-031-36167-8_2

This chapter addresses these debates at a higher level of abstraction, appraising the conditions under which we might expect states in capitalist societies to act in order to prevent ecological catastrophe—or not. It does so by considering two debates in Marxist thought—first, the debate about nature among eco-Marxists, and second, the debate about the state among Marxist state theorists—with attention to the resources they offer for understanding the relationship between the state, capitalism, and nature. Although my own position is that the urgency of climate change renders it imperative to engage with institutions as they presently exist, including with what Andreas Malm describes as the 'dreary bourgeois state, tethered to the circuits of capital as always', this chapter is not primarily an argument for that position (Malm 2020, 151; cf. Battistoni 2018). Nor is it an outline of an ideal state, a just state, or even a post-capitalist state. As such, it does not address criticisms of the state and sovereignty made on normative grounds.[1] Its aims are more modest: to bring two largely distinct theoretical debates into conversation, in order to clarify assumptions about the relationship between the state, capital, *and* nature that often remain implicit or underdeveloped in political arguments.

In Part I, I consider the central question of eco-Marxism: what is the relationship between capitalism and nature? In particular, I focus on accounts of the relationship between ecological and capitalist crises: on the one hand, arguments that capitalism's destruction of nature is also self-destructive; and on the other, arguments that capitalism destroys nature without also undermining its own operations. In Part II, I consider the central debate of Marxist state theory, concerning the relationship between capital and the state. I draw on Raju Das' (1996) distinction between 'structural' and 'class struggle' analyses: structural analyses emphasize the constraints that capitalism sets on the kinds of action the state can undertake; while class struggle approaches see the state as conditioned in part by class conflict and the shifting balance of power

---

[1] Marxist theorists rarely advance normative theories explicitly, but they are often implicit: Mann and Wainwright's (2018) argument in favour of the anti-sovereign 'Climate X', for example, is rooted in an appeal to justice. Political theorists, by contrast, have frequently undertaken normative critiques of the state and sovereignty from a wide variety of perspectives. For a varied but non-comprehensive range of approaches see, for example, Simpson (2014); Pettit (2012); Eckersley (2004); Scott (1998); Brown (1995); Nozick (1974).

between classes, even as those struggles are also constrained by structural limitations. In Part III, I put these debates in conversation in order to explore the interaction between three central terms which are too rarely considered together: state, nature, and capital. I argue that the specific territorial authority of the state makes it particularly important as a mediator between abstract capital and concrete nature. Natural processes happen in specific places, while capital flows around the world in search of profit; but when capital touches down, whether to drill a well or build a wind turbine, it has to go through the state. Theorizing the state, then, has crucial implications for eco-Marxist thought, and vice versa.

1   Capitalism and Nature

Marxists concerned with ecology have largely focused on the question of capitalism's relationship to nonhuman nature. Marx's own relatively sparse remarks on nonhuman nature have been thoroughly documented by eco-Marxists seeking to recuperate Marx as a thinker concerned with capitalism's ecological effects rather than as a Promethean advocate of the domination of nature (Foster 2000; Foster and Burkett 2016; Saito 2016). Other ecologically oriented Marxists have sought to extend Marxist insights to ecological issues not explicitly addressed in his own work (Benton 1996; Moore 2015; O'Connor 1998; Salleh 1998). While the particulars of these accounts vary, however, nearly all Marxist theorists of ecology agree that capitalism tends to destroy what we might think of as 'ecological nature', whether by digging up the earth in search of raw materials, converting biodiverse forests to plantations growing high-yield cash crops, or treating the atmosphere as a free dumping ground for waste, including excess carbon dioxide. While eco-Marxists have frequently parted ways when it comes to ontological questions about what nature *is*—in particular, debating whether a 'monist' or 'dualist' view of nature and society is appropriate (cf. Malm 2017)—I focus instead on a dispute of greater significance in relation to the state: the question of whether capitalism's tendency to destroy nature also constitutes a crisis for capitalism itself. That is, does the ecological destruction caused by capitalism affect profitability and processes of capital accumulation? Or do ecological crises, however devastating for many forms of human and nonhuman life, tend not to have direct or major consequences for capital accumulation?

On the one hand is a Polanyian argument, originally made by James O'Connor, which holds that capitalism—what Polanyi (2001) called market society—tends to destroy its conditions of existence and must be prevented from doing so (O'Connor 1988; 1998). Polanyi's account focuses on the category of 'fictitious commodities', referring to things which are not actually produced for sale: land (nature), labour(human beings), and money. When traded on the market, Polanyi argues, these entities are 'annihilated', ultimately threatening the stability of 'market society' itself. O'Connor's account effectively redescribes 'fictitious commodities' as capitalism's 'conditions of production'—things which are not produced according to capitalism's law of value, but which are utilized by capitalism as part of production, and which are degraded, exhausted, and run down as a result. Significantly, O'Connor notes a disjuncture between the 'conditions of production' and 'means of life': capital needs 'conditions of production', while the 'means of life' are necessary for human and nonhuman existence but may not be essential to capital accumulation (O'Connor 1988; 1998).[2] Yet O'Connor oscillates between, and sometimes conflates, these two terms when discussing the degradation of ecological conditions, with implications for his view of crisis, as discussed shortly. As with Polanyi, O'Connor's account holds that the destruction of the conditions of production eventually poses a threat to capitalism itself: thus capitalism's tendencies are self-destructive.

O'Connor describes this self-destructive tendency as the 'second contradiction of capitalism'. Traditional crisis theory focuses on the contradiction between the productive relations and forces of capitalism, which frequently results in crises of overproduction—a glut of commodities relative to demand. O'Connor's 'second contradiction' gives rise to a different kind of crisis: by degrading the social and environmental conditions of production, he argues, capital will inadvertently increase its own costs and undercut its own profits. Rising temperatures, for example, might lead to droughts and in turn bad harvests, causing the costs of food, and in turn labour, to rise; acid rain might cause buildings to deteriorate, thus diminishing profits from rents; rising seas might destroy the value of vast swathes of real estate; and so on. Economic crisis might therefore

---

[2] Notably, the conditions of production are *always also* means of life, but not all means of life are also conditions of production. Not every human being sells their labour-power; and not every nonhuman species provides 'raw materials' for commodity production or is essential to sustaining the ecosystems from which raw materials are gleaned.

result from the *underproduction* of the conditions of production as well as from the *overproduction* of commodities. Ecologically spurred crises might lead capital and/or the state to restructure the ecological conditions of production such that they remain available: for example, a state forestry department might institute permanent-yield forests to ensure a steady supply of timber; or a city choked by traffic congestion might undertake urban planning to ease commutes. At the same time, as with the traditional crisis of overproduction, these ecological-cum-economic crises are endemic to capitalism but also potentially generative for it: as eco-Marxists following O'Connor have pointed out, ecological crises resulting in shortages of raw materials might also drive capital to innovate technologically, such that it uses 'raw materials' more efficiently; or to undertake a 'spatial fix' by relocating production from an area where ecological conditions have been exhausted (Moore 2010a, 2010b). To sum up, then, O'Connor's influential account, whose core dimensions are reflected in the work of Jason Moore (2015) and Nancy Fraser (2014; 2021), holds that the degradation of the conditions of production tends to cause a crisis for capitalism, which must be resolved in some way.

Is this claim warranted? For John Bellamy Foster and Paul Burkett, the central flaw in O'Connor's thesis is the disjuncture between ecological and economic crises: there is 'no feedback mechanism' between ecological degradation and economic crisis 'demanding an immediate response on the part of capital' (Foster and Burkett 2016, 5–6; Burkett 2016). O'Connor's view of the second contradiction, they argue, and more generally of capitalism's relationship to nature, is overly functionalist. Although certain basic ecological conditions, like a minimally habitable planet, are required for ongoing capital accumulation, it might nevertheless be compatible with levels of ecological degradation devastating to both human and nonhuman life. In other words, the disjuncture between the means of life and the conditions of production suggests a similar disjuncture between crises of society, health, and ecology on the one hand, and crises of capital accumulation on the other. Historically, Foster and Burkett observe, ecological crises have threatened profits in specific places or industries, as in crises of soil fertility, but these localized crises have not translated into permanent or widespread crises of accumulation. The toll of ecological degradation on human and nonhuman life, they argue, must be distinguished from its significance for capital. This, in turn, has significant political implications, as I will discuss in more detail: whereas O'Connor's position suggests a 'second path' to socialism, via ecologically driven capitalist collapse, Foster and Burkett argue that this expectation is unwarranted. The case against capitalism must be made on the basis of its harm to nonhuman and human life in themselves.

Thus far, the empirical evidence regarding ecological crisis and contradiction seems to support Foster and Burkett's position. Although growth appears to be slowing, the proximate cause is not the high costs of ecological goods, resource scarcity, or destruction of value by volatile planetary phenomena, but the lack of investment opportunities promising adequate rates of return (Benanav 2020; Brenner 1998; Summers 2020). If what mainstream economists call 'secular stagnation' reflects a contradiction, it stems from underinvestment in traditional commodity production rather than in the 'conditions of production'. Meanwhile, capital seems capable of weathering many storms: cyclones and typhoons killing thousands in Myanmar and Mozambique; floods displacing millions in Pakistan; and even a global pandemic have not seriously disrupted capital accumulation (Davis 2005; Malm 2020; Wallace 2016). This is likely to change as climate conditions worsen, of course, and some sectors of capital (e.g. insurance) are likely to face serious losses. But history thus far suggests that capitalism can continue to function in the face of severe ecological and social crises.

2   Capitalism and the State

If the central point of contention in eco-Marxist debates concerns the relationship of nature to capital, the central debate in Marxist state theory concerns the relationship of state to capital and class struggle. Here, as with respect to nature, theorists have been faced with a relative paucity of Marx's own writing. Instead, Marxist theories of politics and the state have developed most significantly in relation to distinct political moments, addressing questions of revolution, fascism, and the rise of the welfare state over the course of the twentieth century. My analysis here looks primarily to the most recent major iteration of these debates, which addressed the prospects for socialist and communist politics in the capitalist democracies of Western Europe between the 1960s and 1980s. Although the parameters of this debate are limited by its geographical scope and the historical contexts within which it unfolded, it nevertheless offers an important starting point.

As eco-Marxists typically agree that capitalism is destructive of nature, Marxist state theorists typically share a critique of 'bourgeois' theories of the state, charging that the state cannot simply be seen as an autonomous institution with its own distinctive logic and ends, per Weberian accounts; as an expression of the general or popular will, per Rousseauian democratic theories; or as a 'neutral' terrain which any set of interests may contest and seek to wield towards their own ends, per pluralist accounts (Khachaturian 2019; Smith 2017). Rather, the modern state must be understood as specific to capitalist society, structured by class relations, and oriented towards stabilizing capital accumulation. The state, most Marxists agree, does things that capitalists themselves cannot. The state monopoly on coercive force secures private property and regulates class conflict. States provide the 'conditions of production', including legal relationships governing property ownership, the guarantee of fiat money, and public goods that are necessary but unprofitable for private investors, including many forms of physical infrastructure. States interact with other states to develop frameworks for international cooperation: most notably, establishing the legal foundations for economic activity, including trade agreements, financial institutions and regulations, property rights, and so on, even as individual states also seek to promote the interests of their national capitalist classes. The state mediates between the interests of individual capitalists, whether among distinct industries (e.g. between the interests of fossil fuel and renewable energy producers); those of competing producers (e.g. between different oil companies competing for access to a given reserve); or across temporal imperatives of capital accumulation (e.g. between the immediate profitability of extracting oil as quickly as possible and the long-term interest in conserving oil for future use). The state may also act to resolve capitalist crises—for example, by stepping in to provide liquidity amidst a financial crisis. Finally, states mediate between the interests of capital and those of the general population by developing a social and ideological consensus which affirms its own legitimacy.

State theories nevertheless differ in their accounts of how precisely the state relates to capital. What is most significant for my own analysis is how different theorists understand the extent of political agency within the capitalist state and the degree to which it might be possible to use the state *against* capital, as outlined in Raju Das' (1996) distinction between structuralist and class struggle analyses.

Structuralist accounts, in Das' reading, see the state as strongly constrained by its role in capitalist society. The state is constituted by class society and capital accumulation such that it will not, and in some accounts *cannot*, act in ways that are counterposed to the general interest of capital or oriented towards non-capitalist ends. This view is expressed most forcefully in the state derivationist and related social form traditions of Marxist thought, wherein the economic and the political constitute a 'separation in unity'—discrete elements of capitalist society which nevertheless develop out of the same underlying social relations. Here, the state form is the political expression of capitalism's social relations, and inevitably reproduces those relations and their contradictions. It cannot simply be redeployed for other purposes, let alone serve as a vehicle for the transition to a new social order (Altvater 1973; Clarke 1991; Holloway and Picciotto 1978; c.f. Marx 1973). But other approaches also suggest similar, if less foundational, constraints on the capitalist state. Poulantzas' (1973) more structuralist early texts, for example, emphasize the political role of the state in mediating between different fractions of the capitalist class, as well as between the capitalist and working classes. While Poulantzas emphasizes the state's 'relative autonomy' from capital, this autonomy is not an indication of the state's ability to act independently. Rather, the state's autonomy is functional for capital: it allows for greater flexibility in responding to capital's needs and resolving disputes. Other theorists, like Claus Offe (1984), emphasize the state's economic dependence on capital: states depend on private investment and growth to maintain employment, generate tax revenue, and ensure political stability. Even in the strongest accounts, however, although the state *seeks* to act in the interests of capital, it may not succeed, and cannot resolve capitalism's contradictions altogether. For example, the state may attempt to stimulate the national economy but fail due to underlying conditions, as in the recent experience of lagging capital investment despite low interest rates. Similarly, the state may attempt to act in the long-term interests of capital in general by reducing carbon emissions, but fail to discipline carbon-intensive fractions of capital. These failures, however, do not mean that the state can be intentionally turned against capital or made to serve non-capitalist ends.

Class struggle accounts, meanwhile, share many key elements with the structuralist account: the state still carries out various functions in the interest of capital; it is still constrained by capitalism as a system; and efforts to transform it still face structural limitations. Yet in this view, the structure of the state is also affected by class struggle as it plays out in contingent historical moments. As a result, the state, or elements of it, may act in ways that do not directly serve the interests either of particular fractions of capital or capital in general. This struggle may play out at the level of policies which shift the balance of power between classes—a full employment policy, for example, would bolster workers' position against capital (cf. Kalecki 1944). In some cases, class struggle may even challenge the more basic separation of the political from the economic, as when tenants fight against eviction laws which back landlords' economic power with the police power of the state (Clarke 1991; Das 1996; cf. Wood 1981).

The class struggle account encompasses a wide range of thinkers and traditions, including the later Poulantzas' (1978) treatment (in turn drawing on Gramsci) of the state as a 'condensation' of class forces and corresponding call for the 'transformation' of the state through democratic struggle; Ralph Miliband's (1977; 2015) emphasis on the potential for structural reforms brought about by both internal and external pressure on the state; and Bob Jessop's (2007) 'strategic-relational' approach, among others. Notably, what Das categorizes as class struggle accounts continue to maintain that the state is organized in the interests of capital, dependent on capital accumulation for revenue, and perhaps even generally 'captured' by the ruling class. They do not suggest that instances where the state acts to advance working class or other non-capitalist interests *necessarily* constitute a blow to capitalism's viability. They do, however, hold that there is at least a possibility that the state will act in ways that are not directly oriented towards the reproduction of capital, in either the short or long term.

While the class struggle and structuralist positions are counterposed in Das' typology, there are also points of convergence: class struggle always takes place within structural constraints, while structuralists acknowledge that formal tendencies are always expressed in concrete historical moments, and in relation to specific political conditions. We might consider, then, not only the distinctions which delineate these positions, but the gradient between them: at what point does class struggle run up against the limits of the capitalist state? Conversely, how might class struggle exacerbate or exploit the contradictions of capitalism acknowledged in the structuralist account? Ideas like the 'non-reformist reform', as outlined by André Gorz (1967) and more recently taken up by thinkers like Amna Akbar (2020) and Ruth Wilson Gilmore (2007; 2022), can be read as efforts to bridge this gap, by tackling structural problems through partial gains and ruptures which build on one another (see also Battistoni and Mann 2021; Rooksby 2018).

3   State, Nature, Capital

With the parameters of these two debates in mind, the three key terms of this paper—capital, state, nature—can be brought together. To frame this discussion, I return to O'Connor, who most explicitly develops an account of all three. Recall that for Polanyi, 'market society' has to be restrained from its self-destructive tendency to exhaust its own bases by an external force, which Polanyi figures as 'society': in the famous 'double movement', society pushes back against the market, re-embedding it in a social order and subjugating it to democratic control. For Polanyi, society and the state appear nearly synonymous: the double movement is instantiated in legislation protecting workers, for example. Here, too, O'Connor updates Polanyi: he agrees that the state may act at the behest of society (here, labour and social movements) to stave off the second contradiction of capitalism by protecting the conditions of production from capitalism itself, but also develops the analysis of the state's role more explicitly. Because the conditions of production are not produced by capitalist means, he argues, capital cannot rely on the market to provide them. The state therefore manages capitalism's access to the conditions of production, and in some instances produces the conditions of production directly. For example, the state regulates capital's access to new sources of 'raw materials' through the allocation of mining permits, and 'produces' labour-power by providing public education in order to train future workers, public transportation for commuters, and so on. If, on the one hand, the state provides things that capital needs but does not produce, on the other it also deals with things capital produces but does not need: what O'Connor (2002, 175) describes as the 'unmarketable *social* costs and, more generally, unwanted *social* consequences' resulting from capitalist production, including the likes of pollution and traffic congestion. In O'Connor's view, then, 'the state places itself between capital and nature or mediates capital and nature, with the immediate result that the conditions of capitalist production are politicized...every state agency and political party agenda may be regarded as a kind of interface between capital and nature' (O'Connor 1988, 24). Capital's relationship to nature, then, is always mediated by political relationships rather than exclusively economic ones.

While for O'Connor this means that the state plays a role in reorganizing capital in the face of ecologically spurred crises, I argue that his account of the state's mediating role between capital and nature is compatible with other, non-Polanyian readings of capitalism. That is, the question of *how* the state mediates between capital and nature will vary depending on one's view of (a) capital's relationship to nature; and (b) capital's relationship to the state. To see how, we can combine these two axes of debate, very roughly, into four main configurations, as mapped in the chart below.

		Capital-nature relationship	
		Capital is socially and ecologically destructive but not self-destructive (Burkett, Foster)	*Capital is self-destructive (O'Connor, Moore, Fraser)*
State-capital relationship	*Class struggle (late Poulantzas, Miliband, Jessop)*	State action to prevent or address ecological crises will often cut against the interests of capital, and may be possible depending on the balance of class forces and struggle	State action to prevent or address ecological crises 'saves capitalism from itself' but may also have elements which oppose, or do not directly serve, capital's interests, the extent of which depends on the balance of class forces and struggle
	Structural (early Poulantzas, state derivationists)	State action to prevent or address ecological crises will likely cut against the interests of capital, and will not occur	State action to prevent or address ecological crises 'saves capitalism from itself' by preserving the conditions of production, but does little to protect means of life which do not serve capital; states will undertake only the former

The left-hand column reflects the Foster and Burkett position on capital and nature, wherein capital destroys nature but not itself. While Foster and Burkett do not explicitly analyse the state, from their account we can surmise that state intervention to prevent biodiversity collapse, stabilize atmospheric conditions, etc., would *not* constitute an instance of the state stepping in to protect capitalism from itself or produce capitalism's required 'conditions of production', since capital does not actually need many aspects of nonhuman nature and does not suffer serious consequences from its destruction. Rather, state action to prevent ecological and social crises would constitute action *against* capital—a limitation on its destructive tendencies undertaken not in its own interests, whether short- or long-term, but in the interests of human and nonhuman life.

On strictly structural views, as reflected in the bottom left-hand quadrant, we can surmise that the state will not act in order to protect ecosystemic nature and non-productive human life from climate catastrophe. If the state acts in service of capital accumulation, and ecological destruction does not threaten capital accumulation, the state will not act to prevent or reduce ecological destruction, whether in the form of a carbon tax (in which it is the action of the state itself which causes the 'second contradiction' of rising ecological costs) or a Green New Deal which undertakes costly public investments that are not oriented primarily towards accumulation. Action to prevent ecological destruction of the means of life, then, must escape both capital *and* state by developing entirely autonomous forms of provision or through successful revolution on a global scale (Bernes and Clover 2019; Mann and Wainwright 2018).

Taking the class struggle view of the state, however, as represented in the top left quadrant, it is at least possible to imagine a state acting to preserve human and nonhuman 'means of life' even where they are not also conditions of production. While state action to ward off ecological crisis cannot be understood as staving off a crisis of capitalism, the state might act in non-capitalist ways, and even against the interests of capital, in service of ecological and social wellbeing. The state might, for example, ban harmful products like chlorofluorocarbons, protect old-growth forests from conversion into palm oil plantations, increase corporate taxes to build public transit and social housing, or even nationalize companies responsible for certain ecologically harmful activities and set them on a path of managed decline. These measures may be unlikely, of course; the extent to which the state acts to constrain capital will depend on whether the movements and forces arrayed against (or, at least, existing in tension with) the interests of capital—including not only 'traditional' labour movements and parties, but also 'environmental' and Indigenous movements seeking to defend land from extraction or social movements seeking an expansion of public goods like housing and transit—are able to adequately challenge capital (cf. Cohen 2017; Estes 2018; Huber 2022; Malm 2020; Riofrancos 2020). Moreover, threats to the 'means of life' posed by ecological crises are not universally distributed: the state may act to protect some threatened communities while leaving others vulnerable, enacting what some have called 'eco-apartheid' or 'climate barbarism' (Blumenfeld 2022; Cohen 2019; Pulido

2017). Nor can the unity of the social forces opposed to capital be assumed: to the contrary, different elements of these forces are likely to come into conflict, as in tensions between sectors of the labour movement and environmental and Indigenous movements. In short, this position does *not* suggest that the state will automatically or universally act to protect the means of ecological and social reproduction from destruction by capitalism.

The right-hand column, by contrast, reflects O'Connor's position on nature and capital, wherein ecological crises are also crises for capitalism. If this is the case, we would interpret state action to prevent or address ecological crises as action intended to 'save capitalism from itself'—to limit its self-destructive tendencies in the service of continued accumulation.

Here, given the structural view of the state, as expressed in the bottom right quadrant, we would expect that the state *will* act to preserve the 'conditions of production' from capitalism's self-destructive tendencies, so that capital accumulation can continue. Yet it will likely do so in limited ways, acting to protect the conditions of production for major industries while neglecting socioecological conditions which constitute merely 'means of life'—whether species deemed to be superfluous, human 'surplus populations', or parts of the planet where the 'climate risk' to investment is relatively insignificant. The state might, for example, undertake carbon removal projects in order to permit fossil fuel companies to continue to extract and sell hydrocarbons, invest in the development of new drought-resistant crops with qualities which prevent their use in subsistence farming, or invest in seawalls and levees to protect economically significant industries from flooding, while simultaneously doing little to protect working class and racialized communities (e.g. New Orleans prior to Hurricane Katrina). These efforts to preserve the conditions of production—like other state interventions undertaken in the interests of capital—may not succeed, however, in particular, the combination of global capitalism and planetary biospheric processes is likely to limit the ability of individual states to control ecological conditions of production.

On the class struggle view, by contrast, as reflected in the top right quadrant, we would still expect the state to act primarily in response to threats to the conditions of production. But states may also act in ways that do not *only* serve the interests of capital: they might protect people from climate disasters or preserve unprofitable forms of nonhuman life, potentially even in ways that cut against capital's interests. Here, too, the balance of social forces and conditions of class struggle would shape the contours of state action and the degree to which it protects the means of life, and for whom.

These four possibilities are clearly stylized ideal-types operating at a level of abstraction which cannot capture many of the specific factors at play. The very idea of 'ecological crisis', for example, names a wide range of possible phenomena, materializing at geographical and temporal scales which do not always align with political borders or timeframes (Nixon 2011; Eckersley 2004). The build-up of carbon molecules in the atmosphere, for example, takes place over a period of decades, producing warmer temperatures only gradually; in turn, the effects of temperature change on different biospheric and ecological processes unfold at different speeds: an increase in the number and severity of droughts will happen more immediately than sea level rise. Political and social processes, meanwhile, proceed at their own pace. On the one hand, many electoral processes, like short terms of office, are oriented towards near-term outcomes rather than the longer-term processes which characterize climate change; on the other, the urgency of reducing carbon emissions often comes into conflict with the slow processes of building social movements or undertaking legislative action. Ecological crises, moreover, tend to be 'displaced' rather than solved: measures that states undertake to address one kind of ecological problem frequently generate others (Dryzek 1987). For example, efforts to replace fossil fuels with forms of renewable energy may diminish the threat of climate change while increasing local ecosystemic damage, water pollution, and other harms stemming from the extraction of mineral resources necessary for renewable technologies (Arboleda 2020; Riofrancos 2019).

Climate change also makes particularly clear that ecological crises may manifest most severely in places far removed from either the production or consumption processes which drive them. This adds another wrinkle to the challenges of a now truly global capitalism in which different states occupy different positions in the world system and have disparate capacities to respond to crises of capitalism. The United States, as home of the global reserve currency, can respond to financial crises in ways that Greece cannot, which in turn increases its ability to undertake costly projects aimed at mitigating and adapting to climate change or capitalizing on 'green investment' opportunities (Arboleda 2020; Battistoni 2023; Milanovic 2019; Tooze 2018). Many of the challenges posed by a global-planetary system reflect more complex versions of those identified above. For example, the possibility of implementing international trade deals which integrate and prioritize climate and environmental protection rather than shunting such protections onto the sidetrack of non-binding UN conventions depends at least in part on whether the interests of national capitals can be challenged (cf. Aronoff et al. 2019). Similarly, the question of whether states will share useful technologies, from electric batteries to carbon capture and storage, depends in large part on whether states choose to protect the intellectual property rights held by corporations or override them in the interests of global health and sustainability. The specifically global and international dimensions of these problems therefore demand greater engagement with theories of international law and imperialism.[3] Indeed, the Marxist tradition's long-standing attention to the international dimensions of political economy makes it a particularly useful perspective from which to analyse climate change and other global environmental problems (Ince 2018; Anievas and Nişancıoğlu 2015; Moore 2015; Panitch and Gindin 2013; Wallerstein 1974; Sweezy and Magdoff 1973).

Simplified though this framework may be, it nevertheless suggests a rough guide for thinking through the possibilities before us. Notably, the configuration in the bottom left is the only one which predicts that the state not only will not, but *cannot* act to effectively stave off ecological catastrophes. Conversely, we might note that there is also only one configuration in which state action to address ecological crises constitutes a challenge to capitalism which might lay the groundwork for a more substantial ecosocialist programme. The point is not that each quadrant is equally plausible, of course—simply that positions taken in political debates about climate policy and strategy reflect a more complex set of ideas than are usually articulated. In my view, the fact that certain political projects do not in themselves constitute a break with capitalism is not necessarily an argument against them: given the exceptionally short time horizon of impending climate catastrophe, non-linear nature of the climate system, and disjuncture between present action and future effects, simply buying time, even in ways that do not more substantially challenge

---

[3] Conversely, some eco-Marxist work contains a theory of imperialism, most notably Jason Moore's (2015) 'world-ecology' and John Bellamy Foster and Brett Clark's (2004) critique of 'ecological imperialism'. However, in these works the state is relatively undertheorized.

capital, is an essential element of anti-capitalist climate politics (Battistoni 2018). But assessments of the prospects even for buying time will also depend on one's view of the capital–state–nature relationship.

I suggest two particularly pressing areas for future research. First, it is crucial to consider in greater depth the various dimensions of class struggles with respect to 'environmental' issues. On the one hand, this means attending fractions within the capitalist class augured by the rise of 'green capital', amidst a surge of state-subsidized investments in renewable energy and other 'green technologies,' paired with growing pressure to decrease state support for fossil capital (cf. Hook and Lee 2021; Hook and Sanderson 2021; Meaney 2022; Sanderson 2021). On the other, it requires attention to the dynamics of social forces which might generate struggle within and around the state today, whether in making demands for social provision or challenging state repression. In particular, this entails more detailed analysis of how social forces frequently described in terms of 'new social movements' relate to more traditional labour and working class movements; how the effects of ecological crises are felt across class and how those effects might shape class consciousness; what an 'ecological class struggle' might consist of; what the bases of social power for such movements might be; and what kinds of strategies and organizational forms are appropriate to these particular struggles, as well as what kinds of repressive force such movements might be expected to confront (cf. Huber 2022; Mann and Wainwright 2018; Jessop 2017; Pulido et al. 2016).

Second, the distinctive spatial and temporal dynamics of contemporary ecological crises, as sketched above, demand more analysis of the nationally bounded state in relation to *both* global capitalism *and* planetary ecological conditions—two analytic frameworks which, like the other debates examined here, have largely developed in parallel. This, I suggest, entails analyses corresponding to the multiple scales of both ecological phenomena and inter-state relationships: analysis of domestic struggles over climate policy, extraction, etc., within specific nation-states set in the context of the world system; of global and multinational institutions like the UN and WTO; of relations between nation-states, including ongoing and novel forms of imperialism; and of the internationalist dimensions of ecological organizing and class struggle. Indeed, the high abstraction typical of much state theory to date, often resting on an implicit model of North American and European capitalist democracies, must be supplemented by more empirically informed studies of differently positioned states, and perhaps a turn to state *theories*.

In closing, I want to simply reiterate the importance of studying state, capital, and nature together. The state is an often-overlooked but essential mediating force between the 'logic of capital' and concretely existing nature, rendering political questions crucial to the future of capitalism in the age of climate change. Conversely, both capital and nature are often overlooked in liberal political theories of states and their actions, while Marxist theories of both state and capital typically neglect nonhuman nature. Bringing these terms together is only a starting point—but it is a crucial one for understanding both capitalism and politics in the twenty-first century.

REFERENCES

Akbar, Amna. 2020. 'Demands for a Democratic Political Economy.' *Harvard Law Review Forum* 134: 90–118.

Altvater, Elmar. 1973. 'Some Problems of State Interventionism.' *Kapitalistate*, 1: 96–108; 2: 76–83.

Anievas, Alexander, and Kerem Nişancıoğlu. 2015. *How the West Came to Rule: The Geopolitical Origins of Capitalism*. London: Pluto Press.

Arboleda, Martin. 2020. *Planetary Mine: Territories of Extraction Under Late Capitalism*. New York: Verso.

Aronoff, Kate, Alyssa Battistoni, Daniel Cohen, and Thea Riofrancos. 2019. *A Planet to Win: Why We Need a Green New Deal*. New York: Verso.

Battistoni, Alyssa. 2018. 'States of Emergency.' *The Nation*, June 21, 2018. https://www.thenation.com/article/archive/political-theory-for-an-age-of-climate-change/.

Battistoni, Alyssa and Geoff Mann. 'Was Donald Trump's "War on Coal" Real, or Just the Market at Work?' *The New Statesman*, November 22, 2021. https://www.newstatesman.com/ideas/2021/11/what-kind-of-crisis-is-the-climate-crisis.

Battistoni, Alyssa. 2023. 'Picking Winners.' In *Who Will Build the Ark? Debates on Climate Strategy from New Left Review*, edited by Benjamin Kunkel and Lola Seaton, 218–224. Verso.

Benton, Ted, ed. 1996. *The Greening of Marxism*. New York: Guilford Press.

Benanav, Aaron. 2020. *Automation and the Future of Work*. New York: Verso.

Bernes, Jasper and Joshua Clover. 2014. 'The Ends of the State.' *Viewpoint*, October 12, 2014. https://viewpointmag.com/2014/10/12/the-ends-of-the-state/.

Bernes, Jasper. 2019. 'Between the Devil and the Green New Deal.' *Commune*, April 25, 2019. https://communemag.com/between-the-devil-and-the-green-new-deal/.

Blumenfeld, Jacob. 2022. 'Climate Barbarism: Adapting to a Wrong World.' *Constellations*, Early View.

Brown, Wendy. 1995. *States of Injury: Power and Freedom in Late Modernity*. Princeton: Princeton University Press.

Brenner, Robert. 1998. *The Economics of Global Turbulence: The Advanced Capitalist Economies from Long Boom to Long Downturn, 1945–2005*. New York: Verso.

Burkett, Paul. 1999. *Marx and Nature: A Red and Green Perspective*. Chicago: Haymarket.

Clarke, Simon, ed. 1991. *The State Debate*. London: Palgrave Macmillan.

Clover, Joshua. 2019. 'The Two Greens, Part II.' *Popula*, February 20, 2019. https://popula.com/2019/02/20/the-two-greens-part-2/.

Cohen, Daniel. 2017. 'The Other Low-Carbon Protagonists: Poor People's Movements and Climate Politics in São Paulo.' In *The City is the Factory: Social Movements in the Age of Neoliberal Urbanism*, edited by Miriam Greenberg and Penny Luce, 140–57. Ithaca: Cornell University Press.

Cohen, Daniel Aldana. 2019. 'Eco-Apartheid is Real.' *The Nation*, July 26 2019. https://www.thenation.com/article/archive/green-new-deal-housing-climate-change/.

Das, Raju. 1996. 'State Theories: A Critical Analysis.' *Science and Society* 60: 27–57.

Davis, Mike. 2005. *The Monster at Our Door: The Global Threat of Avian Flu*. New York: The New Press.

Dempsey, Jessica. 2014. *Enterprising Nature: Economics, Markets, and Finance*. Malden, MA: Wiley Blackwell.

Dryzek, John. 1987. *Rational Ecology: Environment and Political Economy*. New York: Basil Blackwell.

Eckersley, Robyn. 2004. *The Green State: Rethinking Democracy and Sovereignty*. Cambridge, MA: MIT Press.

Estes, Nick. 2018. *Our History is the Future: Standing Rock Versus the Dakota Access Pipeline and the Long History of Indigenous Resistance*. New York: Verso.

Foster, John Bellamy. 2000. *Marx's Ecology: Materialism and Nature*. New York: Monthly Review Press.

Foster, John Bellamy and Brett Clark. 2004. 'Ecological Imperialism: The Curse of Capitalism.' *Socialist Register* 40: 186–201.

Foster, John Bellamy, and Paul Burkett. 2016. *Marx and the Earth: An Anti-Critique*. Chicago: Haymarket.

Fraser, Nancy. 2014. 'Can Society Be Commodities All the Way Down? Post-Polanyian Reflections on Capitalist Crisis.' *Economy and Society* 43 (4): 541–58.

Fraser, Nancy. 2021. 'Climates of Capital.' *New Left Review* 127: 94–127.

Gabor, Daniela. 2023. "The (European) Derisking State." SocArXiv. May 17. https://doi.org/10.31235/osf.io/hpbj2.

Gilmore, Ruth Wilson. 2007. *The Golden Gulag: Prisons, Supplies, Crisis, and Opposition in Globalizing California*. Berkeley: University of California Press.

Gilmore, Ruth Wilson. 2022. *Abolition Geography: Essays towards Liberation*. New York: Verso.

Gorz, André. 1967. *Strategy for Labour: A Radical Proposal*. Translated by Martin A. Nicolaus and Victoria Ortiz. Boston: Beacon Press.

Holloway, John, and Sol Picciotto. 1978. *State and Capital: A Marxist Debate*. London: Edward Arnold.

Hook, Leslie and Henry Sanderson. 2021. 'How the Race for Renewable Energy is Reshaping Global Politics.' *The Financial Times*, February 4, 2021. https://www.ft.com/content/a37d0ddf-8fb1-4b47-9fba-7ebde29fc510.

Hook, Leslie and Dave Lee. 2021. 'How Tech went Big on Green Energy.' *The Financial Times*, February 10, 2021. https://www.ft.com/content/0c6 9d4a4-2626-418d-813c-7337b8d5110d.

Huber, Matthew. 2022. *Climate Change as Class War: Building Socialism on a Warming Planet*. New York: Verso.

Hunter, Rob. 2021. 'Capitalism, Depoliticization, and Climate Politics.' *Science & Society* 85 (2): 184–91.

Ince, Onur. 2018. *Colonial Capitalism and the Dilemmas of Liberalism*. Oxford: Oxford University Press.

Jessop, Bob. 1990. *The Future of the Capitalist State*. Cambridge: Polity.

———. 2007. *State Power: A Strategic-Relational Approach*. Cambridge: Polity.

———. 2017. 'Nicos Poulantzas on Political Economy, Political Ecology, and Democratic Socialism.' *Journal of Political Ecology* 24 (1): 186–199.

Kalecki, Michal. 1944. 'Political Aspects of Full Employment.' *Political Quarterly* 14 (4): 322–30.

Khachaturian, Rafael. 2019. 'Bringing What State Back In? Neo-Marxism and the Origin of the Committee on States and Social Structures.' *Political Research Quarterly* 72 (3): 714–26.

Klein, Naomi. 2019. *On Fire: The Burning Case for the Green New Deal*. New York: Simon & Schuster.

Malm, Andreas. 2017. *The Progress of This Storm: Nature and Society in a Warming World*. New York: Verso.

Malm, Andreas. 2020. *Corona, Climate, Chronic Emergency: War Communism in the Twenty-First Century*. New York: Verso.

Mann, Geoff, and Joel Wainwright. 2018. *Climate Leviathan: A Political Theory of Our Planetary Future*. New York: Verso.

Meaney, Thomas. 2022. 'Fortunes of the Green New Deal.' *New Left Review* 138: 79–102.

Marx, Karl. 1973. *Grundrisse: Foundations of the Critique of Political Economy*. Translated by Martin Nicolaus. New York: Pelican.

Milanovic, Branko. 2019. *Capitalism, Alone: The Future of the System That Rules the World*. Cambridge: Harvard University Press.

Miliband, Ralph. 1977. *Marxism and Politics*. London: Merlin Press.

———. 2015. *Class War Conservatism: And Other Essays*. New York: Verso.

Moore, Jason. 2010a. 'Amsterdam is Standing on Norway Part I: The Alchemy of Capital, Empire and Nature in the Diaspora of Silver, 1545–1648.' *Journal of Agrarian Change* 10 (1): 33–68.

———. 2010b. 'Amsterdam is Standing on Norway Part II: The Global North Atlantic in the Ecological Revolution of the Long Seventeenth Century.' *Journal of Agrarian Change* 10 (2): 188–227.

———. 2015. *Capitalism in the Web of Life: Ecology and the Accumulation of Capital*. New York: Verso.

Nixon, Rob. 2011. *Slow Violence and the Environmentalism of the Poor*. Cambridge, MA: Harvard University Press.

Nozick, Robert. 1974. *Anarchy, State, and Utopia*. New York: Basic Books.

O'Connor, James. 1988. 'Capitalism, Nature, Socialism: A Theoretical Introduction.' *Capitalism, Nature, Socialism* 1 (1): 11–38.

———. 1998. *Natural Causes: Essays in Ecological Marxism*. New York: Guilford Press.

———. 2002. *The Fiscal Crisis of the State*. London: Transaction Publishers.

Offe, Claus. 1984. *Contradictions of the Welfare State*. Edited by John Keane. Cambridge, MA: MIT Press.

Panitch, Leo, and Sam Gindin. 2013. *The Making of Global Capitalism: The Political Economy of American Empire*. London: Verso.

Pettit, Phillip. 2012. *On the People's Terms*. Cambridge: Cambridge University Press.

Polanyi, Karl. 2001. *The Great Transformation: The Political and Economic Origins of Our Time*, 2nd ed. Boston: Beacon Press.

Poulantzas, Nicos. 1973. *Political Power and Social Classes*. Translated by Timothy O'Hagan. London: New Left Books.

———. 1978. *State, Power, Socialism*. Translated by Patrick Camiller. London: New Left Books.

Pulido, Laura. 2017. 'Geographies of Race and Ethnicity II: Environmental Racism, Racial Capitalism and State-Sanctioned Violence.' *Progress in Human Geography* 41 (4): 524–33.

Pulido, Laura, Ellen Kohn, and Nicole-Marie. Cotton. 2016. 'State Regulation and Environmental Justice: The Need for Strategy Reassessment.' *Capitalism Nature Socialism* 27 (2): 12–31.

Riofrancos, Thea. 2019. 'Plan, Mood, Battlefield: Reflections on the Green New Deal.' *Viewpoint,* May 16, 2019. https://viewpointmag.com/2019/05/16/plan-mood-battlefield-reflections-on-the-green-new-deal/.

———. 2020. *Resource Radicals: From Petro-Nationalism to Post-Extractivism in Ecuador.* Durham: Duke University Press.

Rooksby, Ed. 2018. "'Structural Reforms' and the Problem of Socialist Strategy Today." *Critique: Journal of Socialist Theory* 46(1): 27–48.

Saito, Kohei. 2016. *Karl Marx's Ecosocialism: Capital, Nature, and the Unfinished Critique of Political Economy,* 2016. New York: Monthly Review Press.

Salleh, Ariel. 1998. *Ecofeminism as Politics: Nature, Marx, and the Postmodern.* London: Zed Books.

Sanderson, Henry. 2021. 'Investors See "Gold Rush on Steroids" for Green Battery Metals.' *Financial Times,* March 12, 2021. https://www.ft.com/content/fb1fa29b-7f2b-448b-ba47-05f16eccad97.

Scott, James C. 1998. *Seeing Like a State: How Certain Schemes to Improve the Human Condition Have Failed.* New Haven: Yale University Press.

Simpson, Audra. 2014. *Mohawk Interruptus: Political Life Across the Borders of Settler States.* Durham: Duke University Press.

Smith, Tony. 2017. *Beyond Liberal Egalitarianism: Marx and Normative Social Theory in the Twenty-First Century.* Chicago: Haymarket.

Summers, Lawrence H. 2020. 'Accepting the Reality of Secular Stagnation.' *Finance and Development* 57(1): 17–20.

Sweezy, Paul M. and Harry Magdoff. 1973. *The End of Prosperity (Economic History as it Happened, Vol II).* New York: Monthly Review Press.

Tooze, Adam. 2018. *Crashed: How a Decade of Financial Crises Changed the World.* New York: Viking.

Wallace, Rob. 2016. *Big Farms Make Big Flu: Dispatches on Influenza, Agribusiness, and the Nature of Science.* New York: Monthly Review Press.

Wallerstein, Immanuel. 1974. *The Modern World-System: Capitalist Agriculture and the Origins of the European World-Economy in the Sixteenth Century.* New York: Academic Press.

Wood, Ellen. 1981. 'The Separation of the Economic and the Political in Capitalism.' *New Left Review* I (127): 66–95.

'Bursting Asunder the Integument': Democracy, Digitalization, and the State

Dimitrios Kivotidis

1   INTRODUCTION

Re-opening the state debate is a contradictory task which involves developing revolutionary theory in a historical context of counter-revolution. Yet that contradiction underlines the urgency of the task. This chapter will focus on the role of the state in the process of reproduction of capitalism, as mediated by technological development, in particular by digital platforms. To begin with, I accept that the state is the political form which ensures the cohesion, organization, integration, and reproduction of the capitalist economy, whose purpose is to accumulate extracted surplus value (Bonefeld 2014, 168, 182). The capitalist state is thus conceived 'not as a neutral instrument but as a form-determined set of institutions within the world market' which 'by virtue of their structural separation

---

A more extensive discussion from a slightly different angle of the issues covered in this chapter can be found in my monograph *The Dialectics of Democracy: Towards a Socialist Constitutionalism* (forthcoming by Routledge).

D. Kivotidis (✉)
Constitutional Law, Goldsmiths, University of London, London, UK
e-mail: D.Kivotidis@gold.ac.uk

© The Author(s), under exclusive license to Springer Nature Switzerland AG 2023
R. Hunter et al. (eds.), *Marxism and the Capitalist State*, Political Philosophy and Public Purpose, https://doi.org/10.1007/978-3-031-36167-8_3

from "the economy" under capitalism, are integral to the crisis-ridden process of capital accumulation' (O'Kane 2019).[1]

In the following sections I intend to examine how digitalization factors in this process—in particular, how digital platforms mediate the masses' political participation in bourgeois institutions. The term 'digital platforms' refers to social network sites, owned by powerful monopolies, which are characterized by the centrality of so-called user-generated content (Gerbaudo 2014, 73; Kaplan and Haenlein 2010, 61). Notwithstanding the reasons for the development of these platforms, the reality is that they have come, in a short period of time, to mediate many aspects of social interaction. Personal and commercial relations, information, as well as employment and political relations, are nowadays largely mediated through social media. My analysis focuses on the effect of social media on political participation and the operation of democratic processes and institutions.

I argue that digitalization exacerbates the reactionary characteristics of the bourgeois state, from repression and surveillance techniques to influencing public opinion and sustaining the false consciousness of subordinate strata. My analysis will focus on the interrelation between the bourgeois democratic state, technological development, and the reproduction of capitalism. On a more abstract level, my analysis aims to contribute to the understanding of the dialectical relationship between the class state, productive forces, and relations of production. Relations of production determine the purpose towards which productive forces are deployed (for profit or towards satisfaction of social needs), and the state plays a crucial mediating role in ensuring the reproduction of these relations. Unless the capitalist state is 'smashed', the emancipatory potential of digital platforms cannot be actualized. Additionally, the development of productive forces in digital capitalism allows us to explore new solutions to problems that earlier attempts at building socialism encountered, such

---

[1] According to Marxist theories of the state, the crisis-ridden pattern of capital accumulation necessitates a constant reorganization of social relations of production and exchange. This process, in its turn, gives rise to new functions and forms of the state. According to Ben Fine and Laurence Harris, 'the capitalist state's economic intervention is fundamentally determined by capital's economic requirements' (Fine and Harris 1976, 99). According to Joachim Hirsch, the tendency for the rate of profit to fall is the determining historical law, 'in responding to which the state takes on new functions, and develops appropriate forms through which to carry out those functions' (Clarke 1991, 14).

as economic management and the antithesis between council democracy and central planning.

On this basis, the chapter is structured as follows. The first section examines the process of digitalization in the context of imperialism, understood as the highest, monopoly stage of capitalism. It focuses on the characteristics of capitalist production at this stage to argue that digital capitalism is not an aberration or distortion of traditional capitalism but a direct result of its contradictions. It also focuses on the role of the capitalist state in this historical period. The next section analyses how digital platforms contribute to the essential function of the capitalist state, i.e. the reproduction of capitalism, by focusing on their effect on social consciousness. These platforms, based as they are on a continuous flow of unrelated information, are doomed in contemporary capitalist societies to produce and reproduce a fragmented worldview and false consciousness which precludes a conscious critique of capitalism and pursuit of a radical alternative. The final section concludes with the argument that the adverse effects of digital capitalism on social consciousness and political participation cannot be ameliorated within the confines of bourgeois institutions through regulation and 'radical reforms'. Only a different kind of state, aimed at superseding the contradictions of capitalism, can actualize the potential of digital platforms for democratic participation and self-governance, addressing problems that earlier historical attempts at building socialism were faced with.

2   Digitalization, Imperialism, and the Capitalist State

Imperialism, the monopoly stage of capitalism, is characterized by the heightening of the totality of capitalist contradictions, central among which is the contradiction between capital and labour. This historical period, which, according to Lenin, began in the late nineteenth century and continues until today, has so far given rise to devastating imperialist wars, severe economic crises, intensified exploitation globally, as well as extreme inequality on a national and international level (Lenin 1976). Recent contributions to the Marxist theory of imperialism reveal the thirst for profit and intensified exploitation as the main characteristic of contemporary imperialism (Callinicos 2009; Wood 2005; Harvey 2003; Foster 2006; Cox 2013; Higginbottom 2018).

In the stage of imperialism, the fundamental changes take place in the *sphere of production*. The real subsumption of labour to capital deepens and the extraction of relative surplus value assumes greater significance. As a result, the balance between absolute and relative surplus value tends to change in favour of the latter. This results in the displacement of living labour (i.e. workers) by machines and the appearance of more complex forms of surveillance and control of labour in the production process (from the 'director' to 'departments of Human Resources' and all the way to 'digital surveillance'). The imperialist stage is the age of Taylorism and Fordism but also the stage of post-Fordism and digital capitalism. Furthermore, the increasing concentration of capital is manifested in the growing role of the financial system and the dominance of the joint-stock company form in the most dynamic parts of capitalist production. What is more, the international system acquires an imperialist character, evidenced in the intensification of politico-economic competition and the upgraded role of money-lending capital, which is institutionalized on an international level.

On a high level of abstraction, it may be argued that the role of the tendency of the rate of profit to fall acquires extreme significance in this stage. This law was discovered by Karl Marx as a manifestation of the contradiction between productive forces and capitalist relations of production.[2] A compelling argument has been made that recurring and regular economic crises and slumps in output, investment, and employment in modern economies are due to the falling profitability of capital (Carchedi and Roberts 2018). It has been argued that the exponential growth of the banking and finance sector should be regarded as a counter-tendency to this law, because this sector enables industrial firms to increase the speed of turnover of their capital, therefore crucially affecting their profitability (Passarella and Baron 2015). One could go even further and advance the hypothesis that the operation of this law is key to explaining most contemporary developments of the capitalist mode of production

---

[2] According to this law, the value of the means of production (machinery, offices and other equipment) will, over time, rise relative to the value of labour power (the cost of employing a labour force). However, since value (and profit) is only created by labour power, then the value produced by labour power will, over time, decline relative to the cost of investing in means of production and labour power. Consequently, the rate of profit will tend to fall; see Roberts and Carchedi (2018).

in its imperialist stage, such as off-shoring, relative de-industrialization, financialization, neoliberalism, as well as digitalization.

Such a hypothesis contradicts analyses such as Shoshanna Zuboff's 'surveillance capitalism'. Zuboff approaches digital capitalism as 'a new economic order' and 'a rogue mutation of capitalism marked by concentrations of wealth, knowledge, and power unprecedented in human history' (2019, v). I argue instead that digital capitalism is the direct result of developing contradictions inherent in the capitalist mode of production.[3] Phenomena like data mining and targeted advertising revolutionize the already-existing processes of the production and realization of surplus value. The radical increase in the velocity of capital's circulation process leads to a radical reduction of turnover time and, thus, operates as a factor that counters the tendency of the rate of profit to fall—the ultimate barrier of the capitalist mode of production.[4]

Furthermore, in the imperialist stage of capitalism, digital platforms contribute greatly to one of the capitalist state's crucial functions: the mediation of the heightened tension between capital and labour. As far as class struggle in the imperialist stage is concerned, the organized working-class movement is a factor that poses a direct threat to the expanded reproduction of capital. The reason is obvious. The working-class struggle for the immediate improvement of working and living conditions translates into the struggle for a limited working-day and a struggle for higher wages. These forms of struggle directly affect the rate of exploitation and thus the ability of capital to extract surplus value from the workers' labour.

---

[3] A growing literature of Marxist approaches to digitalization focuses on the issue of exploitation (Andrejevic 2012, 73). Under this prism, the crucial questions are whether the users of commercial social media are generating value and whether they are exploited (Fuchs and Mosco 2016, 45). According to Christian Fuchs, usage of these platforms is productive labour and platform users create value, because their labour is objectified in the commodities produced by social media corporations (i.e. the portion of a user's screen filled with ad clients' commodity ideologies). This compelling application of the labour theory of value to the analysis of contemporary processes and phenomena offers a more comprehensive account of the processes and phenomena captured by the term 'surveillance capitalism' than the one offered by Zuboff, because it places emphasis on capitalist relations of production and circulation—which Zuboff fails to address—from the standpoint of surplus value realization and profitability. It therefore assesses the growth of social media platforms as a response to capitalist contradictions and not as an aberration of a system that normally corresponds to social needs.

[4] For a more detailed analysis of the role of new media platforms in countering the tendency of the rate of profit to fall, see Kivotidis (2020).

What is more, the class-conscious struggle for socialism, a struggle carried out with firm commitment to social emancipation, requires the supersession of the capitalist mode of production, and poses a direct threat to the very pillars of capitalist production when it assumes a mass character.

Therefore, bourgeois class struggle intensifies, in its political and ideological form, so as to dull the effectiveness of the working-class struggle. The capitalist state plays a crucial role in this process by hindering the development of independent workers' organizations and struggle through a combination of repressive means (such as policies of open hostility and repression against the 'internal enemy', anti-communist legislation attacking the vanguard of the organized workers' movement, as well as a general tendency towards authoritarianism) and consensual means (such as the granting of concessions, the cultivation of a concessionary logic of subordinate classes, the growth of opportunist and reformist currents in the working-class movement, etc.).

In recent years, digital platforms have also assumed a significant role in this process by mediating political participation and ensuring the reproduction of the false consciousness necessary for the reproduction of capitalism. As is generally accepted in Marxist analyses, the reproduction of capitalism depends on the reproduction of labour-power. The latter is not restricted to the reproduction of workers' skills and qualifications through the educational system but extends to their appearing for work every day and not contesting the capitalist relations of production (Althusser 2014, 52). In other words, the rule of a capitalist minority in capitalist society, where the mass of the population is in possession of the political right to vote, relies on the ideological conditioning of subordinate classes before the electoral moment as such.

A false consciousness of social relations and the process of their reproduction is sustained through various means and institutions, but it originates primarily in the relations of production themselves. As Marx showed in *Capital*, the relations of production create and sustain a false perception of the social condition (Marx 1990, 764). The workers' fear and insecurity in the workplace reinforce bourgeois ideology and determine their perception of their social condition (Papadopoulos and Lyddon 2020). Additionally, reference can be made to the capitalist class' control of the means of communication (press, radio, television, new social media) which allows it to promote its worldview. From the initial conditioning by the family and the educational apparatus, to the every-day conditioning by the media apparatus, various and subtle ideological mechanisms operate on many different levels of capitalist society (Althusser 2014). Additionally, the people's trust in bourgeois institutional forms is built and secured through a mixture of concessions, deception, fear, and insecurity.

The bourgeois democratic forms themselves play a significant role in reproducing this false consciousness. This has been referred to as 'the democratic swindle': 'the methods whereby the bourgeoisie utilized (used and abused) democratic forms for the purpose of stabilizing its socio-economic rule'.[5] For instance, the political participation of the masses in bourgeois democratic institutions relies on the assumed existence of a free and general will of the people, whose unmediated expression in elections and plebiscites confirms the democratic character of the bourgeois state. In reality, the idea of the free will of the voters obfuscates the various mechanisms, institutional forms and practices, which ensure the ideological conditioning and sustain the false consciousness of subordinate classes.

The following section examines how digital platforms contribute to the workers' false consciousness by promoting the fragmented and empiricist understanding of reality which precludes any comprehensive critique of the extant social condition. New social media structurally contribute to the translation of economic power into political power in a variety of ways (such as targeted advertising, spread of misinformation, 'echo-chamber function') that will be explored below in more detail. We will see how the structural characteristics of digital platforms promote state ideology, while at the same time favouring populist and reactionary views, in partnership with big capital.

3   DIGITAL PLATFORMS, BOURGEOIS DEMOCRACY, AND FALSE CONSCIOUSNESS

Let us now focus on the effect of digital platforms on the operation of democratic processes and institutions. In recent years, several analyses and evaluations of the role of social media in political processes have emerged.

---

[5] According to Hal Draper, 'the fact that the US had developed the formal structure of the constitutional republic in the most democratic forms meant that its bourgeoisie likewise had to develop to its highest point the art of keeping the expression of popular opinion within channels satisfactory to its class interests' (Draper 1974, 118).

Most positive evaluations tend to focus on social media's potential to enhance the process of democratization, through information dissemination, as well as binding the people through communication—the ancient Greek word for 'binding' is δίδημι, which is the etymological root of the word *demos*. New social media have thus been conceived as new means of communication that may contribute to the realization of a modern version of Athenian democracy. This approach is based on a traditional mode of perceiving new developments in communication media as necessarily positive, invigorating public dialogue and political participation. It has been argued, for instance, that '[t]hese commercially public spaces may not render a public sphere, but they provide spaces where individuals can engage in healthy democratic practices, including keeping a check on politicians, engaging in political satire, and expressing or circulating political opinions' (Papacharissi 2009, 243).

Digital platforms may thus contribute to the process of democratization by reinvigorating the public sphere through the enhancement of dialogue and political engagement. Furthermore, it has been argued that certain characteristics of digital platforms structurally promote political debate and thereby sustain a healthy public sphere. In the case of Facebook, for instance, the absence of time and character limitations arguably has positive effects on the emergence of rational debates (Janssen and Kies 2005). Such approaches stress the potential of new social media to increase the quality of political deliberation and further develop institutional forms of deliberative democracy (Volker 2019).

Parallel to the above, we need to refer to the role of social media in various social movements. In the context of the Arab Spring and the Iran mobilizations of 2009, a discussion about the new media's contribution to the movement for democracy opened with great intensity (Minotakis and Varvaki 2018). Statements like 'the revolution will be Twittered' captured the decisive role to be played by new social media in mass political mobilization (*Atlantic Monthly* 2009). Shortly after, the role of social media platforms in the *indignados* movement was investigated. These protests, which took place predominantly in Spain and Greece, mobilized thousands of citizens for a long period of time. Given the low coverage of these in traditional media, the spontaneous and leaderless character combined with the absence of traditional organizations, as well as the general nature of the claims made, it was argued that the role of social media in these demonstrations was determinant. Indeed, it was argued that these protests could be considered cases of a 'self-organized connective action network, with significant differences when compared to other collective action events' (Anduiza et al. 2014, 761).

According to this view, the role of social media is crucial for the development of alternative ideas and forms of organization that have given rise to a new kind of social movements that are associated with non- or post-representational forms of politics (Rossiter 2012; Tormey 2012). Anti-globalization movements such as 'Social Forums', the 2010–2011 UK student movement, 'Occupy Wall Street', UK Uncut, Black Lives Matter, etc., can be seen as examples of this kind of social movement. In the relevant literature, these social movements have been described in various ways. For example, they have been called 'networked social movements' (Juris 2004), 'the new "crowdsourced" paradigm' (Peters 2010), or 'postmodernism in the street' (Moses 2011). On this basis, the role of social media appears crucial indeed for the organizational form of social movements nowadays—or the absolute lack of organization altogether.[6]

Parallel to the above positive evaluations, there have been several more critical approaches to the role of social media in contemporary societies. As early as 2011, the term 'Twitter mob' appeared in British newspapers, together with allegations that social media incited the riots that broke out throughout England. Integrated with a conservative rhetoric, this approach called for greater surveillance and control on social media, which were considered responsible for the riots (Fuchs 2014, 254). Several other contributions focused on the severe impact of social media on electoral processes and democratic institutions (Taplin 2018; Bartlett 2018; McNamee 2019; Moore 2019). Other studies focused specifically on the role of 'fake news' and social media's contribution to their dissemination (Allcott and Gentzkow 2017).

I argue that the majority of approaches (regardless of being mainstream or critical, positive or negative) to the role of social media seem to reproduce a technological determinist view, whereby social media are detached from the historical and social context in which they evolve and with which they interact (Minotakis and Varvaki 2018). New technologies

---

[6] Based on the above literature, it may be argued that the absence of organization is rooted either in a technological determinist view that the coming of open digital communication has removed the need for organization, or in a process of disenchantment with more traditional representational forms of organization of social movements. See Robinson (2013).

appear thus to have a one-sided effect (positive or negative) on a homogeneous social whole which is transformed accordingly. In this manner, new communication technologies are fetishized in a way that eliminates any discussion of how and under what conditions they could be used differently. Instead, I am interested in showing how their role in political processes, as well as their effect on democratic institutions, is determined by capitalist social relations.

This determination affects the very structure and operation of such digital platforms, including the core function of the algorithm. The term 'algorithm' refers to any computer code that carries out a set of instructions. Algorithms are essential to the way computers process data and constitute a very important framework in the context of consumption of online content. For instance, Facebook's news feed is based on an algorithm which analyses the input—i.e. the 'likes', shared content, registered conversations, groups of closer and farther friends and relatives—in order to profile a user's identity and predict future choices and expectations. This technical feature ultimately serves as a filter which provides users with tailor-made content—a news feed which suits our tastes and supports our views (Solik 2017).

The importance of algorithms for contemporary networks of information and processes of social consciousness formation cannot be overemphasized, as the vast majority of the population uses social media platforms as their primary source of information. It may thus be argued that newsfeed algorithms become determinant in the formation of the general will, to use the fundamental Rousseauean concept of bourgeois democracy. Despite its neutral appearance, the newsfeed algorithm of a social platform can have a severe impact on political decision-making. Such algorithms determine the allocation of information and enable targeted advertising and suggestions for vote based on the profiling of users. The core technical characteristic of digital platforms—the algorithm—may thus seem neutral, but it structurally functions to affect processes of political decision-making and social consciousness formation.

I argue that, from a dialectical materialist perspective, the core function of digital platforms is the reproduction of dominant bourgeois ideology and the hindering of the development of class consciousness. My claim is not so much based on the argument of the 'bias of the algorithm'. According to this argument, algorithms are biased because they 'always start with a question framed by whoever is in charge' and, thus, tend to reproduce the biases of their creators, i.e. 'a bunch of rich white tech guys in Northern California' (Bartlett 2018, 35). My claim is rather based on analyses around the concepts of 'bubble' or 'tribal politics' and 'echo chambers'. It has been argued that social media algorithms create what in political science is labelled as 'elective affinity' or 'selective exposure', i.e. 'a leaning towards spending our time and attention with the people or organisations we already know and like, thereby strengthening our ties with them' (Howard 2016). New social media facilitate the creation of 'echo chambers', where groups of individuals enclose themselves and reproduce their solidified opinions, due to lack of randomly accessed (high quality) information that would challenge their world views (Solik 2017).

The problem, in our perspective, is that these platforms strengthen and sustain layers of false consciousness. This relates to the quality of information and the manner it is disseminated. The function of 'echo chambers' precludes the possibility of a 'radical Twitter' or a 'radical Facebook' because these platforms are not structured to promote the comprehensive and holistic viewpoint that characterizes the socialist worldview. Instead, they are structured to disseminate fragmented information to be used as a commodity, as well as for ideological purposes. Social media platforms are characterized by the continuous flow and overload of unrelated information. This enhances the reproduction of false consciousness because it promotes the fragmented, empiricist understanding of social and political phenomena and accentuates the elements of metaphysical thinking which facilitate the acceptance of posited reality and hinder subversive and revolutionary thought.

With regard to the content promoted by these digital platforms, it has been argued that their design supports the dissemination of populist and right-wing extremist ideas. The structural characteristic of information overload has been linked to the proliferation of populist forces and the phenomenon of 'emotional tribal politics' (Bartlett 2018, 51). Tribalization refers to a politics shaped by the need to belong and is linked to the affective dimension of politics. This dimension has been assessed as a crucial element of populist politics (Mouffe 2018). Moreover, new social media in the context of the Arab Spring case or the Occupy Wall Street movement were seen as opposed to the traditional media, as well as governments and established institutions. It was therefore argued that digital platforms constituted a main tool for populist solutions, as their opposition to traditional media complemented the opposition of populist parties to traditional parties (Solik 2017). Of course, this argument contradicts the fact that digital platforms themselves are run by gigantic digital monopolies, which in various forms and for various purposes cooperate with both established institutions and traditional media (Bartlett 2018, 138–39).

Furthermore, it has been argued that the 'echo-chamber' function of social media platforms has been crucial for the dissemination of far-right extremist content and the creation of online 'armies' which has been co-opted by mainstream political forces. Websites like 4chan cultivated an 'offensive, taboo-breaking and transgressive' culture that would define women, the left, black people, and ethnic minorities as the 'enemy' to be attacked (Moore 2019, 13–25). The cultivation of a reactionary, fascist consciousness is arguably facilitated by the digital platform's 'echo-chamber' design. However, this ideological content has been disseminated by social media platforms in partnership with traditional media. The case of Breitbart is a characteristic example of a partnership where reactionary ideas were cultivated online in order to be directed towards political ends (Moore 2019, 25–25).

One might argue that the 'echo-chamber' function also allows for the growth of online communities that stand for the opposite goals of social justice, gender and racial equality, etc. Indeed, the benefits of online movements, such as the #MeToo movement against sexual abuse and sexual harassment, cannot be denied. Nevertheless, the problem remains that digital platforms' design does not allow for the universal dissemination of ideas promoting such goals. More importantly, the fragmented consciousness promoted by these platforms, as they are based on the model of continuous flow of unrelated information, is incompatible with the comprehensive and holistic viewpoint that is the prerequisite for a conscious critique of capitalism and pursuit of a radical alternative.

I wish to conclude this section with reference to the functions of data collection, data mining, and targeted advertising by digital platforms. These functions influence public opinion, as well as political decision-making processes and ultimately consciousness. A brief reference to the case of Cambridge Analytica is pertinent here. Cambridge Analytica was a British political consulting firm which combined data mining and data analysis to advise on political campaigns. Having analysed data from more than eighty-seven million Facebook users, the company created 'psychographic' profiles to calculate users' motivations and choices. These calculations could be used in order to influence how voters would vote in an election through targeted advertising. The company's services were used in the US presidential election of 2016, as well as the 2016 British referendum on EU membership, by Donald Trump's campaign and the pro-EU campaign, respectively. The processes of data mining and targeted advertising, as manifested in the Cambridge Analytica case, reveal the deep crisis of the private, atomistic bourgeois conception of democracy.

The digital platforms' significance for reproducing bourgeois ideology and systemic solutions, as well as hindering the formation of radical consciousness, is measured by their efficiency in influencing the formation of political consciousness and political decision-making. They are much more efficient than traditional propaganda mechanisms because they are much more subtle. Adopting the latest insights of behavioural science, the goal of companies like Cambridge Analytica was to 'nudge' voters rather than force them to a particular choice (Thaler and Sunstein 2008). As the company asserted on its—now defunct—homepage, 'Cambridge Analytica uses data to change audience behavior' (Moore 2019, 61). Much more subtle than any previous ideological mechanisms, these platforms have become crucial for the transformation of economic into political power as well as the reproduction of the false consciousness of popular strata.

4   The Emancipatory Potential of Digitalization

If digital capitalism is a direct product of capitalist contradictions, while digital platforms, in their existing state, contribute to the reproduction of capitalism through sustaining the subordinate strata's false consciousness, then it follows that the effects of digital capitalism on the masses' political participation cannot be ameliorated, let alone eradicated, by views that distinguish between a benign traditional capitalism and a distorted surveillance capitalism, all while invoking democracy in the abstract as an essential mediation of the adverse effects of this distortion (Zuboff 2019).

If the problematic relationship between digital media and democracy is determined by the capitalist relations of production, then the liberation of the emancipatory potential of the processes of digitalization and automation from the bonds of these relations can only be realized in the context of a radical restructuring of the relationship between the economy, politics, technology, and work, in a communist society governed by the principle of the free and full development of the individual. This understanding necessitates engagement with the vision of communism, a society where capitalist contradictions are superseded, and where production is geared towards the satisfaction of social needs instead of profit. In the context of this study, this engagement translates into the exploration of the potential of digital platforms for the development of socialist relations of production and administration.

The dialectical relationship between productive forces (i.e. instruments of production, machinery, technological development, scientific research, etc.) and relations of production (e.g. ownership of the means of production, the wage relation, capital and labour relation, etc.) is a central element of Marxist analyses of political economy. Marx argued that capitalist relations of production liberated the productive forces which were bound in the chains of the feudal system of rigid, hierarchical relations. For instance, the modern capitalist conception of property, which made land easily alienable, enabled the increase of agricultural production and created the conditions for industrial capitalism (Marx 1990, 873–926; Tigar and Levy 1977, 196–210; Wood 2017). Once capitalist relations of production are established and consolidated, the iron laws of capitalist production, i.e. the law of value and especially the general law of capitalist accumulation (Marx 1990, 762–870), necessitate the further growth of the productive forces. The general law of capital accumulation, which expresses the compulsive quest for profit in the capitalist mode of production, highlights capital's reliance on scientific progress and technological developments which reduce necessary labour time, thereby increasing the surplus labour time and the surplus value expropriated by capitalists as profit.

The dialectic is already evident here. The growth of productive forces in capitalism creates 'a large quantity of disposable time … for society generally' (Marx 1973, 708). This process possesses a great potential for social emancipation. Leisure time, resulting from the growth of productive forces, is a source of wealth enabling the full development of personality, thereby creating the conditions for a communist society governed collectively by the associated producers (Boucas 2020, 50). However, in capitalist reality this growth translates into an increase of exploitation because capitalist wealth consists directly in the appropriation of surplus labour time (Marx 1973, 708). The fact that the growth of productive forces reduces the socially necessary labour time for the production of a commodity does not, in capitalism, aim towards or result in the creation of leisure time for workers. Quite the contrary. This growth is the direct result of capital's thirst for profit which—as it consists

of surplus labour, i.e. labour that is carried out beyond this socially necessary labour time—binds workers to the 'profit-making machine' as long
as possible to increase the rate of surplus value and enlarge this profit.

Therefore, technology in capitalism, far from liberating the mass of the
population, is used to enslave them. Marx argues that 'all means for the
development of production undergo a dialectical inversion so that they
become means of domination and exploitation of the producers' to the
point that 'they distort the worker into a fragment of a man' and 'degrade
him to the level of an appendage of a machine' (Marx 1990, 799).
In particular, he refers to the 'economic paradox' of machinery, which,
despite being 'the most powerful instrument for reducing labour-time',
in the context of capitalist social relations 'suffers a dialectical inversion
and becomes the most unfailing means for turning the whole lifetime of
the worker and his family into labour time at capital's disposal for its own
valorisation' (Marx 1990, 532).

The antagonism between the productive forces and relations of
production in capitalism may thus be expressed in terms of an antithesis
between the potentials for human emancipation from the realm of necessity in a communist society and the fetters on the development of these
potentials posed by capitalism. New forms of cooperation and potentials for collective ownership, new common goods (such as the digital
commons), and the reduction of necessary labour time have all been
described as communist potentials (Fuchs 2020, 15). Nevertheless, these
potentials are subsumed under the commodity form and cannot fully
develop. Indeed, it is in no way assured that these productive forces will
ever be freed; 'they will remain enchained as long as individuals enchain
themselves' (Fuchs 2020, 16). The development of particular productive
forces—such as digital networks—is a possible material condition for a
communist society of free association of individual producers; but it is
a necessary and not an adequate condition. In other words, communist
society will not result automatically from the development of specifically
digital productive forces.

Rather, the deployment of technological developments—in the context
of new developing relations of production—will ultimately depend on
the struggle for state power and the question of class rule. This is where
my argument parts ways with techno-optimist analyses. According to one
such analysis, information technology will soon enable humans to overcome scarcity and to thereby create an abundance of free time, energy,
space, health, and sustainable artificial food. On Aaron Bastani's account,

this abundance will be achieved through new technologies that will serve as the foundation of 'fully automated luxury communism' (Bastani 2019). Yet his manifesto is quite opaque as to how we shall arrive there and silent on the issues of agency and state power. Instead of an analysis of social agency, state power, and class struggle in the transition to communist society, we find superficial calls for a politics of 'luxury populism' that pits an abstract people against the élite, as well as for the need to engage in electoral politics, break with neoliberalism and return to some form of the welfare state based on neo-Keynesian solutions—like an 'ethos of municipal protectionism', universal basic services, and people's banks that break with 'the monetarist policies which have privileged low inflation at the cost of all else' (Bastani 2019, 186, 195–96, 212, 213, 228).

This line of argument has been criticized as a form of 'twenty-first century utopian socialism'. Christian Fuchs argues that, for its adherents, 'there are only positive potentials of technology and he seems to think that when communism comes, the same technologies can be used without humans having to transform and redesign many of them and having to abolish at least some of them' (Fuchs 2020, 18). According to Fuchs, a digitally networked socialist society is possible only on the premise of radical change in social structures and human practices (Boucas 2020, 59). I would add that this radical change presupposes a social rupture and new institutional forms resulting from the overtaking of state power by a new social force.

The issue of state power is also neglected in more sophisticated analyses of the digital platforms' potential for political participation and self-governance, such as James Muldoon's *Platform Socialism* (Muldoon 2022). According to Muldoon, platform socialism strives for social ownership over digital assets and is concerned with expanding the realm of human freedom by enabling communities to actively participate in their own self-governance (Muldoon 2022, 5). It sets the goal of democratizing digital platforms but also concerns itself with broader considerations of economic democracy and participatory planning (Muldoon 2022, 8–9). To achieve these goals, it proposes a strategy of 'radical reformism' which involves 'resisting, regulating and recoding … existing digital platforms' (Muldoon 2022, 135, 9). This includes concrete institutional reforms such as: regulatory action 'to curb the worst excesses of tech companies and to rein in their power'; 'stronger employment law protections for precarious workers'; stricter limits on monitoring and surveillance; investigation of 'predatory and unfair business practices by large tech companies'; 'regulations stipulating absolute size limitations'; as well as designation and regulation of companies that provide a service to the public as public utilities (Muldoon 2022, 143–46).

Yet this strategy seems blind to the interconnection and structural interdependence between digital monopolies and capitalist institutional formations. Muldoon acknowledges these structural relations in a brief reference to the lobbying mechanisms that form an integral part of national and supranational institutional forms of decision-making, but he fails to arrive at general conclusions regarding this (Muldoon 2022, 147). His calls for 'economic democracy', 'democratic ownership of platforms', and 'participatory planning' do not contest existing institutional forms, nor do they pose a revolutionary challenge to the capitalist state. On the contrary, his strategy is designed to be carried out within the confines of bourgeois institutions. Last but not least, his vision of socialized digital platforms which might enable self-governance lacks any engagement with what this process presupposes, i.e. a comprehensive expropriation of the expropriators, the revolutionary smashing of the capitalist state and a different kind of class rule.

Despite the use of socialist terminology and reference to early socialist thinkers, Muldoon's analysis pays a blind eye to Marx's conclusion that capitalist relations of production become a fetter on further development of productive forces, as well as on the actual self-governance of the associated producers (Marx 1990, 929). The promise of a technological utopia is not realizable in capitalism and the development of productive forces does not automatically lead to a different kind of society; rather this development is fettered as long as society itself remains bound in the strict confines of capitalist production. It follows that only a revolutionary change in social relations, i.e. the embedding of productive forces in a qualitatively different system of social relations, may lead to the actualization of the communist potential of these developments.

There have already been significant theoretical elaborations on the potential of information and communication technologies for the process of building a communist society, i.e. a society of self-governance by the associated producers. For instance, Christian Fuchs recognizes the potential of information and communication technologies for democratic economic planning in a communist society. In a networked and computerized society this can take the form of 'a decentralised collection of the goods that individuals and households require', with this information then being sent 'to production units that thereby know how many goods are required during a certain period of time' (Fuchs 2020, 8). According to Fuchs, the networking of production within industrial sectors 'enables the comparison of the available production capacities and productivity levels, which enables the production of the right amount of goods' (Fuchs 2020, 8). Digital platforms can thus be used to facilitate a production process determined by needs and use value instead of profit and exchange value.

Similarly, according to Evgeny Morozov, a 'feedback infrastructure' relying on digital platforms may be recast in a collectively organized production process geared to the satisfaction of social needs. The term 'feedback infrastructure' refers to the data collected by big corporations (Internet service providers, search engines, social media) through countless traces of online activity—or what is commonly termed 'big data' (Morozov 2019). Morozov claims that, instead of being a profit generation mechanism, this infrastructure could be used to collectively identify social problems, either of local or of more general importance, so that 'public and civil society institutions, deploying the free and available to all digital infrastructure, could arrive at better solutions than the logic of the market and competition à la Hayek and neoliberalism' (Boucas 2020, 60).

The above ideas rely on the dialectical understanding that the distorted social function of digital infrastructure is due to the capitalist ownership of such infrastructure, as well as the regulation of production in general by profit. They are also based on the view that the use of this infrastructure could be redirected to the satisfaction of social needs and enhance collective decision-making and democratic participation, as long as the entire system of social production is radically modified. The potential of this digital infrastructure for collectively evaluating, calculating, and anticipating social needs could be a powerful tool for the actualization of the principle of communist society 'to each according to their needs'.

In light of the above, the process of digitalization might prove to be key for the functioning of a socialist democratic state, as well as for the development of institutional forms of workers' rule. The problem of institutional forms for the management of the economy was crucial in the process of building a communist society and the problematic solutions applied to this problem in earlier historical attempts of socialist construction—to an extent—determined the process of restoration of capitalism. The contemporary level of technological development, however, has the potential of solving the contradiction between workplace democracy and central planning by establishing a two-way transmission of information between local and centralized decision-making institutions which might enable the basic units of social organization to not merely manage production but, at the same time and primarily, to be organs for popular self-management in all its aspects (Holman 2018, 136).

It should not be forgotten that in the 1960s the development of productive forces, and of cybernetics in particular, was identified as the means to radically change the managerial system of the Soviet economy and eradicate market methods of calculating labour as an input in the production process and consumption. Automated management systems, as well as the automation of design and construction work, were recognized during that period as creating the prospect for a complete revolution in the management of the economy (Pichorowitz 2005). However, at the historical point when the productive forces reached a level of development that would allow for more efficient and effective central planning mechanisms and, consequently, for the deepening of socialist relations of production, the struggle between market and social relations took a turn for the worse as market solutions were prioritized over measures that would improve and enhance central planning (Bland 1980). Therefore, in the process of socialist construction, which includes the struggle between socialist relations and market relations, automation and digitalization might enable solutions that enhance the former. Therein lies the significance of these processes for the dictatorship of the proletariat—understood as an historical process of struggle under workers' rule and a socialist state to build new relations of production and institutional forms of decision-making. Information and communication technologies might prove valuable for the battle between socialist relations of production (such as central planning) and market relations that survive in the immature stage of socialism—a battle that proved very significant in the process of socialist construction in the Soviet Union.

5   Conclusion

I conclude that the dire effects of digital platforms on political processes and democratic institutions are due to the capitalist framework within which they developed and operated. However, far from embracing neo-Luddism and techno-pessimism, dialectical materialist analysis recognizes the emancipatory potential of digitalization and automation—if they are embedded in a qualitatively different social system of production.

The productive forces developed in capitalism can be geared towards the satisfaction of social needs if the means of production, as well as the digital infrastructure, are socialized. On the other hand, and contrary to techno-optimist analyses, this process of socialization cannot be initiated—let alone concluded—in bourgeois institutional forms. The symbiotic relationship between the capitalist state and digital monopolies precludes this option.

The emancipatory potential of digital platforms can only be realized in the context of different social relations and institutional forms. In the context of a social revolution, digital platforms may have a beneficial effect on democratic practices, as they might enable the overcoming of the contradiction between centralized institutions and democratic forms of decision-making. Embedding the potential of productive forces in a society which has, through a long and arduous process, superseded capitalist contradictions may lead to the actualization of the self-government of the associated producers.

References

Allcott, Hunt, and Matthew Gentzkow. 2017. 'Social Media and Fake News in the 2016 Election.' *Journal of Economic Perspectives* 31 (2): 211–36. https://doi.org/10.1257/jep.31.2.211.

Anduiza, Eva, Camilo Cristancho, and José M. Sabucedo. 2014. 'Mobilization Through Online Social Networks: The Political Protest of the *Indignados* in Spain.' *Information, Communication & Society* 17 (6): 750–76. https://doi.org/10.1080/1369118X.2013.808360.

Althusser, Louis. 2014. *On the Reproduction of Capitalism*. London: Verso.

Andrejevic, Mark. 2012. 'Exploitation in the Data Mine.' In *Internet and Surveillance: The Challenges of Web 2.0 and Social Media*, edited by Christian Fuchs, Kees Boersma, Anders Albrechtslund, and Marisol Sandoval, 71–88. London: Routledge. https://doi.org/10.4324/9780203806432.

Bartlett, Jamie. 2018. *The People Vs Tech: How the Internet Is Killing Democracy (and How We Save It)*. New York: Dutton.

Bastani, Aaron. 2019. *Fully Automated Luxury Communism: A Manifesto*. London: Verso.

Bland, Bill. 1980. 'The Restoration of Capitalism in the Soviet Union.' https://revolutionarydemocracy.org/archive/BlandRestoration.pdf.

Bonefeld, Werner. 2014. *Critical Theory and the Critique of Political Economy: On Subversion and Negative Reason*. London: Bloomsbury.

Boucas, Dimitris. 2020. 'Theory, Reality, and Possibilities for a Digital/ Communicative Socialist Society.' *tripleC* 18 (1): 48–66. https://doi.org/ 10.31269/triplec.v18i1.1140.

Callinicos, Alex. 2009. *Imperialism and Global Political Economy*. London: Polity Press.

Carchedi, Guglielmo, and Michael Roberts, eds. 2018. *World in Crisis: A Global Analysis of Marx's Law of Profitability*. Chicago: Haymarket Books.

Clarke, Simon. 1991. 'The State Debate.' In *The State Debate*, edited by Simon Clarke. New York: Macmillan Press. https://doi.org/10.1007/978-1-349-21464-8_1.

Cox, Anthony. 2013. *Empire, Industry and Class: The Imperial Nexus of Jute, 1840–1940*. London: Routledge.

Draper, Hal. 1974. 'Marx on Democratic Forms of Government.' *Socialist Register* 11: 101–24.

Fine, Ben, and Laurence Harris. 1976. 'State Expenditure in Advanced Capitalism: A Critique.' *New Left Review* 98: 97–112.

Fuchs, Christian. 2014. *Social Media: A Critical Introduction*. New York: Sage.

———. 2020. 'Communicative Socialism/Digital Socialism.' *tripleC: Communication, Capitalism & Critique* 18 (1): 1–31. https://doi.org/10.31269/triplec.v18i1.1144.

Fuchs, Christian, and Vincent Mosco, eds. 2016. *Marx in the Age of Digital Capitalism*. Leiden: Brill.

Foster, John Bellamy. 2006. *Naked Imperialism: America's Pursuit of Global Hegemony*. New York: Monthly Review Press.

Gerbaudo, Paolo. 2014. 'Populism 2.0: Social Media Activism, the Generic Internet User and Interactive Direct Democracy.' In *Social Media, Politics and the State*, edited by Daniel Trottier and Christian Fuchs, 67–87. London: Routledge. https://doi.org/10.4324/9781315764832.

Harvey, David. 2003. *The New Imperialism*. Oxford: Oxford University Press.

Higginbottom, Andy. 2018. 'A Self-Enriching Pact: Imperialism and the Global South.' *Journal of Global Faultlines* 5 (1–2): 49–57. https://doi.org/10.13169/jglobfaul.5.1-2.0049.

Holman, Christopher. 2018. 'The Councils as Ontological Form: Cornelius Castoriadis and the Autonomous Potential of Council Democracy.' In *Council Democracy: Towards a Democratic Socialist Politics*, edited by James Muldoon, 131–49. London: Routledge. https://doi.org/10.4324/9781351205634.

Howard, Philip. 2016. 'Is Social Media Killing Democracy?' Oxford Internet Institute, November 15. https://www.oii.ox.ac.uk/blog/issocial-media-killing-democracy/.

Janssen, Davy, and Raphaël Kies. 2005. 'Online Forums and Deliberative Democracy.' *Acta Politica* 40: 317–35. https://doi.org/10.1057/palgrave.ap.5500115.

Juris, Jeffrey S. 2004. 'Networked Social Movements: Global Movements for Global Justice.' In *The Network Society: A Cross-Cultural Perspective*, edited by Manuel Castells, 341–62. Cheltenham: Edward Elgar. https://doi.org/10.4337/9781845421663.00029.

Kaplan, Andreas, and Michael Haenlein. 2010. 'Users of the World, Unite! The Challenges and Opportunities of Social Media.' *Business Horizons* 53 (1): 59–68. https://doi.org/10.1016/j.bushor.2009.09.003.

Kivotidis, Dimitrios. 2020. 'Break or Continuity? Friedrich Engels and the Critique of Digital Surveillance.' *tripleC: Communication, Capitalism & Critique* 19 (1): 97–112. https://doi.org/10.31269/triplec.v19i1.1213.

Lenin, V.I. 1976. 'Imperialism: The Highest Stage of Capitalism.' In *Collected Works*, vol. 22, edited by V. I. Lenin, 185–304. Moscow: Progress Publishers.

Marx, Karl. 1973. *Grundrisse: Foundations of the Critique of Political Economy*. Translated by Martin Nicolaus. London: Penguin Books.

———. 1990. *Capital: A Critique of Political Economy*. Translated by Ben Fowkes, Vol. I. London: Penguin Books.

McNamee, Roger. 2019. *Zucked: Waking Up to the Facebook Catastrophe*. New York: Harper Collins.

Minotakis, Alexandros, and Archontoula Varvaki. 2018. 'For A Marxist Approach to Social Media.' *Tetradia Marxismou* 7: 75–88 (in Greek).

Moore, Martin. 2019. *Democracy Hacked: How Technology is Destabilising Global Politics*. London: Oneworld Publications.

Morozov, Evgeny. 2019. 'Digital Socialism? The Calculation Debate in the Age of Big Data.' *New Left Review* 116/117 (March): 33–67.

Moses, Jonathan. 2011. 'Postmodernism in the Streets: The Tactics of Protest Are Changing.' In *Fight Back! A Reader on the Winter of Protest*, edited by Dan Hancox, 90–93. London: Open Democracy.

Mouffe, Chantal. 2018. *For a Left Populism*. London: Verso.

Muldoon, James. 2022. *Platform Socialism: How to Reclaim our Digital Future from Big Tech*. London: Pluto.

O'Kane, Chris. 2019. 'Towards a New State Theory Debate.' *Legal Form*. https://legalform.blog/2019/05/24/towards-a-new-state-theory-deb ate-chris-okane/.

Papacharissi, Zizi. 2009. 'The Virtual Sphere 2.0: The Internet, the Public Sphere, and Beyond.' In *The Routledge Handbook of Internet Politics*, edited by Andrew Chandwick and Philip Howard, 230–45. London: Routledge. https://doi.org/10.4324/9780203962541.

Papadopoulos, Orestis, and Dave Lyddon. 2020. 'Deregulation and Institutional Conversion in the Greek Hotel Industry: An Employment Relations Model in Transition.' *Industrial Relations Journal* 51 (1–2): 92–109. https://doi.org/10.1111/irj.12282.

Passarella, Marco Veronese, and Hervé Baron. 2015. 'Capital's Humpback Bridge: "Financialisation" and the Rate of Turnover in Marx's Economic Theory.' *Cambridge Journal of Economics* 5 (39): 1415–441. https://doi.org/10.1093/cje/beu058.

Peters, Aaron. 2010. '2011: The Year Political Activism and Progressive Politics Goes Open Source.' Left Foot Forward, December 20. http://www.leftfootforward.org/2010/12/2011-open-source-political-activism-progressive-politics.

Pichorowitz, V. D. 2005. 'E. V. Ilyenkov's Views on the Economic Nature of Socialism in the 1960s.' *Communist Review*, 5160–177 (in Greek).

Roberts, Michael, and Guglielmo Carchedi. 2018. *World in Crisis; Marxist Perspectives on Crash & Crisis: A Global Analysis of Marx's Law of Profitability*. Chicago: Haymarket Books.

Robinson, Bruce. 2013. 'The Party's Not Over: Network Politics and the 2010–11 UK Student Movement.' *ACME: An International E-Journal for Critical Geographies* 12 (3): 431–42.

Rossiter, Ned. 2012. 'Organized Networks and Non-Representative Democracy.' In *Reformatting Politics: Networked Communications and Global Civil Society*, edited by Jodi Dean, Jon Anderson, and Geert Lovink, 19–35. London: Routledge. https://doi.org/10.4324/9780203957066.

Solik, Mikolaj. 2017. 'A Managed Democracy: Social Media and the Algorithmic Accountability.' https://www.academia.edu/37816159/A_managed_democracy_Social_media_and_the_algorithmic_accountability.

Taplin, Jonathan. 2018. *Move Fast and Break Things: How Facebook, Google and Amazon Have Cornered Culture and Undermined Democracy*. London: Pan.

Thaler, Richard H., and Cass R. Sunstein. 2008. *Nudge: Improving Decisions about Health, Wealth, and Happiness*. London: Penguin.

'The Revolution Will Be Twittered.' *Atlantic Monthly*, June 13, 2009. https://www.theatlantic.com/daily-dish/archive/2009/06/the-revolution-will-be-twittered/200478/.

Tigar, Michael E., and Madeleine R. Levy. 1977. *Law and the Rise of Capitalism*. New York: Monthly Review Press.

Tormey, Simon. 2012. 'Occupy Wall Street: From Representation to Post-Representation.' *Journal of Critical Globalisation Studies* 5: 132–37.

Vargas, Jose Antonio. 2012. 'How an Egyptian Revolution Began on Facebook.' *The New York Times*, February 19. https://www.nytimes.com/2012/02/19/books/review/how-an-egyptian-revolution-began-on-facebook.html.

Volker, Teresa. 2019. 'Deliberative Democracy in the Age of Social Media.' *Revista Publicum* 5 (2): 73–105.

Wood, Ellen Meiksins. 2005. *Empire of Capital*. London: Verso.

———. 2017. *The Origin of Capitalism: A Longer View*. London: Verso.

Zuboff, Shoshanna. 2019. *The Age of Surveillance Capitalism: The Fight for a Human Future and the New Frontier of Power*. London: Profile.

Crisis, Social Reproduction, and the Capitalist State: Notes on an Uncertain Conjuncture

Rafael Khachaturian

1 PANDEMIC AS SOCIAL CRISIS

Even though it did not lead to social collapse—as seemed quite possible for a short time in the spring of 2020—for the better part of two years the coronavirus pandemic threw a major wrench into the reproduction of capitalism across its social, political, economic, and ecological dimensions. Among its most pronounced effects has been how forcefully it reasserted the relationship between social reproduction, social protection, and the state. By exposing the ethical and emotional challenges of practising triage in underfunded, unprepared, and overwhelmed medical systems across the world, the pandemic revealed the degree to which public services and provisions of basic necessities are affected by the constraints of capitalist social relations. It made visible to all the vulnerability of elderly, immuno-compromised, and marginalized populations—harms often concealed by social relations under twenty-first-century capitalism. And not least of all, it laid bare the ideological character of the questionable distinction

R. Khachaturian (✉)
University of Pennsylvania, Philadelphia, PA, USA
e-mail: rafkhach@sas.upenn.edu

between 'essential' and 'nonessential' work and labour, which masks the more foundational capitalist division of labour and the resulting class struggles.

The onset of the pandemic catalysed new attempts to theorize this unprecedented crisis *in medias res*. Ben Tarnoff (2020) pointed to the shock waves that it immediately sent through both the formal and informal economy and the sphere of social reproduction, as well as to the new 'sites of social power' and upsurges of 'proletarian self-activity' soon generated in response. Zachary Levenson (2020) identified it as a moment of an organic crisis, composed of interconnected economic, political, social-reproductive, racial, and ideological crises, which together were causing the deterioration of social stability and exposing cracks in the hegemonic order. Taking an even broader perspective, Salar Mohandesi (2020) characterized that conjuncture as comprised of four interlocking, 'nested' crises, with each one again operating on their own level and on a distinct temporality. For Mohandesi, these articulated moments of crisis were: first, the coronavirus, representing a particular, conjunctural crisis that unexpectedly disrupted normal patterns of life; second, a deeper organic crisis of neoliberalism, marking the 'breakdown of the entire hegemonic system itself'; third, a yet even deeper structural crisis of capitalist social reproduction, in which the 'normal' precarity of life under capitalism was further compounded by the slashing of wages, layoffs and closures, and the withdrawal of public means of social care; and finally, the fourth, epochal crisis: the climate catastrophe, threatening planetary life altogether.

The fusion of these various crises in 2020–2021 made it publicly evident that the capitalist state was either incapable or, or uninterested in, caring for its citizens. The peak of the coronavirus exposed the state's general inability to adequately protect the population—and, for a moment, to ensure the conditions of social reproduction necessary for the accumulation of capital. Today, with the development of effective vaccines and available information suggesting lower infection rates than before, we are no longer in the nadir of the pandemic. However, with most governments prematurely ending mitigations under the combined pressure from both organized capitalist interests and public desire for a return to 'normalcy', the coronavirus continues to circulate globally. It is likely well on its way to becoming an endemic disease, liable to produce new mutations that continue to threaten the most vulnerable and to strain existing medical infrastructure. What is more, apart from the measures taken by governments in coordination with private actors to enable the rapid development of vaccines, the uneven prophylactic response to the coronavirus crisis has exposed the many pathologies, fault lines, and contradictions internal to the state, understood as the political form corresponding to contemporary capitalism. In other words, practically no one would argue that the root causes of the many social contradictions that it brought to the forefront in 2020 have been fundamentally resolved. However, it is just as important to emphasize that among the reasons they have gone unresolved is the capitalist state itself.

This chapter's goal is to help theorize how the unfolding of the pandemic, understood as a new conjunctural crisis, has affected and exacerbated the capitalist state's role. I contend that the state (crucially, a *capitalist* state, not a state *embedded in* capitalism) is largely faltering in its responsibilities for social reproduction and ideological-popular legitimation, even as its role in capital accumulation continues unabated. Contra suggestions that we are witnessing a reassertion of state power *against* the power of capital, the pandemic has actually further exacerbated the inherent contradictions of the decades-long 'authoritarian neoliberal' hegemonic project that spanned from the late 1970s to the financial crisis of 2008 and the subsequent Great Recession. What we now witness is the state's *inability* to convincingly reconcile the competing priorities of capital accumulation, social reproduction, and ideological-popular legitimation. In other words, what we have seen since 2020 is the deepening of a pre-existing crisis and a reaffirmation of, rather than departure from, the capitalist character of the state, expressed here by a crisis of its role in the field of social reproduction.

My argument proceeds as follows. First, I examine a representative recent account that makes both an empirical and normative case for a post-pandemic neo-statist turn, seeing the pandemic as catalysing a social demand to marshal the capacities and resources of the state in order to stabilize the conditions of social reproduction. In contrast to these projections, I then provide a general outline of the purpose and function of the capitalist state, as that entity responsible for capital accumulation, social reproduction, and popular legitimation. I suggest that instead of introducing a new form of state power or inaugurating a new relationship between the state and capital, the post-2020 period has been characterized by the further erosion of both the state's socially reproductive functions, and as a corollary, of its popular legitimation. Turning then to the example of the United States, I argue that the pandemic has revealed how the social order maintained by the neoliberal state is now in a condition of what can best be described as perpetual crisis, as state managers find themselves tasked with the responsibilities of facilitating capital accumulation but increasingly lack both a comprehensive ideology and the political capacities to do so. After proceeding in this manner from the abstract to the concrete, I conclude with some reflections on why, despite these eroding capacities, the present crisis has not led to an imminent collapse of the system but to the period of readjustment and protracted stasis that we are still experiencing today.

2   THE STATE AS SOCIAL PROTECTION?

Among the most prominent questions raised by the pandemic is the responsibility of the state, in its self-representation as a public power, to care for its population in the midst of a novel social crisis. Given the sheer magnitude of the pandemic, this crisis of social reproduction, and the other interlinking crises mentioned above, have renewed calls for the state to play a more active, mitigating role. The most common form of these social democratic and neo-Polanyian arguments is to diagnose the disruptive effects of decades of neoliberal adherence to globalization and free markets, and in response, to posit the state as a means for social protection against the harmful 'disembedding' effects of the market.

In his recent book *The Great Recoil: Politics After Populism and Pandemic*, Paolo Gerbaudo has argued that, while the events of the past decade had already been trending in this direction, the pandemic has turned the post-industrial societies of the capitalist core towards a qualitatively new horizon. Accepting the framework of an organic crisis of capitalist democracies, Gerbaudo calls for the creation of 'new democratic institutions by means of which political communities might recover some control over their destiny and overcome their perception of impotence and despair' (Gerbaudo 2021, 11). Proclaiming the end of the neoliberal era, which he deems the outside-facing 'exopolitics' of the past, Gerbaudo suggests that we are now witnessing the emergence of a new neo-statist 'endopolitics', concerned with the 're-establishment of a sense of interiority and stability', symbolically marked by the key triad of '*sovereignty, control*, and *protection*' (Gerbaudo 2021, 4, 40). At the core of this neo-statism, which may take either a reactionary or progressive form, depending on the outcome of political struggles, are 'attempts to re-internalise capital, to re-embed economic processes in social and political institutions and to reaffirm a sense of interiority, order and equilibrium as a means to confront and navigate a world marked by uncertainty and disruption' (Gerbaudo 2021, 67).

Gerbaudo's account, which marshals the conceptual frameworks of Gramsci, Poulantzas, Laclau, and Polanyi, among others, situates itself in the socialist republican and democratic socialist tradition. It makes a case for today's nascent left to embrace a politics of social protectivism and so-called 'democratic patriotism', 'through the promise of greater social, health and environmental protections; through a politics of care that strengthens social support systems to respond to people's sense of vulnerability while reinforcing social reciprocity and solidarity' (Gerbaudo 2021, 252). Notably, he observes that the pandemic has prompted the demand for a new 'politics of care' on the socialist left, featuring calls for investments in healthcare, social care, education, and environmental protection, to offset the stressors that the pandemic placed upon existing social infrastructure and the looming wide-scale disruptions of climate change in the coming years (Gerbaudo 2021, 107).

However, despite these agreeable goals, Gerbaudo's account falls short of convincingly explaining how and why the state would be in a position to implement them (Jäger 2021). Such progressive and social democratic neo-statist accounts that wish to revitalize the state for the purposes of building an anti-capitalist and anti-neoliberal project suffer from a common problem—that of seeing the state in a relationship of externality to capital and the capitalist mode of production. That is, instead of beginning with the premise of a *capitalist* state, they begin with the idea of the state *in capitalism*. This is not merely a semantic difference. Upon it rest the general parameters of both the role and the limits of the state given capitalist relations of production. In embedding the state within a broader socioeconomic relation called 'capitalism', the latter formulation reverts to an old dichotomy that has run through the history of the Marxist tradition, that of either approaching the state as an instrument or as a subject. As Poulantzas noted, in this schema either the state is a 'passive, if not a neutral, tool totally manipulated by a single fraction' or the state is a subject, one that 'has absolute autonomy and functions of its own will' (Poulantzas 2008, 308). In other words, either the state becomes an instrument in the hands of the ruling class or a particular fraction of it; or it takes on a mystified existence of its own, expressed through the rationality and foresight of its bureaucracy and elites (Poulantzas 1976). Both approaches misunderstand the true link between the state and social classes, treating them in a relationship of externality to each other, where 'either the social classes, subdue the state (thing) to themselves through the interplay of "influences" and "pressure groups", or else the state (subject) subdues or controls the classes' (Poulantzas 1976).

Despite drawing on Poulantzas for other aspects of his analysis, as well as in recognizing that 'capitalist neo-statism is very selective in the things it can allow and cannot allow' (Gerbaudo 2022), Gerbaudo does not extensively grapple with this point in his argument for social protectionism. His account appears to occupy an indeterminate place between these two poles, implying both that the state may be put to use for particular policy goals given a strong enough mobilization of popular social forces, and that it is a subject that can generate a certain sense of interiority for society (hence, endopolitics.) But the state is not equally pliable and conducive to any particular social project, nor is it akin to a contentless vessel whose institutions can be occupied and redirected from exopolitics to endopolitics, or from a reactionary endopolitics to a progressive one. The parameters of the capitalist state are defined by the capitalist relations of production grounded in the extraction of surplus value through persons' exchange of their labour power for wages under conditions of their nominal 'freedom' in bourgeois civil society. The capitalist state is a contradictory terrain that subsumes popular struggles and (unintentionally) reproduces their own contradictions within its institutions; nevertheless, it is structurally weighed towards the reproduction of the dominance of the capitalist classes, for its institutions serve to organize the dominant, capitalist classes and simultaneously disorganize the dominated and subaltern classes.[1] Given this fundamental constraint, accounts that seek to reappropriate and repurpose the state for social protectionism downplay or sidestep a key point: that overcoming capitalist relations of production and domination would have to be, to a significant extent, an overcoming of the capitalist state itself (Smith 2017, 183–90). This raises the contentious question of the nature of the transition from capitalism to socialism and the role of the state therein, which preoccupied Marxist debates in theory and in practice for over a century (and which would take us too far afield in the current analysis). But even more importantly, it requires briefly restating the theory of the capitalist state as developed within that tradition.

---

[1] For a related discussion, see the contribution by Michael McCarthy in this volume.

3   The General Role of the Capitalist State

Although its particular features vary across space and time, we may theorize the state as fulfilling three general roles within the capitalist mode of production: (1) creating the socially necessary conditions for ongoing capital accumulation; (2) ensuring a degree of social reproduction beyond the 'strictly economic' dimension of capitalist social relations; and (3) generating the political and ideological mechanisms of cohesion, through which both capital accumulation and social reproduction are represented and articulated. These three roles are by no means mutually exclusive, nor do they ever appear in a 'pure' form, isolated from the others. They are best thought of as analytical starting points, instead of descriptions of concrete (and complex and contradictory) social formations.

The first of these roles sees the state take up the task of capital accumulation. Among these are establishing and preserving public order; managing fiscal and monetary responsibilities such as establishing and enforcing taxation, printing and regulating currency, and using economic apparatuses such as central banks to set fiscal and monetary policy; establishing and maintaining public credit and favourable investment conditions; building and maintaining physical infrastructure; and perpetuating the commodification of labour power, preservation of private property, and enforcement of contractual obligations via the mediating abstraction of the legal form (Block 1977; Offe 1984; Pashukanis 1983). Taken together, these are the concrete, material processes through which the state is involved in the ongoing valorization and private accumulation of capital. The state provides the physical, legal, and intellectual infrastructure through which different capitalist class fractions can compete in the accumulation process, thereby serving as a stabilizing node for perpetuating the M–C–M' chain of the production and circulation of capital. In this manner, the state is rendered, in Engels' famous phrase, as the 'ideal personification of the total national capital' or the 'ideal total capitalist' (Engels 2010, 319; Walker 2016).

The second dimension of the capitalist state, that of social reproduction, is closely intertwined with the gradually expanding role and capacity of the historically specific form of the social welfare state that emerged over the course of the twentieth century. Social reproduction is a demand in all stages and phases of capitalism—indeed, it is a demand upon human social organization in all modes of production; yet the role of the state in this process has been historically variable and subject to changes based on given relations of production. Through much of the nineteenth century, the high period of liberal-competitive capitalism and the bourgeois-parliamentary state, the basis of social reproduction in the industrial core of the capitalist world-system was the extended family and the social construction of a nominally 'private' sphere that established the bourgeois family and its accompanying gender subjectivities (Fraser 2017; Wallerstein 2011). By no means was the capitalist state absent or passive in these processes, insofar as it facilitated the accumulation process by enshrining and enforcing private property, and even regulating the duration and conditions of the working day.

However, the subsequent development of industrial capitalism during the late nineteenth century in the core, as well as parts of the periphery and semi-periphery, saw a period of intensified class struggle; working-class organization and the efforts of progressive, feminist reformers altered the specific form of social reproduction. Insofar as popular struggles even outside of the state-enshrined, formal spaces of politics nevertheless traverse the state's material institutions, the role of the capitalist state was rearticulated during this new phase (Poulantzas 1980). By the middle of the twentieth century, while social reproduction remained heavily gendered and continued to take place primarily in the domain of the family and the household, the capitalist state acquired a welfarist, socially protective dimension and came to be articulated in part through those new functions (Abramowitz 2020; Fraser 2017). Politically, it was recast as a guardian against capitalist exploitation, even while its 'socialization' of the costs and responsibility of social reproduction nevertheless kept it sustaining and reproducing the labour power that produced surplus value and thus enabled capital accumulation.

On the surface, social measures such as universal public education; expanded health, child and elder care; public housing; state-backed pensions; and unemployment and disability support all came to be seen as hallmarks of a mature stage of capitalism, characterized by a mutually beneficial compromise and symbiosis between a market economy and socially protective state—a social democratic 'capitalism with a human face'. However, when considered from the standpoint of the ongoing compulsion for the valorization and accumulation of capital, the picture that emerges is instead the social reproduction of the labour force, the generative power behind the creation of surplus value. Whereas in the earlier, liberal-competitive phase of capitalism this reproduction of the labour force was almost exclusively the responsibility of the 'private' sphere—the space of the family, along with its patriarchal and gendered relations of power—industrialization and concomitant class struggles displaced part of that role onto the state, albeit in a limited and uneven way.

The third dimension is that of the political and ideological legitimation of these social relations. At the most abstract level, this entails displacing the inequalities of capitalist social relations onto the level of political and legal equality—what Marx called the 'heavenly' life in the universality of the political community counterposed to the 'earthly' degradation of human life in civil society (Marx 2010; Pashukanis 1983). But more than merely instilling this conception of political equality, juridical universality, the rule of law, and the 'public interest', the national-popular dimension of the capitalist state also plays the crucial role of generating the conception of popular sovereignty, as membership within 'the people' and the accompanying political rights and duties of active citizenship that this entails (Poulantzas 1973). This responsibility for popular legitimation puts the state in the position of being the material and institutional terrain upon which a hegemonic bloc—as an alliance between dominant class fractions with the support of the subaltern classes, and which generates a 'state project' that represents the political unity of society to itself—can be formed, consolidated, and reproduced (Jessop 2016, 49–51).

4   Social Reproduction Under Authoritarian Neoliberalism

What has been called the neoliberal period, understood both as a distinct regime of capital accumulation and a corresponding political-ideological hegemonic project, was born out of a period of political and economic crisis that lasted for much of the 1970s. Yet it is now almost a truism to say that, contra popular wisdom about the retreat of the state, this period of falling profits and rapid inflation actually marked a significant persistence, transformation, and even expansion of state power (Jessop 2002). It is important to note the continuities between this regime of accumulation and the tendencies already present during the 'Glorious Thirty' years of the postwar boom—a period during which social democratic parties and trade unions were incorporated into national and global markets that were protected and insulated from democratic oversight and control via the institutions of the state itself (Panitch and Gindin 2013; Cahill and Konings 2017; Slobodian 2018). However, the crisis period of the late 1960s and early 1970s also initiated an important shift in the structure and social power of the capitalist state. Poulantzas' early diagnosis of these tendencies under the concept of 'authoritarian statism' noted that the organizational methods of the capitalist state shifted from political parties to the state's bureaucratic administration; the power of legislatures weakened at the expense of its consolidation in the executive; a set of clandestine 'parallel networks' formed alongside official ones in the state apparatuses; and the reach and use of state violence expanded (Poulantzas 1980, 310). Building on these original insights, recent scholarship on 'authoritarian neoliberalism' has pointed to the tendencies in which contemporary capitalist-democratic states are beset by problems of crisis management stemming from austerity policies, weakened popular-representative capacities, and a general condition of ideological depoliticization and lack of popular-democratic accountability. In turn, these contradictions have led them to enact further repressive legal and political measures as a means of resolving what is a general crisis of legitimacy (Bruff 2014; Bruff and Tansel 2019; Boffo et al. 2019; Flohr and Harrison 2016; Tansel 2017).

Thus, after a vanguard phase of reorientation from 1979 to 1992, and a social regime of consolidation from 1992 to 2007, the neoliberal project can now be said to be in a crisis regime of permanent exception from 2007 to the present (Davidson 2017). In this current phase, this state form continues to find itself hemmed in both by structural incentives and past policy decisions—not least of all the financialization and transnationalization of capital and the ongoing weakness of organized labour—as well as by state economic apparatuses like central banks, which seek to limit the field of political action in the name of fiscal responsibility and market confidence.[2] At the same time, the repressive and surveillance components of the neoliberal state have continued to grow unabated over the past three decades; thus, in the United States, the semi-private policing-carceral complex works in tandem with authoritarian neoliberalism's fiscal-austerity side to perpetuate a heavily racialized form of capitalist domination (Gilmore 2007; Toscano 2021).

Yet even within this authoritarian neoliberal form, whose parameters became exceptionally stark in the twelve years between the financial crisis and the onset of the pandemic, the responsibility of the capitalist state to

[2] On this point, see the contribution by Stephen Maher and Scott Aquanno in this volume.

balance between its contradictory dimensions remains. It still has to fulfil the 'strictly economic' role of capital accumulation, the 'societal' role of reproduction, and the political-ideological-juridical role of legitimation. Especially after 2008, priority had increasingly been given to accumulation at the expense of legitimacy, with the resulting vicious cycle of the state enacting further repressive measures in response to social unrest, thereby further undercutting its representative-democratic character. But it was with the onset of the pandemic that the socially reproductive role of the state became threatened to a higher degree—one that, for a moment, threatened its position as a nodal point in the reproduction of the capitalist social order as such.

Even before the pandemic, theorists such as Nancy Fraser had noted that capitalism's crisis of care was in fact caused by the 'social-reproductive contradictions of financialized capitalism' (Fraser 2017). After first establishing the general tendency of capitalism to destabilize the 'noneconomic' preconditions (not only socially reproductive, but also political and ecological) of the accumulation process, Fraser then suggests that these general destabilizing tendencies are manifested within the current financialized form of capitalism primarily as a crisis of care (Fraser 2017, 22). Treating the heavily financialized regime of capitalism that emerged after the 1970s as distinct from the 'state-managed capitalist order' of the postwar decades, Fraser also sees it as encompassing a new regime of social reproduction.

Prompted by the late twentieth-century shift of women into the workforce, the globalization of capital flows, and state disinvestment and privatization of social welfare, the neoliberal project 'externalized care work onto families and communities while diminishing their capacity to perform it' (Fraser 2017, 32). Even before the novel coronavirus made the crisis of care more visible than ever, the need for renewed capital accumulation out of the 1970s had already generated the preconditions for a crisis of social reproduction. In recent decades, the working class in the capitalist core (and needless to say, in the periphery) has increasingly borne the rising costs and demands of social reproduction, through the defunding and means-testing of public assistance programmes; the push for the further privatization of social services, child, elder, and palliative care, and education; and the rising costs and patchwork coverage of the health care system. Moreover, this has taken place alongside the ongoing stark division between the capitalist core and periphery. As Fraser notes, the scaling back of the postwar, state-managed capitalist order further intensified the incorporation of migrant workers—almost always poor, racialized, and rural women from the periphery—to fill the 'care gap' left open by the growth of the female white-collar labour force, thereby further extending and reinforcing the 'global care chains' through which the reproduction of the labour force now occurs (Fraser 2017, 34). The result has been a '*dualized* organization of social reproduction, commodified for those who can pay for it and privatized for those who cannot, as some in the second category provide care work in return for (low) wages for those in the first' (Fraser 2017, 32). In this manner, the gendered division of the labour of social reproduction has been further traversed by class and racial divisions, with the state once again acting as enabler and coordinator.

Given these conditions, how did the pandemic bring about a crisis of social reproduction and expose the limitations of the capitalist state in its current form? Before moving on to analysing the concrete instance of the United States, it is useful to recall that crises are moments of political change that are both overdetermined and open-ended. They are overdetermined in their origins, insofar as they have complex, multiple causes, and are not caused by a single, primary contradiction, and may occur only in a particular, relatively autonomous domain of social relations (such as that of economics, politics, or ideology). If crises occur in more than one domain, their relationship is more likely to be temporally contingent than a stage-wise, necessary movement from a crisis in one domain to the other—for example from the economic to the social, and then to the political. However, should these crises converge, they give rise to a conjunctural crisis, a fusion of a plurality of contradictions, each with its own pertinent domain. As Stuart Hall noted, conjunctural crises occur when 'these "relatively autonomous" sites—which have different origins, are driven by different contradictions, and develop according to their own temporalities—are nevertheless "convened" or condensed in the same moment. Then there is a crisis, a break, a "ruptural fusion"' (Hall and Massey 2010, 59–60). Furthermore, while crises have both structural and proximate causes, they are moments when structural forces and their relative weight may shift into a new constellation or arrangement of the balance of social forces. Being periods of relative indeterminacy, crises may also be windows of opportunity—the 'nature of their resolution is not given' (Hall and Massey 2010, 57)—but only under certain favourable conditions.

5   CONTRADICTIONS OF THE AMERICAN STATE

With these theoretical and historical premises in mind, we may now turn to the more concrete social formation of the contemporary United States. There, during the regime of permanent exception from 2007 onward (Davidson 2017), the competing priorities of capital accumulation, social reproduction, and popular-democratic legitimation were manifested as the displacement of contradictions from one domain to another.

The 2008 financial crisis and the Great Recession were the greatest economic shock to American society since the Great Depression. The rapid response by the fiscal and legislative apparatuses of the state, which took the form of initiatives like the Troubled Asset Relief Program and the American Recovery and Reinvestment Act, helped avoid the worst possible outcomes of the crash and the recession, restabilizing the financial system (Konings 2010). Yet paradoxically, the successful economic recovery from the crisis also displaced the contradictions of the neoliberal authoritarian mode of governance onto the political level, in the sense that the economic crisis more broadly discredited the bipartisan neoliberal ideological consensus of the previous decades as a form of popular legitimation. While these effects were felt even more sharply in Europe, with the sovereign debt crisis and the decline of traditional parties opening new political windows for encroachments by the far right, the United States was also not immune to this process. From 2009 up through the Capitol insurrection of January 2021 and into the present, the decline of this consensus has facilitated the triumph of the far right within the Republican Party over its establishment wing. Compounded by the emergence of the Trump candidacy and subsequent presidency, Congressional deadlock and obstructionism, a transparently political and reactionary Supreme Court, and domestic undermining of electoral processes, the American political system has been shaken by a growing crisis of political authority (with popular lamentations about 'political polarization' missing the mark).

The conjunctural shock of the coronavirus has further deepened this political and ideological crisis over the past two years, by compounding it as a crisis of social reproduction. The coronavirus was never strictly a biological phenomenon, but always a social one. Despite being the world's lone superpower, possessing immense advantages in wealth and technology, the United States far outpaced other countries in the absolute number of covid deaths (1.136 million as of August 2023), while placing nineteenth in deaths per capita worldwide. In the United States, state-driven messaging established a categorical distinction between 'essential' and 'nonessential' workers almost overnight, exposing millions of health-care workers but also service technicians, transit and sanitation workers, workers in agriculture and food production, workers in critical retail and trades, and public servants, among others, to a deadly virus at a time when we knew fairly little about its transmission. As one could foresee at the time, this distinction exacerbated already-existing divisions within the working class, between those who could pass the critical stages of the pandemic in relative safety and those who were on the front lines. In addition, the pandemic further exposed the racialized and gendered inequalities of access to care, as the patchwork medical system in rural and impoverished urban areas strained under the weight of record numbers of cases and mass deaths. De-regulated nursing homes became spaces of mass contagion, while longstanding financial pressure upon the health-care system left health workers scrambling to save lives in underfunded hospitals filled to capacity (Winant 2020). Just as disturbingly, prisons—the carceral core of the authoritarian neoliberal state—turned into sites of sickness and death intentionally located out of public sight. Absent a robust social safety net, layoffs and furloughs (especially in the service sector) left millions of people already living paycheck to paycheck under tremendous strain, in light of which the two small stimuli sent out by the Trump administration were more insult than relief. Under these conditions of exposure to death, mass precaritization, and an unprecedented strain on existing health and service infrastructure, the working class was once again rendered superfluous in the face of the logic of capital accumulation—the necessity of keeping 'the economy' going so as not to risk an even broader social crisis and collapse. The coronavirus crisis thus affected not only the reserve army of labour, which already bears upon itself the daily violence of capitalist exploitation and marginalization, but the entire working class.

In addition to the pandemic's social impacts, the following two years were marked by the basic unevenness and shortcomings of the American state's response to this crisis. Among these have been the uneven and changing federal messaging on social distancing and masking; the maldistribution of testing and vaccinations in underserved and poor communities; housing insecurity and the temporary nature of the moratorium on evictions, eventually overturned by the Supreme Court; and continuing issues of food insecurity in poor communities. Exacerbating this even further has been the climate emergency, such that without any foreseeable binding global agreement on reducing carbon emissions, and with the high likelihood of missing the 1.5 C benchmark set for global warming by 2100, we will be confronted with a further intensification of this crisis of social reproduction, manifested as declines in agricultural production, mass displacement due to flooding and fires, and crumbling public infrastructure.

Altogether, this confluence of factors is putting an increasing strain on the ability of the American state to manage these crises. Despite the passage of the CARES Act in 2020 and the American Rescue Plan Act in 2021 as necessary stopgaps, as well as the recent passage of the Inflation Reduction Act (a stripped-down version of the Build Back Better Plan that stalled in the Senate earlier in 2022), promising relief on prescription drug, clean energy, and health coverage costs, other parts of the Biden agenda had been met with legislative roadblocks. Thus, the social safety net proposals originally intended with Build Back Better were set aside. Among these were significant investments and revitalizations of physical, transportation, and digital infrastructure; investments in both the manufacturing and service sectors; rebuilding the infrastructure for clean drinking water; the building of affordable housing, educational institutions, and care facilities; and jobs training and workforce development (The White House 2021a). Furthermore, the American Families Plan proposed by the Biden administration, which would have represented a significant state-backed investment into the social reproduction of the labour force, was likewise left aside. Among the Plan's goals for the next ten years were to introduce new spending to help subsidize childcare; make available free and universal pre-kindergarten programmes; allocate money towards government-subsidized paid family and medical leave; invest in education by introducing free community college; allow convicted felons to access SNAP food benefits; and introduce additional health insurance subsidies through the Affordable Care Act (The White House 2021b). None of these initiatives made it through the Senate to be included in the Inflation Reduction Act of August 2022.

At the same time, more than three years into the coronavirus crisis and well past the midway point of the Biden administration, what becomes apparent is that despite straining political, ideological, and social-reproductive relations, the pandemic has not yet significantly affected the processes of capital accumulation. Corporate profits have continued at a record pace, with the new wealth passed along to executives and shareholders, while rising costs due to inflation have been passed on to consumers and the lower and middle layers of the workforce (Daniel 2022; Pickert 2022). And while global supply chains have not yet fully recovered from the strain of 2020 and have been further compounded by Russia's invasion of Ukraine, transnational capital flows remained unimpeded, indicating not a turn to a 're-internalization' of capital under the mantle of social protectionism, but largely the continuation of the post-2008 status quo in terms of capital circulation and accumulation. Under these conditions, the state continues to consolidate, facilitate, and represent the interests of multinational corporate capital and stabilize its mechanisms of accumulation. These policies have also continued to squeeze smaller entrepreneurs, in this manner further contributing to the rise of reactionary politics (Cooper 2022; c.f. Heideman 2022). It remains to be seen how the prolonged fallout from the war in Ukraine and other global conflicts will affect these tendencies, particularly as global ripple waves from conflicts over fossil fuels and rare minerals, food scarcity, and stretched supply chains resonate domestically, especially in terms of the Federal Reserve's goal of curbing inflation and the possibility of a recession. For now, though, the response of the American state, as the linchpin of the global capitalist order, has been sufficient to stabilize the coronavirus crisis—but at the ongoing cost of its popular-democratic and social-reproductive roles.

What, then, does the crisis of social reproduction that has been catalysed and exposed by the pandemic, and the state's role therein, indicate for the coming years—at least in the United States? Considering the absence of revolutionary alternatives, a relatively weakened left following the unsuccessful Sanders presidential campaigns and the repression that followed the anti-carceral uprisings of the summer of 2020, the balance of forces remains strongly on the side of capitalist class interests—even as they are divided among themselves into competing fractions, which are only partially captured by the two parties. Just as problematically, despite the broad public mistrust and disillusionment with the political system, there are no apparent institutional mechanisms for a popular-democratic re-legitimation of the state, given entrenched interests, the resistance of the constitutional order to amendment and change, the anti-majoritarian design of the Electoral College and the Senate, and frequent Congressional legislative deadlock and obstructionism. Lastly, with the shortcomings of the most ambitious parts of the Biden legislative agenda concerning social care, and the enthusiasm for a progressive neo-statism being more wish than reality at the moment, the crisis of social reproduction has continued to undercut the living standards of the working class, in the process creating a 'new normal' in which the social harms of the pandemic become the new baseline.

6 From Crisis to Restabilization?

If we take the common periodization of the neoliberal era as spanning from the late 1970s to 2008, we can say that neoliberalism was born out of a period of capitalist crisis, and now appears to be indefinitely muddling along through another one. Crises are periods where the state's ability to organize class hegemony becomes less effective in the face of sharpening contradictions, both within the hegemonic bloc and between it and the dominated classes—that is, as these contradictions are diffused through the entire social formation. Even absent an economic crisis, social, political, and ideological crises may rupture existing modes of representation between the dominant and dominated classes, leading to the weakening of party systems and the emergence of new forms of representation and modes of organizing political power. Social crises, especially ones that begin to impede the ability of a social formation organized along capitalist relations of production to continue reproducing itself, resonate along other dimensions, with economic, political, and ideological consequences. Does the present crisis of social reproduction, having been exacerbated by the pandemic, and the state's actions to stabilize capital accumulation at the expense of social investment and popular-democratic legitimation, pose a challenge to the system as a whole?

Certainly, the crisis of the neoliberal hegemonic project decidedly does not mean capitalist collapse. As the American example showed, the stabilization mechanisms deployed by the state's economic apparatuses in 2009–2010 were enough to prevent economic collapse, even if it meant that the unresolved social, political, and ideological contradictions of the crisis would outlast the economic effects of the recession itself and manifest themselves in new forms. What remains of it today is the state's ability to facilitate capital accumulation, but now largely shorn of its broader popular-reproductive role, further undercutting the stability of the hegemonic project as it existed during its 'neoliberal' peak. Thus, instead of a passive revolution from above, in which ambitious progressive legislation may have helped cement a new hegemonic order that addressed both the social-reproductive and popular-democratic shortcomings of the present state project, at least for the time being we are left with a prolonged impasse, in which capital accumulation continues unabated even as the social relations that undergird it continue to unravel.

This same project is now in crisis and could very well be transitioning into a new form. Writing at the tail end of the 1970s, Poulantzas noted that political crisis and the crisis of the state 'play an organic role in the reproduction of class domination', by 'establish[ing] the way for the restoration of an unsteady class hegemony and the way for a transformation-adaptation of the capitalist state to the new realities of class conflict' (Poulantzas 2008, 297). Put differently, absent either a revolutionary mobilization of forces or a protracted equilibrium in which no social bloc or constellation of forces has the upper hand, crises may in fact become windows of opportunity for the reorganization of forces among the dominant classes towards a new arrangement for reproducing their power. More often than being revolutionary windows of opportunity, crises present existing powers with opportunities for adaptation, readjustment, and even reinvention. In such a case, the strategies deployed by the state in response to the pandemic may become the basis for a new regime of accumulation and hegemonic order—a 'new normal'—without severing the link between the capitalist state and capitalist class power. The intensifying (perhaps now chronic) crisis of the capitalist state in its neoliberal form does not mean its collapse.

This brings us back to the initial question of social protection under the auspices of a new neo-statism. It is quite likely that the state will play a role within the transition to any emancipatory political project (no matter how remote this possibility seems today). Yet this is all the more reason to diagnose its potential capacities and limitations in the present moment. The capitalist state is neither an object that can be wholly redirected towards progressive ends through staffing and guidance by left technocrats, nor a subject capable of stepping in to shield society from crises, for it remains confined to a specific set of roles within the capitalist mode of production. The revival of interest in Marxist theories of politics and the state since the 2008 financial crisis also makes it an opportune time to continue building on that tradition's insights—among them that if, much like capital, the state is a social relation, then it cannot simply be bent at will, incrementally taken over at its summits, or repurposed in its entirety for social emancipation. Its terrain is much more fraught.

References

Abramowitz, Mimi. 2020. 'Democratic Socialism, Socialist Feminism, and the US Welfare State'. In *An Inheritance for Our Times: Principles and Politics of Democratic Socialism*, edited by Gregory Smulewicz-Zucker and Michael J. Thompson, 261–77. New York: O/R Books.

Block, Fred. 1977. 'The Ruling Class Does Not Rule: Notes on the Marxist Theory of the State'. *Socialist Revolution* 33: 6–28.

Boffo, Marco, Alfredo Saad-Filho and Ben Fine. 2019. 'Neoliberal Capitalism: The Authoritarian Tur'. *Socialist Register* 55: 247–270.

Bruff, Ian. 2014. 'The Rise of Authoritarian Neoliberalism'. *Rethinking Marxism* 26 (1): 113–129.

Bruff, Ian and Cemal Burak Tansel, eds. 2019. *Authoritarian Neoliberalism: Philosophies, Practices, Contestations*. Abingdon: Routledge.

Cahill, Damien, and Martijn Konings. 2017. *Neoliberalism*. Cambridge: Polity.

Cooper, Melinda. 2022. 'Family Capitalism and the Small Business Insurrection'. *Dissent*, Winter. https://www.dissentmagazine.org/article/family-capitalism-and-the-small-business-insurrection.

Daniel, Will. 2022. 'U.S. Companies Posted Record Profits in 2021, Jacking Up Prices as Inflation Surged'. *Fortune*, March 31. https://fortune.com/2022/03/31/us-companies-record-profits-2021-price-hikes-inflation/.

Davidson, Neil. 2017. 'Crisis Neoliberalism and Regimes of Permanent Exception'. *Critical Sociology* 43 (4–5): 615–634.

Engels, Frederick. 2010 [1892]. *Socialism: Utopian and Scientific*. In *Marx and Engels Collected Works*, 24: 281–325. London: Lawrence & Wishart.

Flohr, Mikkel and Yannick Harrison. 2016. 'Reading the Conjuncture: State Austerity and Social Movements: An Interview with Bob Jessop'. *Rethinking Marxism* 28 (2): 306–321.

Fraser, Nancy. 2017. 'Crisis of Care? On the Social-Reproductive Contradictions of Contemporary Capitalism.' In *Social Reproduction Theory: Remapping Class, Recentering Oppression*, edited by Tithi Bhattacharya, 21–36. London: Pluto Press.

Gerbaudo, Paolo. 2021. *The Great Recoil: Politics after Populism and Pandemic*. London: Verso.

———. 2022. 'Neoliberalism, Globalisation and the State.' Verso, February 22. https://www.versobooks.com/blogs/news/5276-neoliberalism-globalisation-and-the-state.

Gilmore, Ruth Wilson. 2007. *Golden Gulag: Prisons, Surplus, Crisis, and Opposition in Globalizing California*. Berkeley: University of California Press.

Hall, Stuart, and Doreen Massey. 2010. 'Interpreting the Crisis: Doreen Massey and Stuart Hall Discuss Ways of Understanding the Current Crisis'. *Soundings* 44: 57+.

Heideman, Paul. 2022. 'Focus On the Family?' *Dissent*, February 9. https://www.dissentmagazine.org/online_articles/focus-on-the-family.

Jäger, Anton. 2021. 'The End of Neoliberalism?' Verso, November 5. https://www.versobooks.com/blogs/news/5194-the-end-of-neoliberalism.

Jessop, Bob. 2002. 'Globalization and the National State'. In *Paradigm Lost: State Theory Reconsidered*, edited by Stanley Aronowitz and Peter Bratsis, 185–220. Minneapolis: University of Minnesota Press.

———. 2016. *The State: Past, Present, Future*. Cambridge: Polity.

Konings, Martijn, ed. 2010. *The Great Credit Crash*. London: Verso.

Levenson, Zachary. 2020. 'An Organic Crisis Is Upon Us.' *Spectre*, April 20. https://spectrejournal.com/an-organic-crisis-is-upon-us/.

Marx, Karl. 2010 [1844]. 'On the Jewish Question.' In *Marx and Engels Collected Works*, 3: 146–174. London: Lawrence & Wishart.

Mohandesi, Salar. 2020. 'Crisis of a New Type'. *Viewpoint*, May 13. http://www.viewpointmag.com/2020/05/13/crisis-of-a-new-type/.

Offe, Claus. 1984. *Contradictions of the Welfare State*. Edited by John Keane. Cambridge: MIT Press.

Panitch, Leo, and Sam Gindin. 2013. *The Making of Global Capitalism: The Political Economy of American Empire*. London: Verso.

Pashukanis, Evgeny B. 1983. *Law and Marxism: A General Theory*. London: Pluto Press.

Pickert, Reade. 2022. 'US Corporate Profits Soar With Margins at Widest Since 1950'. Bloomberg, August 25. https://www.bloomberg.com/news/articles/2022-08-25/us-corporate-profits-soar-taking-margins-to-widest-since-1950.

Poulantzas, Nicos. 1973. *Political Power and Social Classes*. London: New Left Books.

———. 1976. 'The Capitalist State: A Reply to Miliband and Laclau'. *New Left Review* I (95): 63–83.

———. 1980. *State, Power, Socialism*. London: Verso.

———. 2008. 'The Political Crisis and the Crisis of the State'. In *The Poulantzas Reader*, edited by James Martin, 294–322. London: Verso.

Slobodian, Quinn. 2018. *Globalists: The End of Empire and the Birth of Neoliberalism*. Cambridge, MA: Harvard University Press.

Smith, Tony. 2017. *Beyond Liberal Egalitarianism: Marx and Normative Social Theory in the Twenty-First Century*. Leiden: Brill.

Tansel, Cemal Burak, ed. 2017. *States of Discipline: Authoritarian Neoliberalism and the Contested Reproduction of Capitalist Order*. London: Rowman & Littlefield.

Tarnoff, Ben. 2020. 'These Are Conditions in Which Revolution Becomes Thinkable.' *Commune*, April 7. https://communemag.com/these-are-conditions-in-which-revolution-becomes-thinkable/.

The White House. 2021a. 'FACT SHEET: The American Jobs Plan'. The White House, March 31. https://www.whitehouse.gov/briefing-room/statements-releases/2021/03/31/fact-sheet-the-american-jobs-plan/.

———. 2021b. 'FACT SHEET: The American Families Plan'. The White House, April 28. https://www.whitehouse.gov/briefing-room/statements-releases/2021/04/28/fact-sheet-the-american-families-plan/.

Toscano, Alberto. 2021. 'Incipient Fascism: Black Radical Perspectives'. *Comparative Literature and Culture* 23 (1).

Walker, Gavin. 2016. 'The "Ideal Total Capitalist": On the State-Form in the Critique of Political Economy'. *Crisis & Critique* (November): 434–455.

Wallerstein, Immanuel. 2011. *The Modern World-System IV: Centrist Liberalism Triumphant, 1789–1914.* Berkeley: University of California Press.

Winant, Gabriel. 2020. 'Coronavirus and Chronopolitics'. *N+1,* Spring. https://www.nplusonemag.com/issue-37/politics/coronavirus-and-chrono politics-2/.

From Economic to Political Crisis: Trump and the Neoliberal State

Stephen Maher and Scott M. Aquanno

The 2016 election of Donald Trump to the presidency of the American empire sent shockwaves around the world. Just as many on the left saw this as the harbinger of a distinctly American neo-fascism, the political establishment feared that a Trump presidency could destabilize global capitalism (Hedges 2016; Finn 2017; Foster 2017). This was especially the case as Trump came to office espousing a populist attack on 'globalism', expressed most sharply by advisor Steve Bannon, who once described himself as a 'Leninist' (Radosh 2017). Of course, Bannon did not mean that he intended to carry out a socialist revolution that would transfer productive property into common ownership and democratic control. Rather, he was articulating a desire to radically restructure the state apparatus: in his words, to 'deconstruct the administrative state' by challenging the regulations, taxes, and trade agreements that he and

S. Maher (✉)
Department of Economics, SUNY Cortland, Cortland, NY, USA

S. M. Aquanno
Ontario Tech University, Whitby, ON, Canada
e-mail: Scott.Aquanno@ontariotechu.ca

R. Hunter et al. (eds.), *Marxism and the Capitalist State*,
Political Philosophy and Public Purpose,
https://doi.org/10.1007/978-3-031-36167-8_5

99

Trump claimed had inhibited economic growth and infringed on US sovereignty (Rucker and Costa 2017).

Upon taking office, Trump immediately set about hollowing out a host of state agencies by slashing budgets, refusing to make key appointments, and installing loyalists who could attack departments from within. What is more, these efforts did not end with typical targets, such as the Environmental Protection Agency, Department of Education, and Department of Energy, but encompassed more 'sacred' institutions, such as the State Department. If all this appeared to be much more extreme than the usual Republican politics of 'deregulation', still more shocking was the fact that the onslaught extended to the leading agencies of the state economic apparatus, including the Treasury Department and, to a lesser extent, the Federal Reserve. This included, at the very least, an attempt to roll back the tremendous expansion of the powers and functions of these agencies that had taken place in the wake of the 2008 financial crisis.

However, as we will show, the state economic apparatus emerged from the Trump presidency substantially undiminished. We argue that this outcome highlighted the resilience of the structure of authoritarian statism, whereby state power has been centralized within state agencies—especially the central bank—that are substantially insulated from democratic pressures. Just as Nicos Poulantzas had argued, as the state became more 'interventionist' over the neoliberal period, state power had been concentrated in its economic apparatus, defined by its direct integration with the circulation of capital. Poulantzas already saw in the late 1970s that the continual expansion of the state's economic functions was resulting in the emergence of a qualitatively new and more authoritarian state form. As capital accumulation came to depend more and more on the state economic apparatus, so too did the latter become increasingly dominant within the state complex, and more insulated from democratic institutions—particularly as contradictions grew between the state's economic and legitimation functions. It was this pattern of authoritarian statism which subsequently limited the scope of Trump's authority.

In what follows, we first develop a theory of authoritarian statism, drawing primarily on the work of Poulantzas. Yet Poulantzas' conception of the state economic apparatus was rudimentary and focused largely on the French *dirigiste* state, characterized by the nationalization of important industries. He paid practically no attention to central banks, which have become the most important seat of class power across the advanced capitalist states, and the most important components of state economic apparatuses. Indeed, a major frontier for research on the contemporary capitalist state remains situating central banks within the economic apparatus and identifying their functions within financialized capitalism. We take some steps towards doing so by theorizing the *financial branch* as a distinct sub-unit within the state economic apparatus, and tracing its development in the United States from its emergence as a cohesive unit in the 1920s to its dominance within the neoliberal state by the late 1970s.

As we show, the increasing dependence of global capital accumulation on the American state from World War II onwards, and the need to deflect democratic demands on the state, led to the concentration of power within this financial branch of the state economic apparatus, and its significant autonomy from the rest of the state complex. The independence of financial branch agencies was secured by institutional constraints and rules within the state, but more significantly, it was structured by the integration of state power with the capitalist economy. Challenging the agencies responsible for organizing the internationalization of capital would destabilize global capitalism itself. This would entail a major confrontation with capital—which Trump had neither the intention nor the capacity to carry out. Without a viable alternative to globalization, nor anything like the mass movement support or institutional base within the state necessary to implement one, Trump could only go so far.

1   THE NEOLIBERAL AUTHORITARIAN STATE

The neoliberal state is above all characterized by the prominence of the *state economic apparatus* over its *repressive* and *ideological* apparatuses. Importantly, state apparatuses are not the same as state agencies, but are comprised of practices articulated across multiple state agencies. The ideological apparatus is responsible for the legitimation of state power and the capitalist order. It includes not just so-called 'public diplomacy' and 'information' propaganda programmes, but also political parties, elections, parliaments, welfare and social services, agencies protecting workplace rights, and so on. Similarly, the repressive apparatus consists of those 'institutions which actualize bodily constraint and the permanent threat of mutilation' such as law, courts, prisons, army, and the police (Poulantzas 2003). Finally, the state economic apparatus is directly integrated with the reproduction and circulation of capital. It consists of distinctly and immediately economic practices that are directly internalized within the state.

The integration of the economic apparatus with capital means that it suffers from a particular 'rigidity', in that it most clearly expresses the structural constraints imposed by the capitalist economy on state policy. That the state complex overall is relatively autonomous from capital means that the dynamics, rhythms, and contradictions of accumulation significantly escape its direct control. However, since the economic apparatus is organically linked with the process of accumulation in a direct and unmediated fashion, its institutions are especially subject to the disciplines and vicissitudes of capital, which they express in relation to other apparatuses and agencies. As a result, the orientation of the economic apparatus may come into *conflict* with general state policy. In such cases, state policy must ultimately yield to the imperatives of the economic apparatus or face severe economic dysfunction.

This was brilliantly summarized by Poulantzas:

> [The economic apparatus] is directly linked into the accumulation-reproduction process of capital, and is thus the most affected by the rhythm and contradictions peculiar to that process. Suffering the most from the rigidity imposed on the State by the contemporary process of production and reproduction of capital, this apparatus also displays the limits and restrictions of the political options and tactics available for organizing class hegemony. Since it is the least subject to the conjunctural hazards of government policy it often follows a specific logic in partial contradiction with general state policy... It is this apparatus which most clearly demonstrates the *continuity* of the state, even though it is the most directly embroiled both in the internal contradictions of the power bloc and in contradictions between the bloc and the dominated classes. (Poulantzas 2003, 171)

Importantly, Poulantzas' highly general definition of the economic apparatus largely overlooks central banks, which are the primary point at which financial capital directly integrates with state power. This is particularly important in light of the unique international role of the American state. The Fed is much more than a lender of last resort to troubled institutions; it sits at the centre of market-based financial intermediation, providing both the securities and the liquidity that underpin the global capitalist system. In a financial system in which currency has been separated from a metallic base (i.e. gold), it is the Fed's commitment to low inflation that establishes the value of the dollar. Moreover, that the dollar is *the* global currency means that the Fed is effectively the world's central bank. And because of the dollar's role as the global reserve currency, it underpins international debt, derivative, and foreign currency markets, and is at the centre of the short-term funding markets that nearly all financial institutions rely on (Aquanno 2021; Panitch and Gindin 2012).

Like the neoliberal state, the liberal state of the nineteenth century and the New Deal state of the 1930s through the 1970s both extensively 'intervened' in the economy. Nevertheless, the state's role in capital accumulation continuously expanded over the twentieth century. This did not take place through the linear accumulation of economic functions; rather, the emergence of novel state forms occurred through a series of breaks, as new practices, organizational structures, hierarchies of state apparatuses, and modalities of state integration with capital accumulation were established. The state economic apparatus is *qualitatively* distinct within each state form. The development of the economic apparatus is therefore characterized not just by its increasing *extent*, but also by transformations in its *form*. At the same time, the internalization within the state of new economic functions alters and reshapes the relationship between the 'political' and 'economic' itself.

The economic apparatus of the New Deal state was subordinated to the coercive and ideological apparatuses, centered around the 'military–industrial complex' and welfare state programmes. At the core of the military–industrial complex is a nexus of state agencies, especially the Departments of Defense and Energy, and large, capital-intensive manufacturing firms. By taking on the bulk of R&D costs and providing a stable market for high-tech products, the military–industrial complex supported the global competitiveness and market power of industrial corporations while reducing their reliance on the financial sector (Block and Keller 2011; Mazzucato 2013). However, this was a by-product of its role in reproducing the coercive power of the US empire by funnelling investment into corporations to produce military technologies. It was geopolitical interests, determined largely by the military, that played the leading role in industrial policy planning within the state economic apparatus. Meanwhile, welfare state programmes supported growth by sustaining high demand and extending workers limited protections from markets, thereby also serving to legitimate capitalism.

In *ascending* within the hierarchy of state apparatuses beginning in the 1970s, the economic apparatus was also profoundly *transformed*. In place of the grouping of agencies around the military, it came to be dominated by what we have called its 'financial branch'. The financial branch consists of functions located within the Treasury Department (especially the Office of the Comptroller of the Currency), Federal Deposit Insurance Corporation (FDIC), Securities and Exchange Commission (SEC), Commodity Futures Trading Corporation (CFTC), and, above all, the Federal Reserve. These agencies are uniquely characterized by their 'independence' from electoral pressures and democratic oversight. While the Federal Reserve system is an 'independent and non-partisan entity within government', the FDIC, SEC, and CFTC are 'independent commissions', and the OCC is an independent office within the Treasury Department.

The distinct 'independence' of these agencies, and the growing power of the economic apparatus, are emblematic of what Poulantzas termed *authoritarian statism*, or 'the hermetic insulation of power from democratic control' within contemporary advanced capitalist states (Poulantzas 2003, 226). In particular, the 'rigidity' of the economic apparatus demands that its technocratic functions be insulated from 'political' interference—which it is, in any case, frequently unable to accommodate as it expresses the structural constraints of capitalism. Its rise was thus accompanied by 'the precipitate and accelerated decline of parliament and the institutions of representative democracy', and reciprocally, 'the emergence of the administrative and governmental apparatus as the dominant state structure and the major centre for elaborating political decisions'. Rather than capitalists 'striking compromises in the political arena', with the development of authoritarian statism, the bureaucracy became 'not merely the principal site, but also the principal *actor* in the elaboration of state policy' (Poulantzas 2003, 224).

Authoritarian statism therefore depended upon the capacity of the state administration to negotiate consensus among the dominant fractions of capital outside of parliamentary processes. Its ability to do so required 'the direct expression of big economic interests within the administration', with 'whole sections of the administrative apparatus…structurally organized as networks involving the specific presence of hegemonic interests within the state'. Indeed, the 1970s saw the explosive growth of a 'veritable web' of 'committees, permanent or ad hoc commissions, working groups, delegations, working parties' and the like to carry out this function (Poulantzas 2003: 225).[1] Increasingly, it was only relatively weak social forces which sought to compete for influence

---

[1] This is what Maher, drawing on Gramsci, has called the 'integral state'. For a historical account of how this developed in the United States, see Maher (2022).

within the parliamentary arena. The power of the dominant fractions of capital—especially finance, which became hegemonic over the neoliberal period—was secured within 'independent' state agencies that were not subject to electoral whims or popular pressures.

What the rise of the economic apparatus, and the subordination of the ideological apparatus, practically meant was that the legitimation functions that had been so central to the New Deal state would be made to yield before the demands of capital accumulation. Authoritarian statism was an inherent consequence of the movement away from legitimation, as the entire state apparatus was restructured around its accumulation functions. At the same time, the reduced concern with legitimation immediately paved the way for a legitimation crisis, as the imposition of market disciplines and the dismantling of social supports worsened inequality and increased the precarity of working-class life. Meanwhile, the veneer of democratic legitimacy was further stripped away as parliamentary power was hollowed out, while the 'continuity of the state' institutionalized within the economic apparatus secured the hegemony of financial capital regardless of electoral outcomes. Globalization, financialization, and authoritarian statism were completely interlinked.

As this suggests, the growing prominence of the economic apparatus arose not from the instrumentalization of the state by individual capitalists through 'lobbying', but rather from its role in the circulation and reproduction of capital. Similarly, the dominant position of the financial branch *within* the economic apparatus in the neoliberal period points not to 'regulatory capture' by particular firms, but rather reflects the centrality of finance within the overall structure of accumulation. Indeed, the financial branch does not 'intervene' in the economy, but is *part of* the financial system, which depends completely for its routine operation on these state economic functions. It would therefore be expected that changes in the relative power of financial capital would be reflected and anchored in the organization of the state complex, such that the apparatuses with which it is most closely interconnected become more prominent.

The financial branch first began to cohere as a distinct component of the American state economic apparatus in the 1920s and 1930s. In addition to the establishment of the FDIC and SEC, the independence of the Fed can be traced to this period, when the Treasury secretary and Comptroller of the Currency were removed from the Federal Reserve Board. The 1951 Treasury-Federal Reserve Accord fortified this autonomy, 'liberating' monetary policy from the constraints of government debt management (Romero 1951). This would become the basis for the separation of monetary and fiscal policy—as the former was no longer simply subordinate to Congressional spending decisions, but was instead made accountable to financial markets in a new way. The capacities of the financial branch were also expanded through its role in designing and governing the post-war Bretton Woods system, in which it was essential for managing international capital flows and fixed exchange rates.

Both Bretton Woods and the regime of industrial hegemony came apart as the post-war boom finally ran out of steam, before collapsing into a decade-long crisis during the 1970s. The 'productivism' of the post-war era had allowed workers' wages and corporate profits to rise together, as each captured a fixed share of the benefits of productivity gains. Yet as productivity growth slowed, trade union militancy squeezed profits, which was only exacerbated by growing competition from industrial rivals in Europe and Asia. When capital raised prices to increase profit margins, workers responded with further militancy to protect wages, leading to a wage-price inflationary spiral (Shaikh 2016). Declining growth also led to a 'fiscal crisis of the state', as state spending grew faster than GDP, consuming an increasing portion of total economic output (O'Connor 1973). Sustaining state spending would thus require imposing even higher taxes on capital or larger deficits—either of which would be inflationary.

Resolving the crisis required finding a way restore class discipline. Through the 1970s, the Nixon, Ford, and Carter administrations each attempted to impose wage restraint through various wage and price control regimes. Buy-in from labour was sought by granting unions a seat on the corporatist bodies which set such targets, despite the fact that this delegitimated these leaders among some of the rank-and-file. Yet even the limited forms of democratic participation embodied in the institutions of the capitalist state posed a problem. Controls were implemented by elected officials, and such programs had to be authorized by Congress. Not only was it difficult to force workers' to accept cuts to wages and living standards, but state officials also feared that the public might begin to demand the expansion of controls into wider areas of the economy. The solution was to concentrate power in the financial branch of the economic apparatus, which was by then relatively well-insulated from such pressures—accomplished especially through the 1979 'Volcker Shock' (Maher 2022).

Just weeks after his appointment as Fed Chair, Paul Volcker implemented an unprecedented spike in interest rates. This provoked a deep recession and generated skyrocketing unemployment, finally breaking the back of organized labour. As the state's legitimation functions were sacrificed to the imperatives of accumulation, so too was the state's ideological apparatus subordinated to its economic apparatus. State policy in the neoliberal era came to revolve around the Fed's implementation of a low-inflation monetary regime, which imposed strict limits on government spending and the welfare state while disciplining labour by maintaining a substantial reserve army of the unemployed. The turn to 'free markets' thus depended upon the emergence of a *more* coercive state, as new disciplines organized by the economic apparatus were brought to bear on the working class—that is, a shift 'from consent to coercion' (Panitch and Swartz 2003).

The pre-eminence of the financial branch was reinforced by the transition from the 'tax state' to the 'debt state' over the 1970s, whereby state budgets were increasingly financed by bond sales rather than taxation (Streeck 2014). This intensified market discipline on public finances, since state spending was increasingly subject to market interest rates on government debt, and therefore dependent on the willingness of investors to purchase Treasury bonds. As this constrained fiscal policy and increased reliance on monetary policy, it empowered the monetary authorities (i.e., the Fed) within the state complex. The Fed's role as a vector within the state for the structural constraints of capitalism was enormously enhanced in that it was the primary institutional mechanism through which these market disciplines were imposed. The effect was to further circumscribe democratic institutions in the face of the 'rigidity' of an increasingly powerful state economic apparatus. As Bill Clinton famously queried aides during his first term, 'you mean to tell me that the success of the economic program and my re-election hinges on the Federal Reserve and a bunch of fucking bond traders?' (Woodward 1994).

The 1970s crisis was also a crisis of American imperialism, as inflation jeopardized international confidence in the dollar. Inflationary pressures strained the dollar's peg to gold, which was an important foundation of its stability and centrality within the Bretton Woods system, before this peg was abandoned altogether in 1971. The elimination of the capital controls and financial restraints established in the post-war era introduced new forms of volatility, and accordingly required new forms of state supervision. This was especially reflected in the shift in state crisis management strategy from 'failure prevention' to 'failure containment'. As policymakers in the Fed and Treasury understood, preventing financial crises altogether was impossible in a globalized financial system. Instead, they came to see themselves as global firefighters, containing financial crises as they emerged in order to prevent them from threatening the system as a whole (Panitch and Gindin 2012).

In the pre-neoliberal era, the financial branch had played a crucial role in building the basic infrastructure of global finance, and providing support for the banking system by stabilizing currency values and interest rates. Now its role shifted to establishing new modalities of control *within* the structure of globally integrated financial markets in order to maintain stability and fight crises. This pulled the Fed and Treasury more directly into the management of global financial markets. Likewise, the CFTC was created in 1974 in response to the development of financial derivative markets, replacing the Commodity Exchange Authority, which had only regulated agricultural commodities. This established a foundation for the subsequent explosion of derivative markets, as corporations sought to hedge against the risk of devaluations in highly volatile currency markets now characterized by floating exchange rates.

The development of the close ties between the Fed and other central banks necessary to implement the 'dollar standard' that replaced Bretton Woods further enhanced its power and autonomy. Meanwhile, ever-wider areas of economic and social policy were negotiated at forums such as the G8 and G20. Indeed, the replacement of Bretton Woods with the Tokyo Round trade talks (concluded in 1979) entailed the construction of permanent international venues for coordinating economic policy, and the profound restructuring of state institutions to enforce the new regime (Maher 2022). All of this occurred outside the direct oversight of parliaments. In this way, the dominance of the state economic apparatus and the independence of the financial branch were central components of what Robert Cox called 'the internationalization of the state' (Cox 1987; Gill 1998; Panitch and Gindin 2012, 7–12). The post-Bretton Woods trade regime depended upon the internal restructuring of nation-states themselves, as they took on greater responsibility for creating the domestic conditions for international accumulation.

The financial branch presided over the extension of the neoliberal regime over the next three decades, remaining fixed on its anti-inflation orientation as corporations constructed globally integrated production networks, which depended upon the capital mobility afforded by the liberalization of finance. Neoliberalism in no sense amounted to the retreat of the state; rather it depended upon the continuous development of the institutional capacities to regulate global capitalism. New competitive pressures were unleashed as whole sectors of capital were restructured or eliminated. Yet despite the costs for some capitalists, increasing competitiveness strengthened capital *as a class*, as stronger firms replaced weaker ones, and workers were disciplined through the relocation of production to where labour and regulatory costs were cheaper (Botwinick 2018). This dynamic fuelled a further push for 'deregulation', and inaugurated a new era of concessionary bargaining to maintain 'national competitiveness', leading to the precipitous decline of the trade union movement.

Remarkably, this configuration of power contained worker discontent even as communities were devastated by plant closures and working-class life became more precarious than it had been for generations. Both major parties fully embraced the neoliberal consensus, forcefully insisting that 'there is no alternative' but to accommodate the 'new realities' of globalization. Meanwhile, the power of the Fed to manage the economy was seen over the Greenspan years as being just as sacred, and even less partisan, than was the Supreme Court's authority to interpret the law. With the crucial questions of economic policy decided within venues that were largely outside of public view and beyond the reach of elections—and which thereby embodied 'the continuity of the state' regardless of electoral outcomes—politics increasingly focused on cultural and civil rights issues *within* the structure of corporate capitalism.

Then came the 2008 crisis. The dominance of the financial branch reached its apotheosis as the Fed in particular was given extraordinary powers to cope with the worst financial collapse since the Great Depression. As it did, the chaos and dysfunction provoked by the right-wing Tea Party, which had already engaged in hair-raising brinksmanship around raising the 'debt ceiling', now took the form of efforts to derail the financial rescue and block stimulus spending. But the financial crisis also created an opening for the Occupy Wall Street movement to promote a more progressive narrative of class struggle, pointing to the failure of both parties to present meaningful alternatives to the neoliberal immiseration of the working class. All of this sharply accelerated the delegitimization of neoliberal ideology, both political parties, and the media system (Dean 2013).

It was no doubt true that quantitative easing and the government 'bailout' of the banks benefited particular financial firms. Yet this was a by-product of restoring systemic stability, and coincided with the Dodd–Frank Act's vast new regulations on credit intermediation, financial vehicles, commodity and securities contracts, and insurance carriers, which hit particularly hard at federally and state-chartered banks and bank holding companies. This was reflected in the vast restrictions imposed by the Fed, CFTC, and OCC in the wake of the crisis. Furthermore, financial regulations implemented by the financial branch had *already* grown by nearly 20% over the decade before the crisis, despite high-profile 'deregulatory' initiatives such as the Commodities Futures Modernization Act and the Financial Services Regulatory Relief Act. By the 2016 election, Wall Street had largely come to accept Dodd–Frank as a *fait accompli*. Yet reform was on shakier ground than it might have appeared.

2   Trump and the State Economic Apparatus

It quickly became clear after his election that Trump's campaign rhetoric about further regulating Wall Street was merely smoke and mirrors. Instead, he sought to extend his efforts to 'deconstruct the administrative state' to the leading agencies of the economic apparatus. When Congress proved unwilling to simply repeal the Dodd–Frank Act, Trump acted to limit the regulatory powers and capacities of the financial branch through executive orders and by appointing officials to key supervisory positions who shared his objectives (Klein 2018). These efforts aimed both to undermine these agencies, as well as to reorient their policy priorities around a radical deregulatory agenda and sustaining the stock boom. Yet as we shall see, there were clear limits to how far this could go, both as a result of the institutional independence of these agencies as well as the structural constraints imposed by their critical importance for the making of global capitalism.

The main focus of Trump's efforts within the financial branch was the Treasury Department and the OCC. The administration pushed the Treasury not only to gut the extensive restrictions developed in the aftermath of the 2008 crisis, but even to abandon its pre-existing emphasis on controlling bank leverage and capital ratios. Meanwhile, the OCC (which, we recall, is an independent office within the Treasury) faced pressure to reduce its staff of supervisors and broadly pare down its enforcement of financial regulation. Another important target was the FDIC, which faced demands to curtail its regulatory footprint and enforcement of important sections of Dodd–Frank. Similarly, the CFTC was starved of the resources needed to fulfil its responsibilities, and saw its budget for supervision slashed; while at the SEC, insider trading enforcement collapsed to levels not seen since the 1990s (Dreisback 2020).

Trump even appeared willing to directly challenge the independence of the Federal Reserve. Already during the campaign, Trump had lashed out at Fed Chair Janet Yellen in a 'rare, if not unprecedented' move, accusing her of politicizing monetary policy by holding down interest rates to benefit the incumbent Democratic administration (Marans 2016). This continued after the election, when Trump publicly rebuked his own appointee, Jerome Powell, seven times in a single week—which Yellen referred to as 'a first' (Heeb 2019). Nor was this mere rhetoric: as *Bloomberg* reported in June 2019, Trump had explored options for removing Powell and replacing him with a Fed Chair who would more directly serve his political interests. These exceptional challenges to the independence of the central bank led to an equally remarkable public rebuke from all living former Fed chairs in a *Wall Street Journal* op-ed, which condemned the 'short-term political pressures' Trump had unleashed on the institution.

Given the right-wing activists and personal allies Trump had nominated to the Federal Reserve Board, there was good cause for concern. Indeed, Trump's attempts to appoint Herman Cain, Stephen Moore, and Judy Shelton had all been blocked by *Republicans* in Congress for their extreme views and lack of qualifications. Small-time pizza mogul and Tea Party darling Cain, of course, had none of the experience that could qualify him to serve on the Fed's Board of Governors. Moore, meanwhile, was the founder of the anti-tax 'Club for Growth', a precursor to the Tea Party, and had also publicly called for Powell's firing. Yet these choices appeared conventional compared to Shelton, whose views, including returning to the gold standard and even abolishing the central bank—the very institution she had been nominated to oversee—led a former Treasury official to pen a *New York Times* op-ed headlined 'God help us if Judy Shelton joins the Fed' (Rattner 2020).

While his more extreme nominees were blocked by Congress, Trump-appointed Fed officials would still go some way in advancing his political agenda. Randall Quarles was named Vice Chair of Supervision of the Federal Reserve Board in 2017, and 'meticulously completed the job President Trump nominated him to do' by 'ushering in weaker rules' supposedly aimed at enhancing the 'efficiency' of financial regulations (Smialek 2019). Under Quarles' leadership, the budget for supervision at the Federal Reserve Board decreased from $493 billion in 2017 to $368 billion in 2020—a reversal of the trend through the Obama era, during which it had grown steadily. Officials with similar objectives were also appointed to important positions at the FDIC, CFTC, SEC, and OCC. Moreover, when top officials in these agencies failed to implement his priorities, Trump either publicly condemned their actions, openly threatened their replacement, or both.

At the OCC, Trump tapped Keith Noreika, a corporate lawyer who advised major financial firms, to serve as acting Comptroller of the Currency, thereby bypassing the need for Congressional approval for his appointment—a pattern in the Trump administration. Noreika was classified as a 'special government employee', allowing him to avoid certain conflicts of interest and ethics rules, including a prohibition on taking gifts and payments from outside sources. Such 'special' employees typically serve on advisory committees, rather than heading important government agencies. Noreika long overstayed the 130-day limit on such employees, as he aggressively pursued Trump's deregulation agenda while wearing a Make America Great Again cap to work (Dayden 2018). Soon after he took the top job at OCC, he declared that 'there's a lot that can be done' to weaken Dodd–Frank without Congressional action—'even by our agency unilaterally if we had to' (Tracey and Hoffman 2017). This level of fealty to a presidential agenda was unusual for the generally 'apolitical' position of Comptroller of the Currency, in contrast to the more 'political' post of Secretary of the Treasury.

Chief among Noreika's objectives at OCC was implementing the principles laid out in Trump's 2017 Executive Order, *Core Principles for Regulating the United States Financial System*. Under Noreika and his Senate-confirmed replacement, Joseph Otting, the staff of resident examiners working inside major banks to uphold rules and identify violations was reduced, and the operating budget was cut.[2] Enforcement actions against banks declined from 231 in 2016 to 176 in 2019, and the number of supervisory locations was cut nearly in half. Whereas the OCC had focused on 'ensuring a vibrant and diverse federal banking system' and

---

[2] This decline in the OCC's budget was even more significant given that the financial assets it was responsible for supervising increased 11% from 2016 to 2019. See: OCC Annual Reports for the years 2016–2019.

'firmly positioning the OCC to continue operating independently and effectively', it now aimed at 'modernizing' the Community Reinvestment Act (CRA), 'encouraging the federal banking system to meet short-term small-dollar credit needs', and 'reducing the burden of the Bank Secrecy Act and anti-money laundering compliance'.[3] Notably, the OCC's movement from being one of the most important financial regulators to actively pursuing deregulation was accompanied by a reduced emphasis on its 'independence' as well.

Yet Trump's efforts to 'deconstruct the administrative state' and reduce the independence of the financial branch were sharply constrained. Despite the administration's efforts, principal agency functions were preserved, ultimately succeeding only in drawing down some of the capacities developed following the 2008 crisis. Employment levels within the OCC in fact remained much higher than they had been in 2010, and enforcement actions were actually higher at the end of Trump's term than they had been in 2014. Moreover, despite cuts, the OCC's operating budget was left significantly intact, remaining well above pre-crisis levels. This signalled that it had not been absorbed into Steven Mnuchin's Treasury Department, where changes were more drastic—owing in part to the fact that it did not share the 'independence' of the agencies that comprised the financial branch.

Similar barriers limited Trump's restructuring at the CFTC, SEC, and FDIC. The CFTC adjusted its focus from increasing regulation and supervision 'to fostering economic growth', and introduced Project KISS in 2017 to restructure its Division of Market Oversight. While presented as enhancing intra-agency coordination, this actually resulted in the reduction of the budget for supervision by nearly 25% between 2016 and 2020. The number of full-time employees also dropped, reaching a low of 657 in 2019, and agency enforcement actions decreased by roughly 10%. Despite this, the CFTC's overall budget actually increased modestly from 2016 to 2020, while employment in enforcement, oversight, and examination similarly increased from 380 to 404, hardly indicating a total hollowing out.

For its part, the SEC remained focused on 'protecting investors', but placed less emphasis on 'assessing market wide risks', and more on 'information security' and 'financial innovation'—a shift in agency priorities

[3] See: OCC Annual Reports for the years 2016–2019.

towards practices that were friendly to financial firms.[4] This contributed to a decline in certain enforcement actions, yet in key areas, like trading suspensions, enforcement remained relatively steady, declining only relative to the peak of the post-crisis Obama period. Although the SEC rallied against sections of the Dodd–Frank Act, like the OCC and CFTC, it continued implementing and proposing new restrictions and regulations. Only at the FDIC did enforcement take a sharp dive, but this actually reflected a longer-term shift of regulatory responsibilities within the financial branch, dating back to at least the Obama era.

The resilience of the Fed was the most stark of all. While the budget for supervision and regulation declined at the national level, it increased at the regional bank level, from $1.3 billion in 2016 to nearly $1.5 billion in 2019. This reinforced previous changes that saw regional banks, like the New York Federal Reserve, switch from providing services to financial firms and holding companies to regulating and supervising them, and in fact built on the transformations instituted during the Obama era. Fed examinations and inspections of state member banks and small bank holding companies tell a slightly different story, as these declined significantly from 2016 to 2019. But this only accelerated a trend that started in 2010, after the worst of the crisis had passed, and was in any case offset by an increase in examinations of large bank holding and financial holding companies that marked a shift within the Fed towards monitoring 'higher-risk activities'. Moreover, both total expenses and employment in the Federal Reserve System continued to grow at the pre-Trump pace, and while enforcement actions declined in 2019, they increased in both 2017 and 2018, and remained above 2015 levels.

This points to the limits on Trump's restructuring of the financial branch of the state economic apparatus. The formal 'independence' of the agencies comprising the financial branch from the executive and Congress were significant constraints on Trump. As independent agencies, these institutions are not typically subject to executive orders, and their leadership is to an important degree insulated from 'political' pressure. Moreover, with the exception of the CFTC, these agencies are at least partly self-funding. This institutional independence is particularly well established at the Fed, where governors are appointed to staggered 14-year terms, and cannot be removed except 'for cause'. Such

[4] See: SEC Annual Reports for the years 2016–2019.

independence restrained Trump's executive authority and largely limited his interventions to mostly superficial changes in policy priorities and budgets.

Trump's presidential term overlapped with that of Obama-era appointments in the FDIC, OCC, SEC, and CFTC. All of these officials expressed a very different view of regulation and supervision than Trump and resisted his efforts to scale back operations. Additionally, these agencies are formally required to be politically neutral between Democratic and Republican representatives within their governance structure, further curbing Trump's influence. This institutional independence is particularly robust in the case of the regional banks of the Federal Reserve, which are central actors in terms of regulatory authority. Indeed, neither board members nor presidents of the regional banks are directly selected by the president. As such, Trump's efforts were directed at the Federal Reserve Board in Washington and its management of interest rates—and as we saw, these were limited by the Senate, which blocked his more extreme appointments, as well as by the independence of these agencies from presidential authority.

Crucially, the durability of the Fed's independence and insulation from political pressure also bolstered that of the other agencies of the financial branch, thereby limiting Trump's ability to control them as well. The independence of the financial branch agencies is interdependent, since major financial policies have to be coordinated between these different institutions due to the diversified nature of financial firms, the interconnectivity of markets, and the fragmented nature of the US banking system. Such inter-agency coordination was expanded after the 2008 crisis with the establishment of the Financial Stability Oversight Council. Though this technically gave the Treasury a formal veto over the Fed's emergency powers, creating the appearance of political oversight, it functionally *extended* the Fed's authority. As a result of its pivotal role within the financial system, the network of regulators on the FSOC had little choice but to defer to the Fed, facilitating the ongoing concentration of its regulatory power.

These institutional barriers circumscribing 'political' interference were reinforced by the organic linkages between the financial branch and the financial system. As we saw, the liberalization of finance especially served as a constraint on the Fed's politicization, imposing upon it a 'rigidity' that expresses the hard limits on the range of political strategies the state can deploy. Its role in managing liquidity and inflation, and ensuring the monetary conditions for labour discipline and dollar seigniorage, are indispensable to the structure of neoliberal globalization. Similarly, the capacities the Fed developed after 2008 were vital for the explosive growth of global financial markets after the crisis—making it incredibly difficult to roll back even these expansive new powers. The Fed's role as a vector within the state expressing the structural constraints of capitalism, its weight within the state institutional complex, and the globalization of capital are fundamentally intertwined: one cannot be challenged without also impacting the others.

3   NEOLIBERALISM AND TRUMPISM

Clearly, the ways that the 'rigidity' of the state economic apparatus leads it to 'display the limits and restrictions of the political options and tactics available for organizing class hegemony' is important for understanding the limitations on Trump's ability to 'deconstruct the administrative state' (Poulantzas 2003, 171). As we have shown, understanding how this rigidity functions in the American case requires clarifying and building on Poulantzas' sketch of the neoliberal state. Indeed, significant aspects of Poulantzas' theorization fall wide of the mark in describing the structure of power within the contemporary American state. In particular, there can be little question that Poulantzas drastically overstated the extent to which authoritarian statism would result in a 'personalized presidential system' led by a 'single, dominant state party' that would place 'the entire administration in a relationship of strict political subordination to the summits of the Executive' (Poulantzas 2003, 233). Far from being 'strictly subordinated' to the will of the executive, as we have seen the financial branch of the state economic apparatus remains highly insulated from political interventions, including by the president.

Similarly, even after the dramatic expansion of executive power and severe erosion of judicial and Congressional oversight over a ballooning national security state through the so-called War on Terror, it is clear that Poulantzas went too far in predicting that the 'separation of legislative, executive and judicial powers in the bourgeois State is itself subject to final elimination' with the development of authoritarian statism (Poulantzas 2003, 227). Central bank independence has been a primary feature of neoliberal capitalism, and its autonomy from presidential power is a core component of authoritarian statism as it developed in the United States. As we saw, this independence was protected in part by Congress, and thus the formal separation of executive and legislative authority. Indeed, Poulantzas' outline of authoritarian statism in this regard hardly resembles the impersonal technocratic nature of the neoliberal state. Far from being subordinated to the will of an unchecked president, the US state contains significant bulwarks preventing such a unified concentration of political power around an elected president.

Of course, as Poulantzas argued, the neoliberal state does contain elements that could—through a break from 'within' this state—potentially constitute a fascist state, especially its highly sophisticated and secretive military, policing, and intelligence agencies. But we must take seriously the sharp difference between such a hypothetical fascist state and the present neoliberal one, and recognize the significant barriers that the structure of authoritarian statism itself poses to the emergence of such a regime (Fletcher 2016; Traverso 2021). As Panitch and Gindin (2018, 18–19) speculated:

> Perhaps the greatest irony of central bank independence, explicitly designed by states and capital working together to protect the making of global capitalism from the progressive tendencies of democratic pressures on elected governments, is that it may yet come to be seen as saving global capitalism from the chaos of the Trump presidency. The greatest test of this will be the Fed's behaviour in the face of the gathering financial storms abroad.

This test was passed, albeit in relation to a crisis that struck unexpectedly close to home, when the Fed mobilized all the firepower it had accumulated after 2008—and then some—to stabilize global capitalism amidst the Covid-19 pandemic. As the global economy ground to a halt in March 2020, the Fed resumed quantitative easing and developed new emergency spending facilities targeting commercial paper, municipal notes, and corporate bonds. This intervention in corporate debt markets was particularly significant, as it signalled a further expansion of the Fed's role in crisis management from its traditional remit of financial markets to non-financial corporations. It also involved the Fed reinstating unlimited swap lines of credit with foreign central banks, and further backstopping the Treasury bond market. The latter was necessary to respond to unprecedented chaos and dislocation in government bond markets caused by automatic trading and 'the frenzied dash for cash', and involved the most aggressive intervention into public markets in history (Wigglesworth 2020).

Any political attempt to substantially restructure the state economic apparatus can be expected to run up against significant resistance. The integration of this apparatus within the structure of capitalism forces it to embody the 'continuity of the state', and leaves it least subject to the 'conjunctural hazards of government policy'. After four decades, globalization has become deeply entrenched, and cannot simply be reversed without a major confrontation with the multinational corporations which continue to benefit from it. Trump was nothing if not a 'conjunctural hazard' to global capitalism. Yet for all the chaos and disorder it brought to the American empire, Trump's presidency in no way advanced a viable alternative to neoliberal globalization. Consequently, there was no practical option but to continue to rely on the role of the financial branch in stabilizing and reproducing it.

References

Aquanno, Scott M. 2021. *The Crisis of Risk: Subprime Debt and US Financial Power from 1944 to Present*. Northampton: Edward Elgar Publishing.

Block, Fred, and Matthew Keller. 2011. *State of Innovation: The U.S. Government's Role in Technology Development*. New York: Routledge.

Botwinick, Harry. 2018. *Persistent Inequalities: Wage Disparity Under Capitalist Competition*. Chicago: Haymarket.

Cox, Robert. 1987. *Production, Power, and World Order: Social Forces in the Making of History*. New York: Columbia University Press.

Dayen, David. 2018. 'Swamp Watch: Trump's Top Banking Regulator Heads Back to His Wall Street Clients.' The Intercept, January 9. https://theinterc ept.com/2018/01/09/keith-noreika-occ-trump-simpson-thacher/.

Dean, Jodi. 2013. 'Occupy Wall Street: After the Anarchist Moment.' *Socialist Register* 49: 52–62.

Dreisbach, Tom. 2020. 'Under Trump SEC Enforcement of Insider Trading Dropped to the Lowest Point in Decades.' NPR, August 14. https://www.npr.org/2020/08/14/901862355/under-trump-sec-enforcement-of-insider-trading-dropped-to-lowest-point-in-decade.

Fletcher, Bill. 2016. '"Stars and Bars": Understanding Right-Wing Populism in the USA.' *Socialist Register* 51: 296–311.

Finn, Ed. 2017. 'Is Trump a Fascist.' *The Independent*, May 13. https://theind ependent.ca/commentary/the-nonagenarians-notebook/is-trump-a-fascist/.

Foster, John Bellamy. 2017. 'This is Not Populism.' *Monthly Review* 69 (2): 1–24.

Gill, Stephen. 1998. 'New Constitutionalism, Democratisation and Global Political Economy.' *Global Change, Peace & Security* 10 (1): 23–38.

Hedges, Chris. 2016. 'The Revenge of the Lower Classes and the Rise of American Fascism.' *Truthdig*, August 9. https://www.truthdig.com/articles/the-revenge-of-the-lower-classes-and-the-rise-of-american-fascism-2/.

Heeb, Gina. 2019. 'Janet Yellen Told Us Trump's Attacks on the Fed are "a First"—and Stressed the Importance of an Independent Central Bank.' *Business Insider*, August 7. https://www.businessinsider.in/janet-yellen-told-us-trumps-attacks-on-the-fed-are-a-first-and-stressed-the-importance-of-an-independent-central-bank/amp_articleshow/70576727.cms.

Klein, Aaron. 2018. 'No, Dodd-Frank Was Neither Repealed Nor Gutted. Here's What Really Happened.' Brookings Institution Report, May 25. https://www.brookings.edu/research/no-dodd-frank-was-neither-repealed-nor-gutted-heres-what-really-happened/.

Maher, Stephen. 2022. *Corporate Capitalism and the Integral State: General Electric and a Century of American Power*. London: Palgrave Macmillan.

Marans, Daniel. 2016. 'Trump Doubles Down on Personal Attack Against the Federal Reserve.' *Huffington Post*, September 12. https://www.cnbc.com/2018/10/11/trump-doubles-down-on-fed-attacks-saying-its-going-loco.html.

Mazzucato, Mariana. 2013. *The Entrepreneurial State: Debunking Public vs. Private Sector Myths*. London: Anthem Press.

O'Connor, James. 1973. *The Fiscal Crisis of the State*. New York: Transaction Publishers.

Panitch, Leo, and Sam Gindin. 2012. *The Making of Global Capitalism: American Empire and the Political Economy of Global Finance*. London: Verso.

Panitch, Leo and Sam Gindin. 2018. "Trumping the Empire," In Leo Panitch and Greg Albo, eds., Socialist Register 2019: The World Turned Upside Down?. London: Merlin.

Panitch, Leo, and Donald Swartz. 2003. *From Consent to Coercion: The Assault on Trade Union Freedoms*. Toronto: University of Toronto Press.

Poulantzas, Nicos. 2003 [1978]. *State, Power, Socialism*. London: Verso.

Radosh, Ronald. 2017. 'Steve Bannon, Trump's Top Guy, Told Me He Was "a Leninist."' *Daily Beast*, April 13. https://www.thedailybeast.com/steve-bannon-trumps-top-guy-told-me-he-was-a-leninist.

Rattner, Steven. 2020. 'God Help Us If Judy Shelton Joins the Fed.' *New York Times*, July 22. https://www.nytimes.com/2020/07/22/opinion/federal-reserve-judy-shelton.html.

Romero, Jessie. 1951. 'Treasury-Fed Accord.' Federal Reserve Bank of Richmond, March.

Rucker, Philip, and Robert Costa. 2017. 'Bannon Vows a Daily Fight for "Deconstruction of the Administrative State."' *Washington Post*, February 23. https://www.washingtonpost.com/politics/top-wh-strategist-vows-a-daily-fight-for-deconstruction-of-the-administrative-state/2017/02/23/03f6b8da-f9ea-11e6-bf01-d47f8cf9b643_story.html.

Shaikh, Anwar. 2016. *Capitalism: Competition, Conflict, Crises*. Oxford: Oxford University Press.

Smialek, Jeanna. 2019. 'Meet the Man Loosening Bank Regulation, One Detail at a Time.' *New York Times*, November 29. https://www.nytimes.com/2019/11/29/business/economy/bank-regulations-fed.html.

Streeck, Wolfgang. 2014. *Buying Time: The Delayed Crisis of Democratic Capitalism*. London: Verso.

Tracy, Ryan, and Liz Hoffman. 2017. 'The Volcker Rule: How Trump's New Regulator May Unleash Big Banks.' *Wall Street Journal*, May 11. https://www.wsj.com/articles/the-volcker-rule-how-trumps-new-regulator-may-unleash-big-banks-1494495001.

Traverso, Enzo. 2021. 'Twenty-First Century Fascism: Where We Are.' *New Politics* 18 (3): 39–42.

Woodward, Bob. 1994. *The Agenda*. New York: Simon & Schuster.

Soldiers and the State in Marx and Engels

Jasmine Chorley-Schulz

1   INTRODUCTION

This chapter offers a new perspective on class and the coercive force of the capitalist state. Although Marx famously never completed his planned text on the state, Marx and Engels discussed militaries and wars throughout their works. By returning to these texts, this chapter brings into focus a connection between capitalist social relations and the coercive power of the state through the figure of the soldier. Maintaining and using military institutions require people to carry out work. How do people come to perform specifically military work—as militia, conscripts, professional soldiers, officers, and generals?[1] How is this work constituted, and what is specific about it in the broader context of capitalist development, class struggle, and antagonism?

One aim of this chapter is to interrogate the seemingly eternal appearance of the military and soldiers, their historical development, and how

---

[1] As opposed to non-combat military labour.

J. Chorley-Schulz (✉)
Department of Political Science, University of Toronto, Toronto, ON, Canada
e-mail: jasmine.chorleyfoster@mail.utoronto.ca

© The Author(s), under exclusive license to Springer Nature
Switzerland AG 2023
R. Hunter et al. (eds.), *Marxism and the Capitalist State*,
Political Philosophy and Public Purpose,
https://doi.org/10.1007/978-3-031-36167-8_6

social movements might understand and engage with them. While societies around the world—and from ancient to present times—have had militaries or units for fighting, conflating all such units or institutions as being of a similar kind (due to their general, common activity—that is, fighting) presents the risk of accepting the appearances of capitalist institutions at face value. This chapter approaches the military and soldiers by understanding them within the context of historical class antagonism and struggle. Crucially, in capitalist societies, the people tasked with fulfilling the various roles in military institutions—soldiers, officers, generals—are recruited from civilian classes. In a given historical moment, where are the masses of soldiers recruited from? How and why are they available for this role? In this chapter, I limit my attention to the capitalist epoch in Europe and propose an approach from which to analyse the military as part of the capitalist state. The capitalist state I consider in the abstract is primarily the capitalist state as Marx and Engels wrote about it—that is, the industrial, imperial core—but the primary features of the approach certainly travel beyond the narrow scope of the core. Approaching soldiers as people situated within historical social relations, and not merely abstract agents of the state, is a crucial shift in focus that allows us to better understand the material circumstances and contradictions that make military operations possible and may be used to identify potential vulnerabilities in a given terrain of power.

I break the discussion into two main sections. First, I look at Marx's and Engels' writing on productive economic forces and military power. This involves a brief discussion of Engels' materialist conception of the development of the state. I then discuss the cooperative character of both industrial production and industrial militarism, paying particular attention to chapter 13 ('Co-operation') in *Capital*. Second, I explore Engels' idea of the 'human material' of military capabilities alongside Marx's interpretation of the Paris Commune in order to explore the class position of soldiers and their relation to value.

The purpose of focusing on these texts is both historical-interpretive and methodological. This chapter offers an interpretation of Marx's and Engels' own work on soldiers, which is an under-examined aspect of their thought on the state. Even later Marxist state theory on military institutions tends to overlook the role of the ordinary soldier (as opposed to military elites) in the capitalist state and society. This chapter also looks at Marx's and Engels' texts for direction in the method for understanding the soldier in the capitalist state in historical and contemporary cases.

2   ORIGINS OF THE MILITARY

In this section I discuss key points Marx and Engels make about the military in their writing. What I draw out of their texts is that in many ways the military is like other state institutions: it is historical, it emerges from class society, and it shares the underlying social relations of the rest of capitalist society. Its basis in class division and direction from the ruling class mean that it is a necessarily undemocratic form of political power or force. Furthermore, highly militarized countries build that power on the basis of their economic power. I build on my own specific readings, but these main ideas are an important base to begin with.

2.1   State and Military

In his discussions of the growth of the state through different stages of development, in various works, Engels offers a few points on state coercive force that are relevant here. Engels writes that class antagonism necessitates the creation of public or state coercive forces because 'an independent armed organization of the population became impossible with the division of society into classes' (Engels 1940, 140). Such a 'public power of coercion exists in every state', he continues, and it includes also 'material accessories such as prisons and institutions of coercion of all kinds' (Engels 1940, 140–41).

He describes military force as a matter of historical development; 'force is no mere act of the will, but requires the existence of very real preliminary conditions before it can come into operation' (Engels 1962, 229). With the evolution of production and divisions of labour came increased population density, which 'necessitated closer consolidation against internal and external foes', and war and its organization became 'regular functions of national life' (Engels 1940, 135). The role of the military commander as an indispensable, permanent official is one of the first events that occur once kinship groupings amalgamate into one national territory (Engels 1940, 135). This period of development, still located in 'barbarism' for Engels, marks a new phase of war's role: 'once waged simply to avenge aggression or as a means of enlarging territory that had become too restricted, [war] was now waged for the sake of plunder alone, and became a regular profession' (Engels 1940, 135). Although militaries have existed in some form throughout human history, Engels writes, the role they play evolves with the dominant mode of production. For him, the military is not a transhistorical institution but is determined by social relations—whether through the rule of princes, lords, or the modern state.

In the *Peasant War in Germany*, Engels takes to a lengthy analysis of a particular historical period, presenting what is typically thought of as an early modern confessional conflict as, in fact, the regular conflict of politics; war is class war (Engels 2000). Soldiers here are not really distinguishable as professionals or rebels beyond their term of armed service, and he describes the frequent movement of individuals or groups of soldiers between factions and sides. He discusses the recruitment of soldiers from various classes as an important factor in the historical movement of the wars; various groups surrender and abandon their allied classes when minimum concessions are made. For him, this is an example of an earlier stage of development prior to the development of the national army and the citizen-soldier; war is still the clear purview of feudal institutions and classes. The point is that even if we can identify parallel concrete activities of the role of soldiers between different historical periods, the social relation underpinning them may vary. The particularity of the capitalist state is that the economy and the state become *conceptually* separated, despite their mutual underlying social relations, and this is necessary to consider when thinking about the source of state manpower (Smith 2017; Bonefeld 2021).

In *The Civil War in France*, Marx describes the development of the state as a tool of the bourgeoisie to wield against the monarchy and the nobility in their liberation from feudal domination. In developed bourgeois society, the state is finally transformed into a means of rule of capital over labour (Marx 1978a, 631). Over time, state organs (standing army, police, bureaucracy, clergy, judicature) develop a certain autonomy as institutions and pursue their own special interests, transforming themselves from servants to masters of society (Engels 1978a, 627–29). As Engels writes, in class societies, the state emerged out of class antagonisms in order to manage them; because of its origins as such the state belongs to the ruling class (Engels 1940, 141).

Engels grounds the origins of the coercive force of the state in economic production. While certainly not denying the use of organized force and violence in the development of the state and economic development, he emphasizes that the means of violence are products of economic activity. In his preparatory notes for *Anti-Dühring*, he notes that.

And so it is force that creates the economic, political, etc. conditions of life of an epoch, a people, etc. But who creates force? Organized force is primarily *the army*. And nothing depends more on economic conditions than precisely the composition, organization, armament, strategy and tactics of an army. (Engels 1962, 487)

As an example, he argues that weapons were originally an invention of subsistence hunting; the means of war have developed their own independent purposes, but they are rooted in historic and economic development of the means of production (Engels 1940, 20). 'Industry remains industry, whether it is applied to the production or the destruction of things' (Engels 1962, 230).

Of his own historical period, Engels writes that successful force is based on arms production, which is itself based on production in the economy generally. To produce capable late nineteenth-century armies and navies, the state requires firms capable of producing armaments, munitions, ships, and uniforms; a growing pool of taxable capital; a source of public debts; as well as fuel and food. As Engels describes, the level of development in production, including the financial sector and communications technologies, determines armaments and thus matters of military science: force composition, organization, tactics, and strategy. The state of development of a ship-building industry, for example, will determine the possibility of having a navy in addition to an army, the size and strength of a naval force, and what kind of strategies and tactics (and therefore political options) are available to it. He writes,

> ... nowadays any zealous NCO [non-commissioned officer] could explain to Herr Dühring how greatly, besides, the conduct of war depends on the productivity and means of communication of the army's own hinterland as well as the theatre of war. In short, always and everywhere it is the economic conditions and the instruments of economic power which help 'force' to victory, without which force ceases to be force. (Engels 1962, 236–37)

To conclude his section refuting Dühring's theory of force, Engels argues that the 'primary' force is economic, not an abstract 'political force':

> For what in fact does "the primary" in force itself prove to be? Economic power, the disposal of the means of power of large-scale industry. Naval

political force, which reposes on modern warships, proves to be not at all 'direct' but on the contrary *mediated* by economic power, highly developed metallurgy, command of skilled technicians and highly productive coal-mines.… If we put Herr Dühring in supreme command in the next naval war, he will destroy all fleets of armoured ships…without torpedoes or any other artifices, solely by virtue of his 'direct force'. (Engels 1962, 239–40)

This general dependence on economics should not be confused as a dismissal of the political. In his many writings, on Bismarck especially, Engels pays close attention to choices and errors made with political power, in turn hampering, encouraging, or otherwise influencing the progress of economic force. In a letter to Joseph Bloch, Engels writes, 'why do we fight for the political dictatorship of the proletariat if political power is economically impotent? *Force (that is, state power) is also an economic power!*' (Engels 1978b, 765; emphasis added). The point is that military power, and growing militarism across Europe, were part of capitalist development, and not preceding entities or mere problems of ideas.

2.2   Force (Cooperative, Mass, Organized)

While it is dependent on economic production, military force is, in and of itself, unproductive of capital and does not extract surplus value from soldiers. It can only spend and consume state revenues, so the revenues presupposed by armed forces expenditure require production in the general economy, that is, (typically) outside the state. So what are we to make of the soldier's relationship to capital? Although the state does not extract surplus value from soldiers, there is a striking commonality between the concrete activity of capitalist production and state coercive force: cooperation.

Marx defines cooperation in production as the state of affairs '[w]hen numerous workers work together side by side in accordance with a plan, whether in the same process, or in different but connected processes, this form of labour is called co-operation' (Marx 1981, 443). Cooperation is a qualitative change in production that arises from a quantitative change; Marx cites the example of a hundred men who can together easily lift a ton of weight, whereas one man cannot and ten men would strain to do so (Marx 1981, 443, n 5). While the capitalist may pay for each work-er's labour-power, he does not pay for this combined labour-power; the capitalist gets this power at no cost, and it appears as if inherent to capital (Marx 1981, 451). It is 'the fundamental form of the capitalist mode of production' (Marx 1981, 454).

In *Capital*, Marx uses the commonality between capitalist produc-tion and military force to great rhetorical effect. He compares them to demonstrate two crucial qualities: cooperative power of output; and the discipline, authority, and command over that cooperative power. For example:

> Just as the offensive power of a squadron of cavalry, or the defensive power of an infantry regiment, is essentially different from the sum of the offen-sive or defensive powers of the individual soldiers taken separately, so the sum total of the mechanical forces exerted by isolated workers differs from the social force that is developed when many hands cooperate in the same undivided operation, such as raising a heavy weight, turning a winch or getting an obstacle out of the way. (Marx 1981, 443)

In the course of valorizing capital, the cooperative labour process also generates incredible potential revolutionary power, so for the capitalist their command over the power of that productive mass is paramount. Cooperation develops revolutionary potential as the labourer 'strips off the fetters of his individuality, and develops the capabilities of his species', but it does so initially for the purpose of capital accumulation (Marx 1981, 447). The task of controlling this power is again an opportunity for Marx to draw a military comparison: 'That a capitalist should command in the field of production is now as indispensable as that a general should command on the field of battle' (Marx 1981, 448). He elaborates on the various roles subordinate to command: 'An industrial army of workers under the command of a capitalist requires, like a real army, officers (managers) and NCOs (foremen, overseers), who command during the labour process in the name of capital' (Marx 1981, 450).

The military metaphors call to mind a tremendous power of a cooper-ative mass of people and a capitalist's impetus to control that power. 'As the number of [cooperating] workers increases, so too does their resis-tance to the domination of capital, and, necessarily, the pressure put on by capital to overcome this resistance' (Marx 1981, 449). As with a mili-tary leader and his troops, alienation here has to be maintained: 'Hence the interconnection between their various labours confronts them, in the realm of ideas. As a plan drawn up by the capitalist, and, in practice, as his authority, as the powerful will of a being outside them, who subjects their activity to his purpose' (Marx 1981, 450). All this immense cooperative power of labour *appears* as 'a productive power inherent in capital' (Marx 1981, 451). In *The Communist Manifesto* too, Marx and Engels compare the domination in industrial production to the military:

> Modern industry has converted the little workshop or patriarchal master into the great factory of the industrial capitalist. Masses of labourers, crowded into the factory, are organized like soldiers. As privates of the industrial army they are placed under the command of a perfect hierarchy of officers and sergeants. (Marx and Engels 2011, 227)

While rhetorically powerful, comparing the cooperative power of labour to military force also reveals the character of these things in a way that is more than metaphoric. The modern military, just like the capitalist mode of production, requires a mass of people working cooperatively. These masses are alienated from their means of production, do not themselves decide to what use they will be put, and are brought together to labour for a single entity (the state), under the delegated supervision and command of an external entity (officers), including promoted fellow workers (NCOs). Only when they are brought together in this advanced form can they produce a qualitatively new force that is not only more powerful but also 'intrinsically collective' (Marx 1981, 443). The concrete commonality between the productive industrial workplace and the consuming state military is the force of the organized, cooperative labour of a mass of people subjected to the ends of a boss or a king.

In production, workers' cooperative power is developed for the sake of its productive power: that is, for the valorization of capital. But like the productive power of workers threatening the command of capital, the mass of soldiers presents a threat to military and ultimately state command. Furthermore, in both cases, competition and conflict between capitals or national bourgeoisies enlist working people into alignment against one another for the economic or political objectives of their ruling class. Both labour processes embody the power of the mass of expropriated classes—those who produce the economic and state power of their own domination but contain the potential power to overcome it. The force generated by the mass organized force of military labour occurs regardless of its unproductivity of any exchange value. The setting of the army, lacking the direct compulsion of value extraction, shows how it is *labour-power* that produces such great concrete force. Further, the hierarchy of military command, like capital command, produces the illusion of its own necessity.[2] The cooperative heights of their domination contains the revelation of their power. And, the productive, economic power on one side of the comparison structurally underwrites the military power of the other.

In capitalist society, the force of productive power and of state power are similar in fundamental ways: they are generally characterized by the cooperative and organized mass power of the expropriated classes for the enrichment or battles of the ruling class(es). One view of this could be from a liberal perspective: the one produces economic activity and the other state authority, two sides of a well-functioning society providing goods of prosperity and safety. But by accepting the antagonism of class society, we accept that productive economic power is not neutral, but historical and exploitative, and the state itself is a capitalist state. So, what of the soldiers themselves, the masses of state power? Is it sufficient to see military power and their masses as antagonistic to the masses of labour? Is it a similarly exploitative enterprise? In the next section, I introduce Engels' idea of 'human material' to explore these questions and return again to the question of command.

3   HUMAN MATERIAL AND CLASS STRUGGLE

Armed forces of the state are, like the cooperative productive forces, typically characterized by a cooperative, organized mass of people under the direction of a group-external figure: the capitalist and his agents for the latter, and the military leadership and the government for the former. More than a similarity of concrete activity, this shared characteristic contains a political insight into the revolutionary potential of the mass cooperative worker and soldier. To make this point, this section explores the mass of people who comprise a state's armed forces using Engels' concept of 'human material' and Marx's interpretation of the Paris Commune.

---

[2] See the next section for Engels on the myth of the military genius.

In *Anti-Dühring*, Engels introduces the role of 'human material' in a discussion of 'military genius':

> Nothing is more dependent on economic prerequisites than precisely army and navy. Armament, composition, organization, tactics and strategy depend above all on the stage reached at the time in production and on communications. It is not the "free creations of the mind" of generals of genius that have had a revolutionizing effect here, but the invention of better weapons and the change in human material, the soldiers; at the very most the part played by generals of genius is limited to adapting methods of fighting to the new weapons and combatants. (Engels 1962, 230)

As he describes the role of technological advancements in warfare (for example, gunpowder and the flint-lock musket with a bayonet) so too does he describe the role of the 'human material', a term not defined but which appears to contain an assemblage of expected military characteristics (strength, discipline, etc.) and social characteristics (Engels 1962, 230–32). For example, the foot soldiers of the early eighteenth century 'were the mercenaries of princes [consisting] of the most demoralized elements of society, rigorously drilled but quite unreliable and only held together by the rod; they were often hostile prisoners of war who had been pressed into service' (Engels 1962, 231). Forces thus composed were a 'cumbrous mass', a considerable limit upon tactical options (Engels 1962, 231–32). In another example, he argues that the success of the Prussian military against the Austrian Empire in 1866 was the result of a change in both technology and human material. Amidst an economic boom following from the German states' customs union, Prussia was the first state to equip the whole infantry with a rapid-firing breech-loaded rifle. Moreover, the *Landwehr* militia system had increased the number of active duty and reserve personnel, who were continuously trained and drilled. (Engels 1962, 233–34).[3]

Engels describes human material in terms of physical strength, training, and discipline, but also in terms of loyalties, motivations, employment arrangements, and class. He argues that, rather than simple material, soldiers' social characteristics affect the qualities of their individual and

---

[3] For recent historical research on the cultural phenomenon of the Landwehr and peacetime military's social effects see Hewitson (2017) and Frevert (2004). Thanks to Eriks Bredovskis for their helpful input.

combined mass, in a way distinct from more familiar military consider-ations, such as morale and unit cohesion. As I interpret it, the concept of human material points us towards understanding that the cooperative organized mass is not robotic, even when disciplined in the service of a reactionary state. Unlike machines, one soldier is not necessarily equal to another even when they have common training and command. How one fights depends surely on military organization, arms, training, and discipline, but also personal and social characteristics. Indeed, the mili-tary scientific design of training and discipline is an attempt to override these social characteristics to facilitate uniformity and command.[4]

A more familiar text adds further flesh to this idea. Marx writes in *The Civil War in France* that the Commune could only resist the siege of Paris because they had eliminated the standing army and replaced it with a National Guard made up mostly of workers.[5] This substitution of the standing army for armed workers implies that the role of manpower in an armed force is not merely a technical matter of numbers and training, but that it also matters *who* makes up that force. Under siege, the Paris Commune needed to arm and defend itself, and its members worked together in the cooperative sense discussed above. Like the cooperative, social production force in *Capital*, 'Paris mobilized as one man for resis-tance' (Engels 1978a, 622). The Commune abolished conscription and the standing army declared the National Guard (the volunteer citizen militia of the French Revolution) the sole armed force, and all citizens capable of bearing arms were armed (Engels 1978a, 623).

In this interpretation of the story of the Commune, what makes the National Guard different than the conscripted standing army? What is the substance of this substitution? The standing army and conscription are removed not because the Commune did not need military functions, but

----

[4] For example, Foucault makes great use of the soldier as a model for later disciplinary structures: 'By the late eighteenth century, the soldier has become something that can be made; out of a formless clay, an inapt body, the machine required can be constructed … turning silently into the automatism of habit; in short, one has "got rid of the peasant" and given him "the air of the soldier"' (Foucault 1991, 135). For a recent study, see Evans (2020).

[5] 'Paris could resist only because, in consequence of the siege, it had got rid of the army, and replaced it by a National Guard, the bulk of which consisted of working men. This fact was now to be transformed into an institution. The first decree of the Commune, therefore, was the suppression of the standing army, and the substitution for it of the armed people' (Marx 1978a, 632).

because there is something in the quality of the state's repressive apparatus *itself*, other than the violence-potential of 'repression' in the abstract, and there is something distinct in the characteristics of the armed workers.

3.1   The Soldier and Surplus Value

The centrality of class struggle is essential to the Marxist methodological framework. Class struggle emerges out of the unique feature of capitalism, the extraction of surplus value for which time (labouring time) is fought over (Harvey 2010, 141). Soldiering itself is not characterized by the extraction of surplus value, however. As discussed above, the concrete activity of the two may appear similar—as when Marx compares the discipline and command involved in both—or even identical—what distinguishes the activity of an engineer in the Navy from an engineer in a private firm, or a soldier from a private mercenary?

In the *Grundrisse*, Marx describes how the consumption of use values is neither capital accumulation nor wealth-production. Although money is exchanged for a labour service, the money in this exchange is revenue, not capital. The military—and we have also seen Engels describe it as such—consumes direct use values. Marx gives one such an example of 'exchange of mere use values' in 'the old communities': 'The pay [*Sold*] of the common soldier is also reduced to a minimum—determined purely by the production costs necessary to procure him. But he exchanges the performance of his services not for capital, but for the revenue of the state' (Marx 1978c, 258). The key here is that 'there is nothing of wage labour in this relation' (Marx 1978c, 258); that is, the payment exchanged for the work that is performed is *not* that which distinguishes the capitalist mode of production, where one part only of the worker's daily labour is paid, while the other part is unpaid, although it *appears* as if the total day worked is paid. Military work, even amidst a capitalist mode of production, so long as it takes this shape, can be categorized as 'service'. Marx writes, 'In bourgeois society itself, all exchange of personal services for revenue' belong in this category, including:

> labour for personal consumption, cooking, sewing etc., garden work etc., up to and including all of the unproductive classes, civil servants, physicians, lawyers, scholars etc.—belongs under this rubric, within this category. All menial servants etc. By means of their services—often

coerced—all these workers, from the least to the highest, obtain for themselves a share of the surplus product, of the capitalist's *revenue*. (Marx 1978c, 258)[6]

This offers a direction in how Marx and Engels understood military pay in the bourgeois societies they were analysing: 'since bourgeois society is itself only a contradictory form of development, relations derived from earlier forms will often be found within it only in an entirely stunted form, or even travestied' (Marx 1978c, 241). It is not unusual to find these older economic forms, distinct from wage labour:

> The categories which express [bourgeois society's] relations, the comprehension of its structure, thereby also allows insights into the structure and the relations of production of all the vanished social formations out of whose ruins and elements it built itself up, whose partly still unconquered remnants are carried along within it, whose mere nuances have developed explicit significance within it, etc. (Marx 1978c, 241)

For example, in *The Civil War in France*, Marx describes how, as the state developed greater power, it increasingly assumed the character of the national power of capital over labour: 'a public force organised for social enslavement, of an engine of class despotism' (Marx 1978a, 630).

For the state to mount increased capacity for force requires more people to fill the roles of soldiers and officers. This human material has to come from somewhere, and the composition of these forces relates to the concurrent economic development it is entwined with. This will take different forms depending on the historical particularities of the society. The military (and other state functions) can act as a sponge to absorb, for a time, lumpen elements of the economy, such as former petty bourgeois, peasants, nobility, surplus workers, or criminalized classes. In Bonapartist France, for example, Marx writes that this mass of political power in the form of state force masked a weakness of the French economy, only to

---

[6] Note the acknowledgement of this category of work not as being 'better' than wage labour—the distinction of older forms of labour from wage labour is that the former is an expenditure of revenue and the latter a valorization of capital. Marx discusses the unpaid portion of wage labour contrasted with serfs and slaves where it is transparent that only a part of their productive labour is for the worker's own reproduction. It is in capitalist production where this unpaid portion, where the worker is producing solely for the boss, is obscured by the wage form, making it appear as though all the day's labour is paid for by the wage. See the chapter 'Wages' in *Capital* (Marx 1981, 675–682, esp. 680).

be 'laid bare by the bayonet of Prussia' (Marx 1978a, 631). As discussed above, the military is a revenue-spending enterprise, not one of capital accumulation, so it rests on a foundation of production in the general economy. Services rendered to the state by military personnel take place through a pre-wage-labour economic form (that is, a service-for-revenue exchange not involving the production of surplus value) that carries on in various ways but is adapted to bourgeois society. Rather than the attendant feudal political forms—feudal hierarchies and privileges, obligations of service—we see it adapted to a bourgeois political form, the nation-state, which draws on revenues and citizenship rather than local feudal bonds or privileges.

3.2   The Soldier and Class

Where do the 'unproductive' fit into class struggle? While this question has been explored, particularly by Marxist Feminists and others in great detail over the past decades, soldiers have not received much attention relative to other unproductive state workers.[7] This relative absence of soldiers in such discussions is one of the reasons to turn to these original texts by Marx and Engels. In the role of soldier, one may be economically outside a direct capital-labour relation, but this does not mean that individual soldiers themselves are outside capitalism and the political antagonism it generates. Marx distinguishes between roles and individuals, and *Capital* is about roles: 'the characters who appear on the economic stage are merely personifications of economic relations [commodities]; it is as the bearers of these economic relations that they come into contact with each other' (Marx 1981, 179). The population available for the work of war—from enlisted men to officers—has a relationship to the general economy and society.

While variously defined, the proletariat encompasses an ever-widening group of society, both wage-labourers and others, united by not owning the means of production.[8] Individuals move between classes, most

---

[7] See Kirstin Munro's chapter in this volume, particularly the critical overview of the redefinitions of 'social reproduction' in pursuit of a recognition of the revolutionary potential of 'unproductive' workers, particularly women workers.

[8] The proletariat is variously defined in the works of Marx and Engels, for example: 'The class of modern wage-labourers who, having no means of production of their own, are reduced to selling their labour power in order to live'; 'that class in society which

frequently downwards: the 'proletariat is recruited from all classes of the population'; 'small peasants and petty bourgeois...are in the process of falling into the proletariat' (Marx and Engels 2011, 228; Engels 2005). This occurs to whole classes in transitional periods. For example, in *The Eighteenth Brumaire*, Marx describes the proletarianization of the countryside in the transition from feudal to bourgeois rule and the corresponding state form (Marx 1978b, 606–608).[9] Also, capitalism regularly makes workers 'surplus'. This downward force within capitalism is due to the development of new means of production making old skill-specialisms redundant (Marx and Engels 2011, 228; Marx 1981, 781–88). The production of surplus populations is a uniquely capitalist phenomenon— no other mode of production sees this 'law' of population (Marx 1981, 783–84). The surplus population provides a 'reserve army of labour' for the capitalist to replace workers who are unable to work, and are used to exert downward pressure on workers' bargaining power and wage. As well, the 'extraordinary increase in the productivity of large-scale industry', the fact that the economic output and exploitation per worker increases so much, 'permits a larger and larger part of the working class to be employed unproductively' (Marx 1981, 574). Marx seems to suggest here that the military, now a state function and not one of the feudal ties, can employ more bureaucrats and soldiers in the course of its consuming economic function by using various surplus populations.[10]

Engels thought a great deal about how the development and increased strength of the Prussian military over the second half of the nineteenth century had major implications for the prospects of revolution in that

lives entirely from the sale of its labor and does not draw profit from any kind of capital' (Marx and Engels 2011, 219; Engels 2005).

[9] First, the old authority of feudal ties is broken to create bourgeois national unity. The new smallhold property transformation creates a uniform level of relationships and persons over the whole country, permitting uniform action from the supreme centre on all points of the mass, annihilating aristocratic mediation between the state and the people. This moves the countryside from self-sufficiency and into the nation, completing proletarianization by absorbing the newly emancipated peasants into new economic roles (Marx 1978b, 612). Like the bourgeois economy, the bourgeois state is a 'regulated plan of state authority whose work is divided and centralized as in a factory' (Marx 1978b, 606).

[10] On this point, Martin Berger writes that Engels believed that a socialist economy of the future would use resources so efficiently that they could afford to expend even greater amounts of labour-power on defense to their advantage against capitalist offensives (Berger 1975). https://doi.org/10.1111/j.1540-6563.1975.tb00035.x

country (Wangermann 1968, 23). He wrote that 'an unarmed people is a negligible force against the modern army of today' and therefore, in a militarist country such as Germany, 'revolution could only take place if it began in the army itself' (Wangermann 1968, 23). In that context, Engels advocated for policies that would undermine a 'human material' problem, what he saw as the 'spirit of absolute submissiveness of the rank-and-file of the Prussian regiments, which were still recruited largely from the oppressed masses of rural labourers' (Wangermann 1968, 23). His target here—political subjectivity—is notable. As discussed already, class society stems from the expropriation and alienation of an ever-greater mass of people from the means of production and the concentration of the same in the hands of the few resulting in the expropriated being compelled to sell their labour-power. But while someone may belong to the working class as determined by their status as a labourer condemned to exchange their labour-power for money, they may not know themselves as such—as someone already facing enemy fire in a class war.

In light of this problem, Engels offered an unusual solution in a series of letters to August Bebel: that the Social Democratic Party should put forward a resolution to demand 'the lease of Crown [lands] to co-operatives of rural labourers for common cultivation' (Engels 1968, 23).[11] An economic solution is proposed, hitting the problem at the source by diverting labour from the unproductive military to the productive and collective work. But this was not the *purpose* of his proposal, which he did not expect to be implemented. 'This proposal will not be carried out by any *Junker* or bourgeois government', he wrote. Its purpose was rather

> to show the rural proletariat of the eastern provinces the way to end *Junker* and tenant exploitation; to put the means to do this in their hands; to set in motion the very people whose enslavement and stultification produces the regiments which are the foundation of Prussia; in short, to destroy Prussia from within at the root. (Engels 1968, 24)

His proposal is a political and educational tool of class struggle with which to undermine the rural proletariat's 'submissiveness' by showing

---

[11] For a different translation, see Engels (1884). https://www.marxists.org/archive/marx/works/1884/letters/84_12_11.htm

them, through economic not moral argument, what could be. This course of action was not taken up by the Party.

What Engels' concept of human material shows us is the variability of armed forces and of class formation. The soldier is a formal role, but soldiers are drawn from capitalist society, and the masses increasingly over the nineteenth century were none other than the expropriated classes, productive and unproductive workers alike. Like the industrial workers, soldiers embodied the power of the mass of expropriated classes, where the site of their domination contained its opposite: their power, skills, and abilities to rule for themselves. In conducting analysis of any given historical moment, the formal-ideal role of soldiers should be considered in relation to broader economic and political dynamics. Classes are not stagnant, particularly as political subjects; 'every class is always caught up in a process of reconstitution and deconstitution, variation and transformation, emergence or disappearance' (Mohandesi 2013, 75). Soldiers have historically been drawn from feudal relations, from peasants, and from proletarians and have variously taken different sides in class struggle—we should attend to changes in the human material and their broader context as we seek to understand those historic and contemporary struggles and the diverse roles soldiers have played.

4   Conclusion

Militaries, like states, are not outside history. State force in the capitalist state contains both relics of earlier social forms and uniquely capitalist characteristics. General economic production makes possible production for arms, infrastructure, and other assets, which makes a successful state force possible. Likewise, the labour-power required to put those assets into action is drawn from social classes subject to the social forces of capitalism. The state does not extract surplus value from soldiers in its employ, but the labour-power necessary for both mass militaries and capitalist production share a cooperative quality. The distinctiveness of capitalism lies in the fact that the masses of people are expropriated and alienated from the means of production, and with them are brought together not in a self-directed, active, collective practice or to fulfil feudal obligations, but in order to produce for a single entity under an external command. When workers are brought together in this form they can produce a qualitatively new destructive or productive force that is not only more powerful but also intrinsically collective.

A particular military is shaped by the particular historical development of economic forces and associated class struggles. Military practices, including matters of organization, bureaucracy, and military science, are influenced by technological development but also, crucially, by human material. Highlighting the processes of class struggle in which people move between the army and the masses by situating both the institutions and the servicemembers in their employ in the broader context of class struggle, opens up a productive Marxist approach to understanding war in capitalist society. The class struggle shapes military institutions in class societies and, politically, we should be interested in these institutions not just when they are deployed, but also as they are reproduced and particularly in who is reproducing them. The military capabilities of a state are determined by technological and human material and will therefore take different forms depending on the historical particularities of the society in question. To analyse the human material that the state can draw upon therefore requires looking at the broader state of class struggle, the forces of labour and capital at a given moment in time, and the opportunities already located therein to evolve beyond them.

References

Berger, Martin. 1975. 'Engels' Theory of the Vanishing Army: A Key to the Development of Marxist Revolutionary Tactics.' *The Historian* 37 (3): 421–35. https://doi.org/10.1111/j.1540-6563.1975.tb00035.x.

Bonefeld, Werner. 2021. 'On the State as Political Form of Society.' *Science & Society* 85 (2): 177–84. https://doi.org/10.1521/siso.2021.85.2.177.

Engels, Friedrich. 1865. 'The Prussian Military Question and the German Workers' Party.' https://www.marxists.org/archive/marx/works/1865/02/12.htm.

———. 1884. 'Engels to August Bebel in Berlin.' https://www.marxists.org/archive/marx/works/1884/letters/84_12_11.htm

———. 1940. *The Origin of the Family, Private Property and the State.* Moscow: Foreign Languages Publishing House.

———. 1962. *Anti-Dühring*, 3rd ed. Moscow: Foreign Languages Publishing House.

———. 1968. *The Role of Force in History.* Translated by Jack Cohen. London: Lawrence & Wishart.

———. 1978a. 'Introduction to The Civil War in France.' In *The Marx-Engels Reader*, edited by Robert C. Tucker, 2d ed., 618–29. New York: Norton.

————. 1978b. 'Letters on Historical Materialism.' In *The Marx-Engels Reader*, edited by Robert C. Tucker, 2d ed., 761–68. New York: Norton.

————. 2000. *The Peasant War in Germany*. https://www.marxists.org/arc hive/marx/works/1850/peasant-war-germany/index.htmhttps://www.mar xists.org/archive/marx/works/1850/peasant-war-germany/index.htm New York: International Publishers.

————. [1847] 2005. 'The Principles of Communism.' https://www.marxists. org/archive/marx/works/1847/11/prin-com.htm.

Evans, Dan. 2020. 'Basic Training.' In *Making War on Bodies: Militarisation, Aesthetics and Embodiment in International Politics*, edited by Catherine Baker, 31–53. Edinburgh: Edinburgh University Press, 2020. https://www.marxists.org/archive/marx/works/1847/11/prin-com.htm or https://www.marxists.org/archive/marx/works/1865/02/12.htm

Foucault, Michel. 1991. *Discipline and Punish: The Birth of the Prison*. London: Penguin Books.

Frevert, Ute. 2004. *A Nation in Barracks: Modern Germany, Military Conscription and Civil Society*. Oxford: Berg.

Harvey, David. 2010. *A Companion to Marx's Capital*. London: Verso.

Hewitson, Mark. 2017. *The People's Wars: Histories of Violence in the German Lands, 1820–1888*, 1st ed. Oxford: Oxford University Press.

Kay, Geoffrey. 1988. 'Right and Force: A Marxist Critique of Contract and the State.' In *Value, Social Form and the State*, edited by Michael Williams, 115–33. London: Palgrave Macmillan UK. https://doi.org/10.1007/978-1-349-19393-6_7.

Marx, Karl. 1978a. 'The Civil War in France.' In *The Marx-Engels Reader*, edited by Robert C. Tucker, 2d ed., 629–52. New York: Norton.

————. 1978b. 'The Eighteenth Brumaire of Louis Bonaparte.' In *The Marx-Engels Reader*, edited by Robert C. Tucker, 2d ed., 594–617. New York: Norton.

————. 1978c. 'The *Grundrisse*.' In *The Marx-Engels Reader*, edited by Robert C. Tucker, 2d ed., 221–93. New York: Norton.

————. 1981. *Capital: A Critique of Political Economy*. Translated by Ben Fowkes. Vol. I. London: Penguin Books.

Marx, Karl, and Friedrich Engels. 2011. *The Communist Manifesto*. Translated by Samuel Moore. New York: Penguin Books.

Mohandesi, Salar. 2013. 'Class Consciousness or Class Composition?' *Science & Society* 77 (1): 72–97.

Smith, Tony. 2017. *Beyond Liberal Egalitarianism: Marx and Normative Social Theory in the Twenty-First Century*. Leiden: Brill.

Wangermann, Ernst. 1968. 'Introduction.' In Engels, Friedrich, *The Role of Force in History*, Translated by Jack Cohen, 11–28. London: Lawrence & Wishart.

To Embrace or To Reject: Marxism and the 'War-Emergency Paradigm'

Eva Nanopoulos

Following the outbreak of the COVID-19 pandemic, several national leaders mobilised the language of war to frame their response to the crisis. The United Kingdom vowed to 'win the fight' against the 'deadly' enemy, France announced its nation was at war, and the United States rang alarm bells about the unprecedented threat posed by this new 'invisible' enemy. Across the globe countries declared formal emergencies, typically allowing for greater executive power and more sweeping restrictions on human rights.

Particularly in the early stages of the pandemic, the war–emergency paradigm—the deployment of the language of war, security, and threats coupled with access to an 'exceptional' legal arsenal—was met with suspicion, if not alarm, building as it does on the well-known script that has characterised the various endless wars usually associated with US imperialism, from the war on drugs to the wars on the poor, crime, and, infamously, terror. With time, however, a more favourable outlook on war and emergency emerged, with some going as far as to call for a form of

E. Nanopoulos (✉)
Queen Mary, University of London, London, UK
e-mail: e.nanopoulos@qmul.ac.uk

© The Author(s), under exclusive license to Springer Nature
Switzerland AG 2023
R. Hunter et al. (eds.), *Marxism and the Capitalist State*,
Political Philosophy and Public Purpose,
https://doi.org/10.1007/978-3-031-36167-8_7

141

'war communism' as an antidote to 'disaster capitalism' (Žižek 2020). A similar ambivalence and polarisation about the paradigm emerged in the context of the ecological crisis[1] with Malm's lockdown-produced book urging us to stay 'with the dilemma' of 'how to execute control measures' without trampling on democratic rights and apply the paradigm to the climate crisis (Malm 2020).

The dilemmas underlying these debates in our age of crises and catastrophes are both real and urgent. As a discursive frame, the war–emergency paradigm has contributed to the construction of imagined threats, crises, and enemies, obscuring the real causes of violence, and polarising society along racial, class, gender, and spatial lines. As a political and legal modality of state power, it has played a crucial role in normalising authoritarian and illiberal institutions and measures, most notably the concentration of power in the executive and the erosion of civil and political rights. Yet, in contexts like the pandemic or climate change, there are also risks that these crises may not be over-blown, but underplayed, and that our response may not go too far, but rather not far enough—indeed, we see this with climate change, which is among the few emergencies that have been declared without attracting any formal action (Greene 2020). More generally, crises such as the pandemic or climate change are directly linked to the logic and functioning of capitalism, including its hyper-extractive exploitation and commodification of nature, and its attendant laws and institutions. As such, tackling them requires a rupture with the 'normal' order of capital accumulation, including the capitalist state and capitalist legality. The question then arises: in conditions where crises require urgent and radical action, how do we best secure the interests of the exploited and oppressed as well as (re)build the social ties of solidarity required to enact progressive change? Is the answer to embrace the war–emergency paradigm or to reject it?

The purpose of this chapter is not to provide a definite answer to the question whether in the context of the pandemic or the climate crisis, but to offer some general observations about how we should approach these dilemmas informed by Marxist theories of war and emergency. Marxist scholars have reflected on how the ambivalence towards the state revealed by the pandemic 'mirrors a broader antinomy that is written into the very structure of capitalist society', namely 'the *desire for the state* and the

---

[1] For a summary of the debate see Albert (2022).

(often all-too-justified) *fear of the state*, on the one hand, and between the (momentary) *primacy of the state* and the (structuring) *primacy of the economic*, on the other' (Toscano 2020, 15). A similar line of thinking could be applied to the ambivalence underpinning the debate about the war–emergency paradigm. As we shall see, the paradigm builds on a long history of war and emergency as colonial and counter-revolutionary tools. Yet, neither have wars nor emergencies been invariably associated with conservative and imperial practices. Many revolutions sprung out of the ashes of war or repression, even if few were ultimately successful. The Paris Commune of 1871 emerged out of the long siege of Paris and the French defeat in the Franco-Prussian war. The Russian Revolution was fuelled by the inter-imperial rivalries that defined the post-1848 revolutionary period and the autocratic policies of the tsarist regime. And there are histories of the emancipatory deployment of the war metaphor by grass-roots movements in such contexts as the AIDS epidemic or the fight against cancer. Answering the question of whether to embrace or to reject the war–emergency paradigm thus partly requires us to better understand the deeper antinomy at the heart of the relationship between war, emergency, and capitalism.

To think through this antinomy, I juxtapose two different bodies of work. The first section reads the war–emergency paradigm through the lens of pacification theory, as developed, most notably, by Neocleous, Rigakos, and other members of the anti-security collective, which views the state's war and emergency powers as forms of policing that have been and remain crucial to the production and stabilisation of capitalist (dis)order. Having outlined the benefits and limitations of this approach, Sect. 2 goes back to the writings of Marx and Engels on the problem of war, which, Balibar has shown, combines reflections on both the war metaphor and 'empirical' wars i.e. the eruption of actual physical violence, as expressions of capitalist contradictions and crises. Contrary to pacification theory, which invariably refuses to engage in either a politics of rejection or a politics of embrace, for Marx and Engels, I argue, the choice would ultimately involve a 'pragmatic decision about what tactics are most likely to achieve a specific strategic end at any particular point in time' (Barrow 2021, 6). In the final section, I outline some of the ways in which Marx and Engels thought about the relationship between the class struggle and bourgeois democracy (i.e. the politics of rejection), on the one hand, and between the class struggle, wars, and emergency powers on the other (i.e. a politics of embrace). The analysis is necessarily schematic.

My aim is merely to highlight the value of broadening, and re-centring the class struggle in, our understanding of the relationship between war, emergency, and capitalism in a manner that links the tension between the fear of, and the desire for, the war–emergency paradigm to the broader tension between the primacy of capital versus the primacy of the class struggle.

1   NEITHER REJECT NOR EMBRACE: PACIFICATION THEORY

1.1   *Critique of Security and Pacification Theory*

Although there have been various Marxist analyses of the war–emergency paradigm, particularly in the context of the pandemic, pacification theory is the closest example of a systematic examination of the question drawing on Marx's writings. Pacification theorists' starting point is the critique of security, which builds on Marx's brief—but in their view critical—remark in *On the Jewish Question* that '[s]ecurity is the highest social concept of civil society, the concept of *police*, expressing the fact that the whole of society exists only in order to guarantee to each of its members the preservation of his person, his rights, and his property' (Marx and Engels 1973, 3:163). From this, pacification theorists conclude (a) that security, rather than liberty, is the epicentre of bourgeois society; (b) that security is ultimately about policing, understood not in the liberal sense of law enforcement but in the wider and more productive sense of fabricating social order, and more specifically, the order of wage labour; and (c) that this policing function underwrites all institutions and practices of bourgeois society.

The idea of pacification is then used to unearth the historical and structural connections between war, police, law, emergency, and accumulation (Neocleous 2018). The result is a framework which, contrary to liberal perspectives in which these concepts appear as separate, sees them as intrinsically linked and as mutually implicated in policing/pacification, i.e. in the production of capitalist order. This applies to war and policing:

> Holding on to the idea of war as a form of conflict in which enemies face each other....and the idea of police as dealing neatly with crime, distracts us from the fact that it is far more the case that the war power has long been a rationale for the imposition of international order and the police

power has long been a wide-ranging exercise in pacification (Neocleous 2011, 156).

But it also applies to law and emergency, which are but different forms of state violence designed to secure the order of wage labour. From that perspective, like the actual empirical wars of accumulation that preceded them, the many metaphorical wars and emergency regimes of the last few decades, including the war against COVID-19, are but forms of policing/ 'class war from above' (Neocleous 2018) in the name of capital accumulation and contemporary expressions of the role of war and emergency in the production of the bourgeois (imperial) order.

Production, it should be noted, is not merely understood as repression, coercion, or the suppression of dissent, but has a more positive constitutive meaning. Pacification is about building 'secure foundation[s] for capital accumulation'. Historically, it has been key for domestic and colonial dispossession and today, it continues to ensure the reproduction of capitalist social relations. In that process, it not only secures the separation of workers from their means of subsistence and their exploitation by capital. War as policing also helps to constitute pacified legal subjects and subsume struggles in ways that secure the submission of labour to the order of capital. This is particularly prevalent in the contemporary age of neoliberal marketisation and securitisation, where 'security-conscious subjects' are at once made to obey and continuously re-enact the logic of capital security through resilience and suspicion (Neocleous 2018).

The result is not only de-politicisation, i.e. the displacement of alternative emancipatory language. Worse, security's logic of obedience, submission, and exclusion suppresses rebellion before it even arises, pre-empting the very possibility of a politics of solidarity. At this level, too, there is no alternative. And the answer, then, is a project of 'anti-security', that is, a rejection of security, and by extension of the war–emergency paradigm (Neocleous and Rigakos 2011), but also of anti-legality, i.e. a rejection of the 'normal' status quo and law, in favour of alternative discourses and extra-legal revolutionary practices.

1.2   *Beyond the Dichotomy: Prospects and Limitations*

Pacification theory has long warned against—and was arguably developed as a critique of—a politics of rejection based on advocating a 'return' to some mythical 'normality' and 'legality' (Neocleous 2008, 69). Such a strategy is not only conservative, in the sense of seeking to preserve the status quo, but also fundamentally misplaced. It wrongly locates the problem in war and emergency, rather than the 'all-encompassing' logics of policing, security, and accumulation, and it wrongly assumes a distinction between war and peace, law and exception, and ultimately, between law and violence: to 'criticize the use of emergency power in terms of a suspension of the law' is to 'make the mistake of counterpoising normality and emergency, law and violence' (Neocleous 2006, 206). Law is not 'designed to protect human rights from state violence' but is foundational to capital's violence. This explains why pacification theorists foreground the language of emergency rather than Schmitt's exception: emergency powers do not operate 'outside the law' (Neocleous 1996, 72), as the language of the exception or of suspension implies, but emerge out of the state's legal structures, as distinct moments and forms in the reproduction of capital.

If liberal peace is a myth, however, so is war communism. Embracing the war–emergency paradigm is not only tantamount to embracing the 'fallacious notion' that the state is somehow '"outside" of capital' (Toscano 2020, 16), but to fundamentally underestimate the relationship between state violence and capitalism. At a moment when the state has become the epicentre of capitalist (re)production, there just is no scope for 'mutual trust between the people and state apparatuses' (Žižek 2020, 12) or for pushing the state to go against the interests of capital.[2] Even if, as Malm argues, there is no 'other form of state on offer', engaging with the capitalist state would be as 'delusional and criminal' (Malm 2020, 151) as simply waiting for the emergence of a form of dual power or a workers' state. The war–emergency paradigm—and indeed the state more generally—cannot be severed from its entanglement with the reproduction of capital. This is a war 'the [capitalist] state cannot win, for to win it would mean abolishing the condition of private property that gives rise to it, and thus abolishing itself as a state' (Neocleous 2000, 82).

Pacification theorists bring important insights into contemporary debates about the war–emergency paradigm, highlighting its connection to capital accumulation in a manner that rightly warns against the pitfalls of both a politics of rejection and a politics of embrace. Yet, there are

---

[2] For a discussion of various positions on this claim, see Alyssa Battistoni's contribution to the present volume.

two limitations with their approach. The first relates to the object of their critique. The critique of security is ultimately a critique of political liberalism and its imposition of 'banal dichotomies' between war, peace, law, and emergency that mask its connections to capital accumulation and produce 'a set of what are ultimately liberal concerns', such as the militarisation of the police. In seeking to retrieve those connections, however, pacification theory focuses mainly on wars of accumulation. It does not explore other forms of war (e.g. anti-colonial, revolutionary, or inter-imperialist wars) or counter-hegemonic discourses or practices of war and emergency. As a result, their conclusion that the war–emergency paradigm is invariably a new form of war/policing for the purpose of accumulation and/or that there is nothing positive to hold onto 'in the idea of security' (Neocleous and MacQuade 2020, 8) or, by extension, the paradigm, derives from a narrow understanding of war and emergency.

The second concerns the subject of their theory. In principle, pacification aims to offer not only a theory of war and policing but also a theory of the (capitalist) state. Neocleous' early work, for example, placed his account of the role of the state in constituting and administering civil society between Foucauldian accounts, which he claims collapse the distinction between state and civil society, and instrumentalist Marxist accounts that disregard the relevance of civil society (e.g. Neocleous 1996). Leaving aside whether this is a fair representation of Foucault and/or Lenin, in seeking to retrieve (and rethink) the role of the state, pacification theory is less a theory *of the state*—or indeed *of war and emergency*—than a theory *of state power* and of the *state's war and emergency powers*. As such, it pays less attention to the ways in which civil society is not only constituted or policed by the state but itself continuously acts through and upon the state.

The result is that pacification theory runs into some of the difficulties that it was seeking to overcome. For example, Neocleous criticises Foucauldian and instrumentalist accounts of the state for neglecting the class struggle: Foucauldians because they dissolve society into a system of full domination and subjection, and more generally neglect the question of labour; Marxist instrumentalist accounts because they tend to rely on a 'crude base-superstructure analysis' in which the state is merely a tool 'for oppressing the working class' (Neocleous 2000, 155). Yet, a similar process of elision at times returns in pacification theory. In theory, pacification theorists view the state, alongside law, as elements of a 'totality subject to continual struggle' (Neocleous 1996, 164) which have developed 'in response to class struggle' (Neocleous 1996, 45). But when they speak of the state as a 'product of class struggle' they chiefly refer to the ways in which the state has absorbed and pacified the class struggle. Partly because of their attention to political administration, they pay less attention to how the state and law *always remain* sites of class struggle. The result is a theory of the state that does not ignore, but somewhat suspends and brackets away, the class struggle. Temporally, class struggle seems always something of the past; spatially, it can only take place outside the state. Like Foucauldian and instrumental approaches, then, this tends to present a unidimensional and undialectical account of the capitalist state.

This framework has implications for the strategy of anti-security. Foucauldian and instrumentalist approaches have been criticised for their stance on the problem of agency, the former for foreclosing it, the latter for over-simplifying it. Commenting on Žižek's conception of 'war communism' in the context of the pandemic, for example, Sharma asks: '[h]ow can we create the conditions for such a transformation?' and who will seize 'the emergence of global solidarity in the crisis and [give] it an *enduring* form outside the crisis as well?' (Sharma 2022). Pacification theory's approach to agency would seem to fall somewhere between these two approaches. In the realm of the state, workers have lost their revolutionary potential. Political administration has taken 'working class struggles and [transformed] them into bodies constituted by the state, abstracting them into an administrative form and nullifying their revolutionary potential' (Neocleous 1996, 165). In the realm of civil society, however, their revolutionary agency persists. The two, however, can be hard to reconcile. If the conjoint logics of marketisation and securitisation have become so pervasive, if they structure, even colonise, both our individual subjectivity, the ways we think of ourselves, and our inter-personal and social relations, the ways we relate to one another, in ways that foster individual responsibility, separateness, and exclusion, how exactly is anti-security to be enacted? Beyond offering discursive spaces—themselves often located in the very disciplinary institutions like the university which are embedded in and subject to the logic of capitalist civil society—where 'critical scholars and activists can discuss security without creating more security intelligence', how can these discussions translate into concrete struggles (Manolov and Rigakos 2014, 1)? How can pacified subjects develop revolutionary agency?

Pacification theory builds directly on Marx. The primacy they assign to security and policing, as we saw, draws from his essay *On the Jewish Question*. Their connection to war is derived from Marx and Engels' use of the war metaphor, which shows they want us 'to think of capital as war' (Neocleous 1996). And more generally, their prescriptions, they claim, align with Marx's critique of bourgeois rights. However insightful, however, this is only one possible reading of Marx. Below, I chart a different path through his writings, one that begins, not with his critique of security and hence of bourgeois society, but with his own deployment of the war metaphor and hence with his theory of historical change, and one that leads, not only to a critique of the war–emergency paradigm, but to a consideration of its relationship to the class struggle and revolution.

2   BACK TO MARX AND ENGELS: SOMETIMES REJECT, SOMETIMES EMBRACE

2.1   *The War Metaphor: War as Class War*

The war metaphor first appears in *The Poverty of Philosophy* in a passage that describes the process of class formation and the emergence of the class struggle under capitalism. There, Marx distinguishes between three phases: (a) spatial concentration, when 'large-scale industry' concentrated 'in one place a crowd of people unknown to one another'; (b) individual combinations, when their 'common interest' against their bosses unites the workers 'in a common thought of resistance' with both the economic aim of maintaining wages and the (pre)political aim 'of stopping competition among the workers, so that they can carry on the general competition with the capitalist'; and (c) association when 'combinations at first isolated, constitute themselves into groups' and the 'second aim overtakes the first' as capitalists 'unite for the purpose of repression' and 'the maintenance of the association becomes more necessary to them than that of wages'. This is when Marx introduces the war metaphor: at this point, the masses unite as a class against capital, 'association takes on a political character' and 'in this struggle—a veritable civil war – all the elements necessary for a coming battle unite and develop' (Marx and Engels 1976b, 6: 211).

Already in this text, we see that the metaphor is used to denote not only the politicisation of the class struggle—what Marx describes as the transformation of the working class from a 'class in itself' to a 'class for itself'—but a *'new concept'* (Balibar 2010, 10), one that we may even say constitutes the *very essence*, of the political. What we have here is neither Clausewitz's conception of war as politics by other means, nor Foucault's conception of politics as war by other means, but, as Balibar highlights, (class) war *as politics*, as the *'becoming visible'* of the class struggle (Balibar 2010, 10), which is produced and sustained through the continuous (re)constitution, interaction, and antagonism between classes and whose 'highest expression is a total [i.e. socialist] revolution'.

The metaphor appears even more prominently in *The Communist Manifesto*, which not only further developed the connections between the class struggle, politics, and revolution, but also added to the specificity and significance of the class struggle under capitalism. Indeed, the *Manifesto* not only put the class struggle (and hence class war) at the centre of Marx and Engels' theory of historical change. It also used the language of war—as opposed to struggle or fight—with specific reference to the character of the class struggle in bourgeois society, which 'simplified' and hence deepened class antagonism, dividing society 'into two great hostile camps...directly facing each other'. And it also connected the class war i.e., the class struggle under capitalism, to the notion and possibility of *total* revolution, i.e. communism, defined as the abolition of classes.

In contrast to pacification theory, then, first, the class war, rather than security, is the epicentre of bourgeois society. Second, the war metaphor is not used only to describe the war of capital *against* labour, or of the state against labour, but a particular moment in the struggle *between* capital and labour. Thirdly, that moment does not (necessarily) mark the depoliticisation of the class struggle, but the unification and political subjectivisation of working people, even though, of course, Marx and Engels were all too aware of capitalist tendencies and historical conditions that produced divisions among the (global) working class, including along racial, gender, and spatial lines, and that would be further developed in Marxist theories of imperialism, race, and gender, as well as analyses of class formation and class consciousness under late (neoliberal) capitalism. And finally, the class war does not necessarily mark the deepening of class domination but opens the possibility of revolution, indeed of socialist revolution.

2.2   To Embrace or to Reject? From Strategy to Tactic

Is the decision of whether to embrace or to reject the war–emergency paradigm then part of the class struggle? The war–emergency paradigm usually follows one of two models, although they often overlap in practice: the separation model, under which the threat is seen to emanate from, and the response is primarily directed at, a specific group within the population (e.g. the 'terrorist') and a unitary model, under which the threat emanates from the outside (e.g. the coronavirus) and the response (seemingly) targets the population at large. Both locate the cause of the crisis and direct their responses outside the structures of global capital—the first personalises it, while the second externalises it. But if there is one unifying characteristic of the many crises of the last two decades it is that they all have roots in capitalist crises and provide an area for gendered and racialised class wars. This was evident in the context of the pandemic, whether in terms of its causes, its targets (e.g. the 'unproductive' elements of society, such as the elderly and vulnerable as well as 'key' or 'essential' racialised and gendered workers), the responses it triggered (e.g. 'herd immunity' which was effectively willing to accelerate the biological and social death of vulnerable groups), or its effects. The question of the class struggle, and class war, in other words, remains all too relevant.

How we decide to frame or respond to those crises, as well as what kind of legal intervention we demand, is likewise part of the class war. In *The German Ideology*, Marx and Engels highlighted that the class struggle is not limited to the struggle between labour and capital in the workplace but encompassed 'all struggles within the state, the struggle between democracy, aristocracy, and monarchy, the struggle for the franchise' which 'are merely the illusory forms in which the real struggles of the different classes are fought out among one another'. And although Marx never developed a theory of law, he did view law as an important site of class struggle, and indeed of class war. Legal battles were seen both as the *product* of, and *vehicle* for, the politicisation (i.e. of the becoming visible) of the class struggle and hence both a product of and vehicle for the class war. For example, for Marx, the struggle for the limitation of the working day both resulted from the 'protracted and more or less concealed civil war between the capitalist class and the working class' (Marx 1990, 412–13) and facilitated 'the constitution of the working class as a political subject' (Knox 2010, 218).

The war–emergency paradigm does not in itself suspend the class war. Clausewitz, who famously inspired much Marxist thinking on war, stressed that his model of war as a continuation of politics by other means was not to be read as meaning that war 'suspends political intercourse' or replaces it with a 'wholly different condition' (Clausewitz 87, 705–6). And if anything, the class war model of politics would suggest that war is itself the language of politics. Similarly, emergency laws may not pass through ordinary bourgeois processes, but as pacification theory (and multiple other studies of emergency laws) shows, neither do they operate according to the extra-legal model of the exception. If anything, contemporary emergencies tend to be distinctively legal—that is legally enacted and regulated phenomena. Neither does the war–emergency paradigm preclude the tactical deployment of legal arguments for strategic goals. It is perfectly possible to contest particular interpretations of the war metaphor and uses of emergency powers, including those that identify imagined enemies and restrict their rights—all the while pressing for framings and measures that advance the interests of labour and other oppressed classes and/or seek to address the root causes of crises. Indeed, the war–emergency paradigm does not suspend but merely redefines the boundaries of politics and legality and alters the range of available political and legal argumentation, with all the risks but also possibilities that this may entail.

The result is that, contrary to pacification theory, the question of whether to reject or to embrace cannot be determined in the abstract, even if a theory of the state and law and their limitations as vehicles for the class struggle remains essential and, as we will see, played a part in how Marx assessed the revolutionary potential of legal struggles. Instead, the question is fundamentally one of tactics, a theoretically informed but also political calculation about whether to embrace or reject the war–emergency paradigm, which may yield different answers in different contexts, conjunctures, or places.

3   Thinking Tactically

3.1   Reject?

How would Marx and Engels have navigated some of the dilemmas that the question of the war–emergency paradigm raises today? There certainly is evidence that Marx would not have supported many of the practices that have come to be associated with the paradigm when wielded by the state and/or the ruling classes, such as the bolstering of the executive or the curtailment of rights. As several scholars have argued, Marx not only saw bourgeois democracy and rights as 'improvements' over the old feudal order, but also stressed their significance for the class struggle and hence for revolution. Just as the exploitation of waged labour under capitalism laid the foundation for the abolition of all classes, so did political emancipation open the door to human emancipation:

> The fundamental contradiction of [the 1848 French] constitution, however, consists in the following: The classes whose social slavery the constitution is to perpetuate, proletariat, peasantry, petty bourgeoisie, it puts in possession of political power through universal suffrage. And from the class whose old social power it sanctions, the bourgeoisie, it withdraws the political guarantees of this power. It forces the political rule of the bourgeoisie into democratic conditions, which at every moment help the hostile classes to victory and jeopardise the very foundations of bourgeois society. (Marx and Engels 1978, 10:79)

It did so not only because political emancipation created new sites for the working class to advance their interests, whether by constituting themselves as organised political formations and parties or by invoking liberal rights, but also because, by 'unchaining the class struggle', it operated at the deeper level of political, that is class, consciousness, and class formation.

At times, Marx even conceived of the class struggle as a struggle for democracy and of communism as an expansion of democracy and rights— 'the first step in the revolution by the working class', according to *The Communist Manifesto*, 'is to raise the proletariat to the position of ruling class to win the battle of democracy', leading some Marxists to argue that the struggle for rights and liberties, including their extension into 'economic domains from which capitalism has excluded them' (Wood 2020, 68), should be part of the class struggle, and/or that rights should have a place in communist society.

At the same time, Marx was often critical of practices that we would today associate with the war–emergency paradigm. His early journalistic writings contain sharp critiques of crackdowns on civil rights and liberties, particularly restrictions on the freedom of the press or freedom of assembly. His early polemics with Hegel and his writings on France consistently criticised monarchical forms of power and constitutional/institutional devices shifting power away from representative bodies (see generally Draper 1977). And *The Eighteenth Brumaire* remains one of the most detailed and powerful critiques of 'Bonapartism', laying the ground for a long tradition of Marxist analyses of the role of dictatorial and/ or authoritarian forms of power in the reproduction of class rule (Marx 1963).

Yet, Marx was far from an unequivocal defender of *liberal* rights and democracy. As pacification theory indeed reminds us, he never drew a rigid distinction between war/peace, law/emergency or, to use terms that were closer to his time and register, between democracy and dictatorship. Indeed, the class war metaphor itself captures the fact that, for Marx, the 'normal' bourgeois order is in a permanent, albeit latent, state of war, characterised, not by some Hobbesian war of all against all, but by the class struggle. Further, for Marx and Engels, authoritarianism was not a state 'policy' but a 'sharper expression of the class conflict', i.e. of class war, that arose in situations that threatened the bourgeois order and which Gramsci would later link to crises of hegemony, when ordinary modes of rule are no longer sufficient to maintain class domination. The differences between democracy and dictatorship, in other words, are a matter of degree, rather than kind: in the final analysis, both are 'expressions of the dictatorship of the bourgeoisie', i.e. both serve to 'reproduce a regime of power relations which safeguard specific social interests' (Kivotidis 2021). To see them as opposite social forms, as Pashukanis would later emphasise, would be to follow 'bourgeois theorists of the state' in conflating 'characteristics relating to the form of government and characteristics relating to the class nature of the state' (Pashukanis 1980, 280). The 'whole question of "democracy" versus "dictatorship"', in other words, 'is profoundly rooted in legal ideology' (Balibar 1977, 67).

More generally, as an equally substantial body of scholarship has demonstrated, Marx never quite embraced bourgeois democracy and rights, particularly as vehicles for emancipatory change. His philosophical and theoretical writings repeatedly highlighted the connections between capitalism, law, and the modern state. *On the Jewish Question* unmasked the bourgeois character of the rights of man, as well as the limits of political emancipation. *Capital* hinted at the specifically legal character of exchange relations, an insight which would later ground Pashukanis' commodity-form theory of law. More generally, bourgeois democracy may have abolished feudal privileges, but in doing so, it also '*abolished the political character of civil society*' (Marx 1990b, 232). In that sense, just as formal freedom pre-supposed freedom from the means of production and hence unfreedom, so did political emancipation pre-suppose the 'emancipation of civil society from politics', i.e. the insulation of the realm of unfreedom from political contestation. As Jessop put it, where 'exploitation takes the form of exchange', 'dictatorship takes the form of democracy' and formal (or legal) equality (Jessop 2001, 160).

These connections imposed concrete limits upon the class struggle. Legally, the separation of the political/public sphere of the state and the economic/private sphere of market exchange, made entire areas at least partially immune to the class struggle through the ordinary means of bourgeois democracy. Ideologically, it promoted an individualistic ethos that isolated individuals, thwarting the development of class consciousness and the class struggle. Ad hoc working-class gains, moreover, often just shifted the form and modalities of exploitation. For example, while the struggle for the working time 'drew the working class together as a political subject, weakened the power of the bourgeoisie, and lessened the rate of exploitation', it 'did not end exploitation, but encouraged capitalists to increase the "productivity" of their workers through mechanisation and increased labour discipline' (Knox 2016, 321).

The counter-revolutionary dimension of bourgeois social forms was even more forcibly denounced in Marx's political and historical texts. In his writings on France, Marx highlighted how the republic proclaimed following the 1848 revolution was 'no revolutionary weapon against the bourgeois order, but rather its political reconstitution' (Marx and Engels 1978, 10:66), how universal suffrage was no 'magic power', and how constitutional rights only applied to the extent that they 'harmonized with the rule of the bourgeoisie' (Marx and Engels 1978, 10:65, 91). These contradictions would erupt out in the open after the February revolution, when the bourgeois republic eventually turned against the very people that brought it into being, namely the proletariat. Thus 'the comedy was played out', he observed: the Assembly 'had decreed that the violation of the letter of the constitution was the only appropriate realization of its spirit' (Marx and Engels 1978, 10:91). This led him to qualify the significance of bourgeois democracy for the class struggle, for, if it demanded that the bourgeoisie do not 'go back from social to political restoration' it also required that 'the workers do not go forward from political to social emancipation' (Marx and Engels 1978, 10:79). Under these conditions, he warned, even 'the slightest improvement' to the position of the proletariat 'remains a utopia *within* the bourgeois republic' and he deplored the workers' inability to see beyond this bourgeois horizon (Marx and Engels 1978, 10:69). Many of these criticisms recurred in the *Eighteenth*

Brumaire and culminated in a more forceful indictment of the bourgeois state in his writings on the Paris Commune, where he concluded that 'the working class cannot simply lay hold of the ready-made state machinery and wield it for their own purpose. The political instrument of their enslavement cannot serve as the political instrument of their emancipation' (Marx and Engels 1986, 22:533).

As Balibar remarks, moreover, Marx's notion of 'the conquest of democracy' identified 'the revolutionary anticapitalist process' not only with 'democratization (if need be, with a democratization of democracy itself, under the limited forms it has taken on until now)', but *also* with a 'destruction of the class structure and its juridical, political, and economic conditions' (Balibar 2009, 59). Similarly, Wood has emphasised that 'socialism emerged out a growing realization that the liberties [Marx] sought to defend required something more than democratic legal forms and political rights abstracted from the realities of social power' (Wood 2020, 52). It is not clear, therefore, that Marx's analysis implied that human emancipation must be seen as, and fought for, in terms of an extension of bourgeois democracy and rights and that he would therefore have necessarily rejected support for the war–emergency paradigm.

3.2   Embrace?

More generally, even if they never 'developed a comprehensive theory' of the relationship between war and revolution (Balibar 2010, 12), Marx and Engels never foreclosed any role for either war—here understood in the empirical/literal sense of armed struggle rather than the metaphorical sense—or exceptional powers in the process of social transformation.

Unsurprisingly, perhaps, war and crises did not feature prominently in Marx and Engels' early writings; indeed, *Anti-Dühring*, which sealed Engels' reputation as a military thinker, was not written until the 1870s. By placing war and conflict as the essence of the political and the class struggle, the war metaphor implicitly subordinated questions of war to the social question. Only when class exploitation would be eradicated would (social) peace become possible. The class struggle and the proletarian revolution were the answers to the problem of war, not war the answer to the problem of social revolution. Their central concern, then, was not so much how to address or respond to capitalist wars (themselves the product of crises), but how to ensure the success and universaliation of the class struggle.

This changed with the failed revolutions of 1848. From that moment, communism was to be derived 'less by the internationalization of proletarian revolution, as from defeat in interstate wars' (Teschke 2020, 310). War, in other words, could be a catalyst for class war, helping to bring the class struggle out in the open. And from then on, the problem of (empirical) war and the problem of the class war merged into the question of 'how to "bring back" class struggle (and thereby politics) into civil war' (Balibar 2009, 64), which Lenin would subsequently transpose to the international level by calling for the transformation of 'imperial war into a civil war/class war'. Indeed, having considered Marx and Engels' use of the war metaphor alongside their understanding of war, Balibar remarks:

> In a sense, we arrive only now at what constitutes the 'heart' of the problem. The two lines that we have considered separately: class struggle as a (generalized) 'civil war', and militarism as an expression of capitalism, merge into one single practical question: how to 'make' the revolution (Balibar 2010, 13)?

This did not mean that Marx and Engels actively supported imperialist wars. After 1870, for example, Engels rejected the 'assumption that European wars could be regarded merely as springboards for socialist revolution' (Gallie 2008, 90). As both expressions of, and vehicles for, capitalist crises, wars created 'all-or-nothing' conditions (e.g. hunger) that could 'hasten the revolutionary process' and/or force the ruling classes 'to appeal to the proletariat, to ask for help', dragging 'it into the political arena' and 'providing it with the weapons (literally and figuratively) to launch its own revolutionary assault'. In addition, the role of war in 'unleashing' the class struggle gained significance as awareness grew that capitalist crises would not in themselves lead to capitalism's demise and that the class struggle was less the originator than the executor of crises (Callinicos 2020). But there was also growing concern that war could create conditions that posed a threat, or could be turned against, the working class, including nationalism and chauvinism. Neither did Marx and Engels treat all wars the same. As Gallie recalls, they viewed wars 'now as causes or catalysts of revolutionary activity, now as skilfully contrived moves by reactionary governments to forestall revolutionary unrest, now as desperate gambles between rival capitalist powers, now as tests which the revolutionary movements had to survive, and now as supplying the very agency—in the form of a mass citizen army—through which alone the existing order could be overthrown' (Gallie 2008, 72). Yet, it did mean that they always also thought about how wars and revolution could be exploited i.e. be turned to 'promote or hasten revolution' (Draper 1996, 10).

Elsewhere, Marx and Engels also considered the connections between emergency powers and revolution. *The Communist Manifesto* placed 'exceptional' forms of rule and laws at the centre of the socialist transition to communism and offered an indicative list of measures that could redirect society away from the profit imperative towards the fulfilment of human needs: abolition of the rights to property and inheritance, confiscation of property, adjustments to the taxation system, the nationalisation and centralisation of banking, transport and communication, free education, abolition of geographical differentiation between countryside and towns, etc.

This model echoes a longer 'left' tradition of emergency rule traceable to the proto-communist Conspiracy of the Equals, a secret organisation founded by Babeuf which sought to overthrow the French Directory during the French revolution. Pre-figuring Schmitt, the revolutionaries envisaged the emergency not as a 'backward looking' institution designed to restore the status quo, but as a 'forward looking' institution designed to constitute a new order. Unlike Schmitt's conservative and counter-revolutionary model of the sovereign (as opposed to the commissarial) dictatorship, however, theirs did not aim to fight the enemy within but to 'assist an oppressed majority of people to fight the injustice of the Ancien Régime' (Kivotidis 2021). More generally, the model aligns with Marx and Engels' conception of the political as (class) war and the state of exception as the 'law of politics' in which, as Balibar explains, 'the institutional form of power disappears under the struggle for power or naked violence incarnated in the confrontation' between the state and the masses (Balibar 2009, 70).

Marx and Engels, as would Lenin, were writing about actual/empirical rather than metaphorical wars. Their support for emergency powers presupposed the establishment of a proletarian transitional state. And as of today, few wars actually led to revolution. But seeking to apply some of their insights to our understanding of the war–emergency paradigm today and its transformative potential is not necessarily mistaken. Like 'real' wars, metaphorical wars can both express and deepen crises of capital—indeed, the pandemic or the climate emergency are such examples. Even absent a transitional workers' state, they can force the bourgeois state to adopt measures which might still benefit the working classes and politicise the class struggle, particularly when the 'normal' conditions of neoliberal capitalism have deepened the de-politicisation and de-democratisation of the market. Posing the question of whether to embrace or reject the war–emergency paradigm in revolutionary terms, moreover, does not need to be limited to revolutionary moments or contexts. On the contrary, Marx and Engels always stressed that the transition to socialism (i.e. the revolution) entailed a long and arduous process of building class consciousness through continuous agitation and struggle.

4   Conclusion(s)

This chapter aimed to chart a path for thinking about the question of how to engage with the war–emergency paradigm, both as a prevalent, if not the de facto, mode of governing of the capitalist state and as an expression of our current age of capitalist catastrophe. I have argued that the answer should be approached as a tactical decision derived from an understanding of both the structural limitations and opportunities that the paradigm opens in terms of politicising the class struggle and of creating the conditions for the overcoming of capitalist social relations. This is not to dismiss the important insights of pacification theory. As Balibar reminds us, at the time of Marx and Engels, the 'revolutions and counter-revolution of 1848 to 1851 displayed a pattern of *actual "civil wars"* in which the proletariat was not only defeated but experienced the inadequacy of its representations of the relationship between crises and class politics' (Balibar 2010, 11). Pacification theory goes some of the way towards remedying these inadequacies and its insights should be incorporated in our approach to the war–emergency paradigm. But it also lapses into the other extreme, treating all wars and crises as if they were the same, and foregoing any role for the state and war-like crisis conditions in building class consciousness and bringing the latent class war of civil society out in the open. This is where returning to Marx and Engels' more expansive and dialectical reading of war and the state can help us decide whether to incorporate the language and practices of war and emergency in our political practice.

In thinking further about our engagement with the war–emergency paradigm the works of Marx and Engels also call attention to three broader issues. First, the importance of combining structural with political analyses of the limitations but also possibilities that the contradictions and resulting crises of capitalism produce at any given historical moment. As Battistoni recalls earlier in this volume building on Raju Das's works, a distinction can be drawn between 'structuralist' and 'class struggle' analyses of the state, with the former emphasising the 'constraints that capitalism sets on the kinds of action the state can undertake' and the latter seeing the state as conditioned at least in part 'by class conflict and the shifting balance of power between classes'.[3] Yet, the two could be helpfully brought together. Indeed, for Marx, the class struggle was as much the 'executor' as the 'originator' of crises, meaning structural contradictions can act not only as a limitation to, but also as a vehicle for, the class struggle (Callinicos).

Second is the importance of applying such analyses to all institutions of bourgeois society. In the face of growing nationalism and authoritarianism threatening the bourgeois model of democratic and liberal statehood, increased attempts have been made to demonstrate Marx's commitment to liberal rights and democracy, or at least to refute the view that he rejected such rights, whether as part of his revolutionary strategy or as part of his views on the communist horizon. This chapter, however, pointed to the need to explore not only to the antinomies of law, rights (Shoikhedbrod 2019), or the state, but also of war and emergency, refraining from reducing an engagement with the state 'articulated in martial terms' to a symptom of 'our cramped political imaginaries and rhetoric' (Toscano 2020, 9).

Last is the value of re-centring the Marxist revolutionary tradition and military thinking (Keucheyan 2016) to our understanding of the capitalist state and revolution. Several key Marxist figures deployed the war metaphor not merely to describe the politicisation of the class struggle, but, even more explicitly than Marx and Engels, as an analytical tool to consider different questions of revolutionary strategy and tactics (Egan 2016). Lenin is a well-known example, but so is Gramsci. In particular, by stressing the significance of cultural struggles/wars, i.e. of building counter-hegemonic discourses that challenge the 'common sense' of

---

[3] See Battistoni in this volume.

bourgeois society, alongside 'direct attacks against the state' intended to seize state power, Gramsci's distinction between wars of manoeuvre and wars of position added an important ideological component to the class war. Certainly, just as Marx and Engels, these writers were writing for a different time. But in this age of crises and catastrophe, rethinking the capitalist state requires also rethinking the revolution which has perhaps rarely felt as necessary and urgent, and yet as distant.

REFERENCES

Albert, Michael. 2022. 'Climate Emergency and Securitization Politics: Towards a Climate Politics of the Extraordinary.' *Globalizations*. https://doi.org/10.1080/14747731.2022.2117501.

Balibar, Étienne. 2010. 'Marxism and War.' *Radical Philosophy* 160 (2): 9–17.

Balibar, Étienne. 2009. 'On the Aporias of Marxian Politics: From Civil War to Class Struggle.' *Diacritics* 39 (2): 59–73.

Balibar, Étienne. 1977. *On the Dictatorship of the Proletariat*. London: Verso Books.

Barrow, Clyde W. 2021. 'Legal and Illegal Political Tactics in Marxist Political Theory.' In *Research Handbook on Law and Marxism*, edited by Paul O'Connell and Umut Özsu, 375–98. Cheltenham: Edward Elgar.

Callinicos, Alex. 2023. *The New Age of Catastrophe*. Cambridge: Polity.

———. 2020. 'Class Struggle.' In *The Marx Revival: Key Concepts and New Interpretations*, edited by Marcello Musto. Cambridge: Cambridge University Press.

Clausewitz, Carl. 1992. *On War*. Princeton: Princeton University Press.

Draper, Hal. 1977. *Karl Marx's Theory of Revolution, Volume I, State and Bureaucracy*. New York: Monthly Review Press.

———.1996. *War and Revolution: Lenin and the Myth of Revolutionary Defeatism*. Humanities Press.

Egan, Daniel. 2016. *The Dialectic of Position and Maneuver: Understanding Gramsci's Military Metaphor*. Leiden: Brill.

Gallie, Walter Bryce. 2008. *Philosophers of Peace and War: Kant, Clausewitz, Marx, Engels and Tolstoy*. Cambridge: Cambridge University Press.

Greene, Alan. 2020. *Emergency Powers in a Time of Pandemic*. Bristol: Bristol University Press.

Jessop, Bob. 2001. 'Bringing the State Back in (yet again): Reviews, Revisions, Rejections, and Redirections.' *International Review of Sociology* 11 (2): 149–173.

Keucheyan, Razmig. 2016. 'Le Marxisme et les Guerres du Climat: Les Théories Critiques Face aux Evolutions de la Violence Collective.' *Raisons Politiques* 61 (1): 129–43.

Kivotidis, Dimitrios. 2021. *Dictatorship: New Trajectories in Law*. Abingdon: Routledge.

Knox, Robert. 2016. 'Marxist Approaches to International Law.' In The *Oxford Handbook of The Theory of International Law*, edited by Anne Orford and Florian Hoffman. Oxford: Oxford University Press.

———. 2010. 'Strategy and Tactics.' *Finnish Yearbook of International Law* 21: 193–229.

Knox, Robert, and David Whyte. 2023. 'Vaccinating Capitalism: Racialised Value in the COVID-19 Economy'. *Mortality* 28 (2): 329–345.

Malm, Andreas. 2020. *Corona, Climate, Chronic Emergency: War Communism in the Twenty-First Century*. New York: Verso.

Manolov, Martin V. and George S. Rigakos. 2014. 'Anti-Security.' In *The Wiley-Blackwell Encyclopedia of Globalization*, edited by G. Ritzer. https://doi.org/10.1002/9780470670590.wbeog613

Marx, Karl. 1963. *The Eighteenth Brumaire of Louis Bonaparte*. New York: International Publishers.

———. 1978. 'The Civil War in France.' In *The Marx-Engels Reader*, edited by Robert C. Tucker, 2d ed., 629–52. New York: Norton.

———. 1990. *Capital: A Critique of Political Economy*. Translated by Ben Fowkes. Vol. I. London: Penguin Books.

———. 1990b. 'On the Jewish Question.' In Karl Marx, *Early Writings*. Translated by Rodney Livingstone and Gregor Benton. Harmondsworth: Penguin.

Marx, Karl, and Friedrich Engels. 1973. *Marx and Engels Collected Works*, Vol. 3. London: Lawrence & Wishart.

Marx, Karl, and Friedrich Engels. 1976a. *Marx and Engels Collected Works*, Vol. 5. London: Lawrence & Wishart.

Marx, Karl, and Friedrich Engels. 1976b. *Marx and Engels Collected Works*, Vol. 6. London: Lawrence & Wishart.

Marx, Karl, and Friedrich Engels. 1978. *Marx and Engels Collected Works*, Vol. 10. London: Lawrence & Wishart.

Marx, Karl, and Friedrich Engels. 1986. *Marx and Engels Collected Works*, Vol. 22. London: Lawrence & Wishart.

Marx, Karl, and Friedrich Engels. 2011. *The Communist Manifesto*. Translated by Samuel Moore. New York: Penguin Books.

Neocleous, Mark. 1996. *Administering Civil Society: Towards a Theory of State Power*. London: Macmillan Press.

———. 2000. *The Fabrication of Social Order: A Critical Theory of Police Power*. London: Pluto Press.

———. 2006. 'The Problem with Normality: Taking Exception to "Permanent Emergency."' *Alternatives* 31 (2): 191–213.

———. 2008. *Critique of Security*. Edinburgh: Edinburgh University Press.

———. 2011. 'The Police of Civilization: The War on Terror as Civilizing Offensive.' *International Political Sociology* 5 (2): 144–159.

———. 2018. 'Security and Police.' In *The SAGE Handbook of Frankfurt School Critical Theory*, edited by Beverley Best, Werner Bonefeld and Chris O'Kane. London: SAGE Publishing.

Neocleous, Mark, and Brendan MacQuade. 2020. 'Beware: Medical Police.' *Radical Philosophy* 208: 3–9.

Neocleous, Mark, and George S. Rigakos, eds. 2011. *Anti-Security*. Ottawa: Red Quill Press.

Pashukanis, Evgeny. 1980. *Selected Writings on Marxism and Law*. London: Academic Press.

Pashukanis, Evgeny B. 1989. *Law and Marxism: A General Theory*. Translated by Barbara Einhorn. London: Pluto Press.

Sharma, Sukriti. 2022. Review of *Pandemic! Covid-19 Shakes the World*, by Slavoj Žižek. *Marx & Philosophy Review of Books*. https://marxandphilosophy.org.uk/reviews/20149_pandemic-covid-19-shakes-the-world-by-slavoj-zizek-reviewed-by-sukriti-sharma/

Shoikhedbrod, Igor. 2019. *Revisiting Marx's Critique of Liberalism*. Bristol: Palgrave Macmillan.

Slavoj, Žižek. 2020. *Pandemic!: COVID-19 Shakes the World*. New York: Polity.

Teschke, Benno. 2020. 'War and International Relations.' In *The Marx Revival: Key Concepts and New Interpretations*, edited by Marcello Musto. Cambridge: Cambridge University Press.

Toscano, Alberto. 2020. 'The State of the Pandemic.' *Historical Materialism* 28 (4): 3–23.

Wood, Ellen Meiksins. 2020. 'Democracy.' In *The Marx Revival: Key Concepts and New Interpretations*, edited by Marcello Musto. Cambridge: Cambridge University Press.

Socially Reproductive Workers, 'Life-Making', and State Repression

Kirstin Munro

1 Introduction[1]

Social Reproduction Theory (SRT) is a recent off-shoot of Marxist feminism (Arruzza 2016; Bhattacharya 2017; Ferguson 2019) that argues for the revolutionary capacity and working class position of unproductive but *socially reproductive* workers whose waged and unwaged work is involved in the reproduction of the commodity labour power. SRT borrows from Dalla Costa and James (1975) and Silvia Federici (2012) the idea that women who perform tasks (on an unwaged basis) related to the reproduction of labour power are members of the working class and thus capable of

[1] Many thanks to the panellists and participants in the New Research in the Critical Political Economy of Labour session at the Eastern Economics Association Meetings in 2021 for useful comments and questions, in particular Hannah Archambault, Luke Petach, Luke Pretz, and Anastasia Wilson. I would also like to thank Alex Mach for valuable research assistance locating employment statistics, and Rob Hunter, Sam Menefee-Libey, Chris O'Kane, Paddy Quick, and Lise Vogel for conversations and comments that strengthened the manuscript.

K. Munro (✉)
Department of Economics, New School for Social Research, New York, NY, USA
e-mail: munrok@newschool.edu

participating in class struggle. From Lise Vogel (2013), SRT borrows the notion that labour power is reproduced not only in the family-household on an unwaged basis by mothers and wives, but also on a waged basis by unproductive workers—disproportionately women of all races and racialized men, and disproportionately employed by the state.[2] In combining these two insights from twentieth-century Marxist feminist scholarship to argue for the revolutionary potential of workers outside the 'productive' economy, SRT has done much to overturn Marxist orthodoxy and shed light on the importance of 'socially reproductive' labour to the economy and society.

While Bhattacharya and Ferguson gesture towards it in places, SRT does not specifically examine how the reproduction of labour power relates to the crisis-ridden reproduction of capitalist society. What Ferguson and Bhattacharya offer instead is a foreshortened account in which exploitation and domination are extrinsic to the organization of production and reproduction. My critique of SRT is based on my view that exploitation and domination are inherent to the organization of production and reproduction in capitalism, and that the reproduction of capitalist society proceeds by perpetuating these forms of organization. 'Socially reproductive' workers are complicit in the reproduction of capitalist society as a whole, just as productive workers are. Furthermore, the state is not a neutral instrument overseeing the economy that can promote regressive or progressive laws or economic and social policies that distribute the proceeds of labour on the basis of the balance of class forces. The state is the 'organized force of society' (Marx 1976, 915). Since this society is capitalist society, the capitalist state is a force for 'social enslavement' (Marx 2010, 23) and the object of the critical theory of society.[3]

Thus, Social Reproduction Theory is *not* a critical theory of society. SRT can be best described as a revolutionary strategy aimed at correctly identifying the working class on the assumption that the correct definition—along with transitional demands (Trotsky 1981) connected to this correct identification of the working class—can help to bring about communism. While the term 'social reproduction theory' has recently

---

[2] See Moraitis and Copley (2016) for a social form approach to the concepts of productive and unproductive labour. Other critical engagements with SRT include Best (2021), De'Ath (2018, 2022), and Vishmidt and Sutherland (2020).

[3] This is discussed in greater detail in O'Kane & Munro (2022).

been co-opted by non-Marxists—for example in the liberal/progressive sub-field of feminist economics[4]—SRT, as originally conceived by Trotskyist scholars such as Arruzza, Bhattacharya, and Ferguson, theorizes the revolutionary capacity of 'socially reproductive' workers, focusing on occupations such as teachers, nurses, and social workers who are disproportionately women who are disproportionately employed by the state. In doing so, SRT overlooks the contradictory and antagonistic role of the state in the lives of the working class, as the reproduction of labour power in capitalism takes place via state repression domination.[5]

In this chapter, I argue that the task of teachers, nurses, and social workers is the production of not just any 'life' but that of a docile, exploitable worker, and that this reproduction of labour power by employees of the state cannot be divorced from state repression.[6] First, I provide an overview of the reproduction of labour power in capitalist society building on my previous work (Munro 2019, 2021, 2023), arguing that the accumulation and reproduction of capital cannot be divorced from the reproduction of labour power and vice-versa. Next, I critique the recent adoption of the term 'life-making' by Social Reproduction Theorists on the same basis. Finally, I discuss the contradictory but repressive nature of institutions such as schools, healthcare facilities, and social service agencies, and I argue that professional state employees whose work involves the reproduction of labour power—disproportionately women of all races and racialized men—have a state repressive function in capitalist society.

---

[4] See for example Agenjo-Calderón and Gálvez-Muñoz (2019); Austen and Sharp (2020); and Moos (2021).

[5] What I mean by domination is not 'the domination of people by other people, but ... the domination of people by abstract social structures that people themselves constitute' (Postone 1993, 30) and reproduce.

[6] Liberal feminist economists appear to make the same error in their veneration of 'caring professions', though a complete analysis of liberal/progressive feminist economics is outside the scope of this book chapter. For further discussion of liberal/progressive feminist economics and SRT, see Munro (2023, 24–27).

2   Is Reproducing Labour Power a Good Thing?

Labour power is 'the aggregate of those mental and physical capabilities existing in... a human being ... which he sets in motion whenever he produces a use-value of any kind' (Marx 1976, 270).[7] Labour power only becomes a commodity when it is offered for sale on the market. The commodity labour power is sold by the bearer of labour power—the free labourer—because he has nothing else to sell as the result of the historical process of forcible expropriation. The existence of the capitalist necessitates the existence of the seller of labour power, and the imperative of accumulation necessitates that labour power remain constantly available on the market. While he viewed the reproduction of labour power as a key component of the reproduction of capitalist society, Marx 'never provided a thoroughgoing exposition of just what it entailed' (Vogel 2013, 188).

A central contribution of Marxist feminism has been the insight that the wage is not exactly equal to the full amount of labour time necessary for the reproduction of labour power (day-to-day or intergenerationally) because of the unwaged time involved in transforming commodities into use-values and raising children (Quick 2018; Vogel 2013)—what Lise Vogel calls the 'domestic component of necessary labour' (2013, 158). State programmes such as public education, healthcare, and other welfare state benefits also contribute to the non-equivalence of the worker's wage and the worker's subsistence level (Conference of Socialist Economists 1977, 4). Understanding the cultural norms that prescribe working class 'needs' (Marx 1976, 275), the specific proportions of inputs (Munro 2019), the social assignment of tasks (Cowan 1983), and the living arrangements of people (Netting 1984) are empirical questions for historians—the reproduction of labour power has been carried out in a variety of ways during the history of capitalism (Vogel 2013, 154).

The imperative of accumulation means that capital must 'tend to socialise (that is turn into a collective activity) the general conditions of capitalist accumulation', (Cockburn 1977, 63). While the focus in Marxist feminism is frequently on women, households, and household production and their role in the reproduction of labour power, labour power can be replenished via other means—such as proletarianization—and in

---

[7] In order to successfully produce use-values, the capacity to produce use-values that exists in a human being—actualized as labour—must be combined with means of production that likewise must possess the capacity to produce use-values.

other sites, such as schools, 'labour-camps, barracks, orphanages, hospitals, prisons, and other such institutions' (Vogel 2013, 159). Marx writes that to be a productive worker is 'not a piece of luck, but a misfortune' (Marx 1976, 644)—the same misfortune is also true for unproductive workers whose work, whether waged or unwaged, contributes to the reproduction of labour power.

In their Trotskyist analysis, class struggle for Social Reproduction Theorists involves workers attempting to recapture for their own use and enjoyment a portion of the value created through their labour that had been 'stolen' by capitalists (Munro 2019).[8] Transitional demands calling for redistribution (the minimum programme) are seen as a stepping stone towards the ultimate end of workers—now broadly defined to also include those engaged in the work of reproducing labour power—seizing power and centrally planning an equitable form of distribution (the maximum programme). However, *contra* the traditional Marxism[9] of SRT, '[e]xploitation and domination are intrinsic to any conceivable arrangement of capital accumulation... [W]e are all compelled to participate in the reproduction of capital as a social relation', (Hunter 2021, 404–405). If exploitation and domination are inherent to the organization of production and reproduction in capitalism, then the reproduction of capitalist society proceeds by perpetuating these forms of organization, no matter the rates of exploitation or the amounts of redistribution.

3   'Life-Making' and the Reproduction of Capitalist Society

More recently, Social Reproduction Theorists such as Alan Sears (2016, 2017), Susan Ferguson (2019), and Tithi Bhattacharya have moved away from redefining social reproduction as the reproduction of labour power, and have begun to use the term 'life-making'. Ferguson argues that capitalism proceeds by 'reorganizing and devaluing all of people's life-making activities, most of which have been the tasks assigned to women' (2019, 2). Social reproduction itself is defined by Bhattacharya as 'life-making' activities' (Bhattacharya 2020a). Others in this niche define social

[8] For a different view of class struggle, see the chapter on 'Class and Struggle: On the False Society' in Bonefeld (2014), which argues that '[t]he critique of class society finds its positive resolution only in the classless society, not in a "fairer" class society' (102).

[9] For an overview of the critique of traditional Marxism, see O'Kane (2018).

reproduction as 'the domain of life-making' (Thompson 2020, 278); 'the under-remunerated effort of producing use-values essential to "life-making"' (Rao et al. 2021, 2); or 'the renewal and maintenance of life and of the institutions and work necessary therein' (Arruzza 2016, 10). Social reproduction is said to give 'a name to the activities that constitute life making … in capitalist society', (Miranda and Lane-McKinley 2017). The shift by Social Reproduction Theorists from redefining social reproduction to refer to the reproduction of labour power to redefining social reproduction to refer to 'life-making' generically divorces these concepts from their explicit relationship to capitalist society as a whole.

Rather than seeing life-makers as complicit in the reproduction of capitalist society, for SRT:

> capitalism develops only by trapping and distilling the generalized capacity of humans to labour. But it does so not simply—or even primarily—by feeding off the productive potential of waged labourers. It does so equally by reorganizing and devaluing all of people's life-making activities, most of which have been the tasks assigned to women. (Ferguson 2019, 2)

To articulate this supposedly contradictory antagonism between capital and life-making, SRT further draws on peculiar readings of the Lise Vogel and Sylvia Federici. Following Ferguson's interpretation of Vogel's 'deep and abiding contradiction', Ferguson contends that 'capitalists do not directly control the (re)production of labour power … They do, however, pay the wages and some of the taxes through which workers gain the means of subsistence to reproduce themselves'. However, 'competition compels capitalists to keep wages and taxes as low as possible' which means that the 'social reproduction of labour presents them with a dilemma: they require human labour power but must constrain the conditions of life that generate it'. Hence, Ferguson, citing Vogel, 'from the point of view of capital, the social reproduction of the workforce is simultaneously indispensable and an obstacle to accumulation'.[10] For Ferguson,

---

[10] A thorough critical discussion of SRT's questionable interpretation of Lise Vogel's work stands outside the focus of this chapter. However, it is important to note that Ferguson's characterization of Vogel's 'deep and abiding contradiction' and Ferguson's citation of this sentence mischaracterizes Vogel. This is ironic because Ferguson's characterization here does not account for the aspects of Vogel's theory Ferguson praises elsewhere: Vogel's interpretation of Marx's theory of value and Vogel's argument that reproductive labour should not be conflated with the domestic household labour because it occurs in various

'Capitalism thus exists only by consistently thwarting the flourishing of human life under which it nonetheless depends' (2019, 112).

Ferguson further develops the implications for revolutionary strategy of the contradictory antagonism between capitalism and reproductive life-making by citing a passage of Federici's (2012, 99):

> Highlighting the reproduction of 'labour power' reveals the dual character and the contradiction inherent in reproductive labour and, therefore, the unstable, potentially disruptive character of this work. To the extent that labour power can only exist in the living individual, its reproduction must be simultaneously a production and valorisation of desired human qualities and capacities, and an accommodation to the externally imposed standards of the labour market.[11]

sites and is performed by different types of labour. The sentence Ferguson cites comes in the context of Vogel's discussion of the 'highly contradictory' role of domestic labour within capitalist social reproduction; to wit, that '[o]n the one hand, it forms an essential condition for capitalism ... On the other hand, domestic labour stands in the way of capitalism's drive for profit, for it also limits the availability of labour-power' (Vogel 2013, 163). In other words, for Vogel (and *contra* Ferguson), it is not 'the social reproduction of the workforce' as whole that 'is simultaneously indispensable and an obstacle to accumulation' (Vogel 2013, 163). Rather, because domestic labour is unproductive, '[o]ver the long term, the capitalist class seeks to stabilise the reproduction of labour-power at a low cost and with a minimum of domestic labour', (Vogel 2013, 163). The 'working class, either as a united force or fragmented into competing sectors, strives to win the best conditions possible for its own renewal, which may include a particular level and type of domestic labour' (Vogel 2013, 163). *Profit,* rather than 'constraining the conditions of the life that generate labour power' (Ferguson 2020, 112) is the primary concern of capital and, for that reason, it is also the focus of Vogel's analysis of domestic labour and social reproduction.

[11] As with SRT's mischaracterization of Lise Vogel's work, a thorough critical discussion of SRT's selective interpretation of Federici exceeds the focus of this chapter. However, it is important to note an important distinction between the sorts of contradictions Federici and Ferguson each use this passage to illuminate. Federici argues that domestic reproductive labour is already organized by capital, specifically because capital is reliant upon reproductive labour producers. For Federici it is then 'impossible to draw a line between' these 'two corresponding aspects of reproductive work, but maintaining the concept brings out the tension, the potential separation, it suggests a world of conflicts, resistances, contradictions that have political significance' (Federici 2012, 99). This is because 'it tells us that we can struggle against housework without having to fear that we will ruin our communities, for this work imprisons the producers as well as the produced' (99–100). In other words, in contrast to Ferguson's interpretation of her passage, Federici is drawing this distinction to *critique* domestic labour and disrupt the reproduction of capital, not to morally valorize domestic labour.

However, Ferguson then proceeds to go against the implications Federici herself draws from this passage. Ferguson first contends that, '[l]abour resists total subsumption by capital precisely because there can be no labour without life—without a living human being, whose life needs can and will assert themselves against capital time and again' (Ferguson 2020, 126). Moreover, Ferguson holds that these 'desired human qualities and capacities' that are created and sustained by reproductive life-making constitute an 'immense well of "practical human activity" from which new societies can be forged—societies that put human need ahead of profit' (130). Finally, 'for both historical and systemic reasons ... "unproductive" social reproductive labour *tends to be* less fully subsumed to capital than "productive" labour' (126).

On these bases, SRT argues for the working class position and revolutionary capacity of people outside the 'productive' economy—those engaged in either waged or unwaged work related to the reproduction of labour power, if not surplus value directly. For,

> [i]n attending to the duality of work—its concrete and abstract forms—social reproduction feminism emphasizes the contradictions between value creation and life creation; it draws attention to the fact that while work is always subject to capitalist disciplines, it also always exceeds them. As a result, those engaged in social reproductive labour can and do defy the alienating and life-crushing tendencies of capitalism to assert and create new forms of relations with each other and with the natural world. This is what teachers, hospital workers, community activists, among others, do every day. And when they do it collectively, with a consciousness of building solidarities among oppressed groups whose aim is to take life back from capital, they have a powerful potential to thwart the system that constantly diminishes and degrades the very lives it depends upon. They have the potential, that is, to organize work for life, not capital. (Ferguson 2020, 141)

While Social Reproduction Theorists may speak about 'life-making' in order to paint these 'life-making activities' (and the people who perform them) in a virtuous light, the life that is made is that of a worker who must compete with other workers for the opportunity to sell her labour power, spending the majority of her life maximizing surplus value. Seen in this way, the task of reproductive workers is the reproduction of not just any life but that of this race of peculiar commodity-owners (Marx 1976, 275), the sellers of labour power. Thus, the reproduction of labour power in capitalist society is not virtuous 'life-making', but rather one aspect of a larger process that perpetuates the capitalist organization of society. After all, 'the reproduction of labour-power... [is] a factor in the reproduction of capital itself. Accumulation of capital is therefore multiplication of the proletariat' (Marx 1976, 763–64).

In conventional Marxist usage, 'social reproduction' properly refers to the reproduction of capitalist society as a whole, a process shaped by the imperative of endless accumulation. Accumulation and the reproduction of capital cannot be divorced from the reproduction of labour power, and the reproduction of labour power cannot be divorced from the reproduction of capitalist society, nor from the class antagonism and social misery inherent to it.[12] Indeed, capitalist society as a 'whole... maintains itself only through antagonism' (Adorno 1973: 311).

4   STATE REPRESSION VIA HEALTH, EDUCATION, AND SOCIAL SERVICES

An understanding of the repressive functions of state institutions involved in the reproduction of labour power—and the extent to which employees of these institutions are implicated in state violence and repression—is largely absent from SRT. In this section, I would like to argue something a bit more nuanced than to merely say that teachers are cops, nurses are cops, and social workers are cops—which is not to say I would entirely disagree with that sentiment. Rather, I wish to emphasize the contradictory nature of these occupations (London-Edinburgh Weekend Return Group 1980)—both from the perspective of the workers carrying out this work and from the perspective of the working class people being worked upon.

Althusser's essay 'Ideology and Ideological State Apparatuses' was a key influence on many Marxist feminists of the 1980s. In this essay, he argues that schools serve an ideological function in capitalism—they are what he calls an Ideological State Apparatus—and while it is not emphasized or elaborated upon (Barrett 1980), Althusser (2001, 149) suggests that schools may simultaneously serve a repressive function,

---

[12] What I mean by social misery is the types of harm inflicted on people by the specific organization of society.

meaning they secure 'by force (physical or otherwise) the political conditions of the reproduction of relations of production'. I would like to
suggest that health clinics and social service agencies similarly serve repressive functions, with employees of these institutions serving as agents of
state repression while at the same time providing—at least to a limited
extent—services to the working class.

Schools, social service agencies, hospitals, and health clinics are examples of sites outside the family-household where labour power is reproduced, and the repressive nature of these institutions in capitalism has
been extensively theorized,[13] as has the role of professional women in
these institutions.[14] For example, Foucault (1989) argues that medical
practitioners have power over and objectify patients, with Lawler (1991)
and May (1992) arguing that these insights apply not only to physicians
in the past, but also to present-day nurses. Diers and Molde (1983) and
Allen (2015) discuss the gatekeeping functions of nurses—that is, the
extent to which it is part of nurses' jobs to deny access to services rather
than provide services. Dyer (2002) discusses this gatekeeping function in
the context of government austerity, and Khalil (2009) discusses nurses'
classification of patients as 'good' and deserving of health services and
'difficult' and thus subject to rationing and denials of care. Dale and
Foster (1986) discuss the historical case of health inspectors and health
visitors, largely women, whose role was to teach modern hygiene practices
to the working class, as 'middle class women became involved in judging
working-class mothers' (37), while Neocleous (2000) links the history
of sanitation reform and health visitation explicitly to state administrative violence and the repression of the working class. Wilson (1977) and
Dale and Foster (1986) discuss the history of women in the social work
profession, pointing to the repressive functions of this work. Ellis (2011)
discusses the gatekeeping functions of workers in social welfare agencies,
and the limits to the use of discretion by these workers—updating the

---

[13] The repressive nature of the family-household has also been theorized, for example
by Barrett and McIntosh (1982). The capitalist state's seeming fixation on enforcing the
family-household is discussed in Munro (2021) with an emphasis on the UK case. For
the US case, see Melinda Cooper (2017).

[14] A theme in much of this literature is that state repression via schools, social service
agencies, and health clinics proceeds on an uneven basis, with special scrutiny reserved for
members of racialized groups, immigrants, disabled people, gender and sexual minorities,
single parents, the childless, and others who are unwilling or unable to conform to social
norms related to the white, heterosexual bourgeois family-household.

results from Lipsky (2010), in which public servants are portrayed as having decision-making power over scarce resources. And the repressive qualities of schools and teachers are discussed by Schmidt (2001), Taylor (2013), Rancière (1991), and Illich (1971), to cite a few examples in an extensive literature. The role of teachers in maintaining and exacerbating inequality is discussed in Vaught and Castagno (2008) and Fergus (2016). Public education as a repressive state institution is an explicit emphasis in Betasamosake Simpson (2014), Shange (2019), and Hill (2010).

Professionals employed by the state in occupations related to the reproduction of labour power—disproportionately women[15]—are tasked with carrying out the commands of the state and enforcing its rules. This entails both denying services as well as providing services, often with only paltry resources available to do so and punishment or redundancy if regulations are not followed. They decide who receives healthcare and who is dismissed as a malingerer or drug-seeker; who is prioritized for housing, food, and cash benefits, and who has their children seized by the state; who is provided with educational support services for learning difficulties and who is punished with detention, expulsion from school, or even arrest by a 'School Resource Officer'. While some well-meaning state employees may wish to subvert the repressive qualities of education, healthcare, and other social services, the extent to which this is truly possible is limited.

> As [socialist] workers in those occupations that are termed 'professional', such as social work, or teaching, we are often given impossible problems to solve arising from poverty or from the powerlessness of our 'clients'. The resources available to back up our intervention the welfare provision of the state—are a drop in the ocean of need. And besides, it is clear that many other actions of the state and of the economy itself are pulling in the opposite direction, making things worse for the poor. We often feel that we are being asked to manipulate people, to use women's pride in their home or love of their children, for instance, as well as their need of the practical resources we partially control and can give them access to, to induce co-operation, (London-Edinburgh Weekend Return Group 1980).

---

[15] Women are the majority of public sector employees in the United States (United States Bureau of Labour Statistics 2021), the United Kingdom (United Kingdom Office for National Statistics 2019), Canada (Statistics Canada 2021), and Australia (Australia Bureau of Statistics 2021).

Interviews described in *In And Against The State* suggest that members of some working class households feel they require state services for survival, and must accept reductions in freedom and intrusions into day-to-day life in order to obtain these meagre state services. 'State provision leaves a bad taste in our mouths. State institutions are often authoritarian, they put us down, tie us up with regulations' (London-Edinburgh Weekend Return Group 1980). Furthermore, the task of dealing with the state on behalf of the working class family is assigned to working class women: 'Who answers the door when the social worker calls? Who talks to the head teacher about the truant child? Who runs down to the rent office? The woman, wife, and mother' (Cockburn 1977, 58). Thus, professional women act as the intermediaries between the state and working class households, while working class women act as the intermediaries between their households and the state. Repressive state institutions such as education, healthcare, and other social services are women on both sides (Wilson 1977; Munro 2021).

5   Conclusion

Contra SRT, capitalist production does not consist in 'an immense well of "practical human activity" from which new societies can be forged—societies that put human need ahead of profit' (Ferguson 2020, 130). This is likewise the case with the activities and the acts of reproductive life-making that create and sustain this practical human activity. One virtue of SRT is that it points to the multiple sites in which 'socially reproductive' labour occurs. However, the conceptualization of these socially reproductive activities as the life-making of the proletariat—and the contention that in creating and sustaining people as bearers of the commodity labour power, reproductive labour cultivates and sustains the desired human qualities and capacities' that capitalism simply appropriates for profit—abstracts from these activities, the qualities and capacities they cultivate, and from the particular institutions in which they take place. As a consequence, SRT does not grasp how these activities, capacities, and institutions are integral to the reproduction of the negative totality of capitalist society, socializing and disciplining individuals so that people are compelled to reproduce capitalist society.

Schools, healthcare facilities, and social welfare agencies are contradictory institutions, at once providing needed services to members of the working class, while at the same time charged with restricting or denying these services—for the purpose of reproducing capitalist relations of production and thus capitalist society as a whole. Furthermore, we can see that public employees—who are disproportionately women—serve as intermediaries between the state, via its repressive institutions, and the working class. Women in the United States and United Kingdom remain overrepresented in public sector employment as a whole, but are specifically overrepresented in many professions related to the reproduction of labour power, such as teachers, social workers, and in healthcare professions other than physicians (United Kingdom Office for National Statistics 2019, United States Bureau of Labour Statistics 2021). These occupations are described by liberal-progressive scholars in the field of feminist economics as 'caring professions' (Folbre 2012) and by Social Reproduction Theorists as waged workers involved in the reproduction of labour power or 'life-making activities' (Ferguson 2020). While their roles and relationship to the working class is complex and contradictory, I would like to offer the following provocation: teachers, healthcare workers, and social workers in capitalism do bear a resemblance to the police—tasked by the state with the enforcement of laws and norms, providing but also denying services, and guilty of inflicting psychological and sometimes physical violence on members of the working class.

The current popularity of SRT has driven a surge in scholarly interest in Marxist feminism, unproductive/'socially reproductive' labour, and the reproduction of labour power—frequently neglected and overlooked topics. Social Reproduction Theorists such as Arruzza, Bhattacharya, and Ferguson have made important contributions that question and overturn Marxist orthodoxies, and shed light on current events such as teacher's strikes (Bhattacharya 2019) and the COVID-19 pandemic (Bhattacharya 2020a, 2020b; Marxist Feminist Collective 2020). However, SRT overlooks the contradictory role of professional women in public sector employment related to the reproduction of labour power, as well as the antagonistic role of the state in the lives of the working class. Is it possible to separate the state's social provisioning functions from its functions related to violence and repression? My answer to this question is no. The reproduction of capitalist society depends on the worker continually reproducing herself as a worker—compelled to do so both 'physically and socially' (Clarke 1995, 19–20) as she is at once produced by the capitalist production process and reproduced by it. Rather, the supposedly virtuous 'activities of life-making' carried out by professional women state employees such as teachers, nurses, and social workers perpetuate the antagonism and social misery inherent to capitalism.

References

Adorno, Theodor W. 1973. *Negative Dialectics*. Translated by E. B. Ashton. New York: Continuum.

Agenjo-Calderón, Astrid, and Lina Gálvez-Muñoz. 2019. 'Feminist Economics: Theoretical and Political Dimensions'. *American Journal of Economics and Sociology* 78 (1): 137–166.

Allen, Davina. 2015. 'Inside "Bed Management": Ethnographic Insights from the Vantage Point of UK Hospital Nurses'. *Sociology of Health and Illness* 37 (3): 370–384.

Althusser, Louis. [1971] 2001. 'Ideology and Ideological State Apparatuses: Notes Toward an Investigation.' In *Lenin and Philosophy and Other Essays*, 85–126. Translated by Ben Brewster. New York: Monthly Review Press.

Arruzza, Cinzia. 2016. Functionalist, Determinist, Reductionist: Social Reproduction Feminism and Its Critics. *Science & Society* 80 (1): 9–30.

Austen, Siobhan and Rhonda Sharp. 2020. 'Feminist Economics and Retirement Income Savings Policy'. In Martin Sawer, Fiona Jenkins, and Karen Downing, eds. *How Gender Can Transform the Social Sciences: Innovation and Impact*, 127–136. Camden, UK: Palgrave Macmillan.

Australia Bureau of Statistics. 2021. Labour Force Survey January 2021 Table 26b. Employed Persons by Sector (Public/Private) of Main Job, Age and Sex. Accessed 1 March 2021. https://www.abs.gov.au/statistics/labour/employment-and-unemployment/labour-force-australia-detailed/jan-2021.

Barrett, Michèle. 1980. *Women's Oppression Today: Problems in Marxist Feminist Analysis*. London: Verso.

Barrett, Michèle and Mary McIntosh. [1982] 2015. *The Anti-social Family*. London: Verso.

Best, Beverley. 2021. 'Wages for Housework Redux: Social Reproduction and the Utopian Dialectic of the Value-form'. *Theory & Event* 24 (4): 896–921.

Betasamosake Simpson, Leanne. 2014. 'Land as Pedagogy: Nishnaabeg Intelligence and Rebellious Transformation.' *Decolonization: Indigeneity, Education & Society* 3 (3): 1–25.

Bhattacharya, Tithi. 2017. 'How not to Skip Class: Social Reproduction of Labour and the Global Working Class.' In *Social Reproduction Theory: Remapping Class, Recentering Oppression*, edited by Tithi Bhattacharya, 68–93. London: Pluto Press.

———. 2019. 'Caring Enough to Strike: U.S. Teacher's Strikes in Perspective.' *Monthly Review* January 15, 2019. Accessed 28 February 2021. https://mronline.org/2019/01/15/caring-enough-to-strike-u-s-teachers-strikes-in-perspective/.

———, interview by Sarah Jaffe. 2020a. 'Social reproduction and the pandemic.' *Dissent Magazine* April 2, 2020a. Accessed February 6, 2021. https://www.dissentmagazine.org/online_articles/social-reproduction-and-the-pandemic-with-tithi-bhattacharya.

———. 2020b. Social Reproduction Theory and Why We Need it to Make Sense of the Corona Virus Crisis. April 2, 2020b. Accessed 2 March 2021. http://www.tithibhattacharya.net/new-blog/2020b/4/2/social-reproduction-theory-and-why-we-need-it-to-make-sense-of-the-corona-virus-crisis.

Bonefeld, Werner. 2014. *Critical Theory and the Critique of Political Economy: On Subversion and Negative Reason*. New York: Bloomsbury.

Brenner, Johanna. 2000. *Women and the Politics of Class*. New York: Monthly Review Press.

Brenner, Johanna, and Barbara Laslett. 1991. 'Gender, Social Reproduction, and Women's Self-Organization: Considering the US Welfare State.' *Gender & Society* 5 (3): 314.

Clarke, Simon. 1991. 'The State Debate: Introduction.' In *The State Debate*, edited by Simon Clarke, 1–69. London: Palgrave Macmillan.

———. 1995. 'Marx and the Market.' https://homepages.warwick.ac.uk/~syrbe/pubs/LAMARKW.pdf.

Cockburn, Cynthia. 1977. *The Local State: Management of Cities and People*. London: Pluto Press.

Conference of Socialist Economists. 1977. *On the Political Economy of Women*. CSE Pamphlet no. 2, London: Stage 1.

Cooper, Melinda. 2017. *Family Values: Between Neoliberalism and the New Social Conservatism*. Cambridge, Massachusetts: Zone Books.

Cowan, Ruth Schwartz. 1983. *More Work for Mother: The Ironies of Household Technology from the Open Hearth to the Microwave*. New York: Basic Books.

Dale, Jennifer, and Peggy Foster. 1986. *Feminists and State Welfare*. London: Routledge.

Costa, Dalla, and Mariarosa, and Selma James. 1975. *The Power of Women and the Subversion of the Community*. Bristol: Falling Wall Press.

De'Ath, Amy. 2018. 'Gender and Social Reproduction'. In Beverley Best, Werner Bonefeld, and Chris O'Kane, eds. *The Sage Handbook of Frankfurt School Critical Theory*, 1534–1550. London: Sage.

De'Ath, Amy. 2022. 'Hidden Abodes and Inner Bonds: Literary Study and Marxist-feminism'. In Colleen Lye and Christopher Nealton, eds. *After Marx: Literature, Theory, and Value in the Twenty-First Century*, 225–239. Cambridge: Cambridge University Press.

Deacon, Desley. 1989. *Managing Gender: The State, the New Middle Class and Women Workers, 1830–1930*. Melbourne: Oxford University Press.

Diers, Donna, and Susan Molde. 1983. 'Nurses in Primary Care: The New Gatekeepers?' *The American Journal of Nursing* 83 (5): 742–745.

Dyer, Owen. 2002. 'BMA Suggests Nurses could Become Gatekeepers of the NHS.' *British Journal of Medicine* 324: 565.

Ellis, Kathryn. 2011. '"Street-level Bureaucracy" Revisited: The Changing Face of Frontline Discretion in Adult Social Care in England.' *Social Policy and Administration* 45 (3): 221–244.

Federici, Silvia. 2012. *Revolution at Point Zero: Housework, Reproduction, and Feminist Struggle*. Oakland: PM Press.

Fergus, Edward. 2016. 'Social Reproduction Ideologies: Teacher Beliefs about Race and Culture.' In *DisCrit: Disability Studies and Critical Race Theory in Education*, edited by David J. Connor, Beth A. Ferri, and Sbini A. Annamma, 117–130. New York: Teachers College Press.

Ferguson, Susan J. 1999. 'Building on the Strengths of the Socialist Feminist Tradition.' *Critical Sociology* 25 (1): 1–15.

Ferguson, Susan J. 2020. *Women and Work: Feminism, Labour, and Social Reproduction*. London: Pluto Press.

Folbre, Nancy, ed. 2012. *For Love or Money: Care Provision in the United States*. New York: Russell Sage Foundation.

Foucault, Michel, and [1963]. 1989. *The Birth of the Clinic: An Archaeology of Medical Perception*. London: Routledge.

Hill, Dave. 2010. 'Class, Capital, and Education in this Neoliberal and Neoconservative Period.' In *Revolutionizing Pedagogy: Education for Social Justice Within and Beyond Global Neo-Liberalism*, edited by Sheila Macrine, Peter McLaren, and Dave Hill, 119–143. New York: Palgrave Macmillan.

Hunter, Rob. 2021. 'Critical Legal Studies and Marx's Critique: A Reappraisal.' *Yale Journal of Law & the Humanities* 31 (2): 389–412.

Illich, Ivan. 1971. *Deschooling Society*. London: Calder & Boyars. https://www.dissentmagazine.org/online_articles/social-reproduction-and-the-pandemic-with-tithi-bhattacharya

Khalil, Doris D. 2009. 'Nurses' Attitude Towards "Difficult" and "Good" Patients in Eight Public Hospitals.' *International Journal of Nursing Practice* 15 (5): 437–443.

Lawler, Jocalyn. 1991. *Behind the Screens: Nursing, Somology and the Problem of the Body*. Edinburg: Churchill Livingstone.

Lipsky, Michael, and [1980],. 2010. *Street-level Bureaucracy: Dilemmas of the Individual in Public Services*. New York: Russell Sage Foundation.

London-Edinburgh Weekend Return Group. 1980. *In and Against the State: Discussion Notes for Socialists*. Edited by Seth Wheeler. London: Pluto Press.

Marx, Karl. 1976. *Capital: Volume I*. Translated by Ben Fowkes. London: Penguin Books.

———. 2010. *The Civil War in France*. https://www.marxists.org/archive/marx/works/download/pdf/civil_war_france.pdf.

Marxist Feminist Collective. 2020. 'On social Reproduction and the Covid-19 Pandemic.' *Spectre Journal*. April 3, 2020. Accessed March 2, 2021. Available at: https://spectrejournal.com/seven-theses-on-social-reproduction-and-the-covid-19-pandemic/.

May, Carl. 1992. 'Nursing Work, Nurses' Knowledge, and the Subjectification of the Patient.' *Sociology of Health and Illness* 14 (4): 472–487.

Miranda, M., and Lane-McKinley, K., 2017. 'Artwashing, or, Between Social Practice and Social Reproduction.' *A Blade of Grass*. February 1, 2017. Accessed February 6, 2021. Available at: https://abladeofgrass.org/fertile-ground/artwashing-social-practice-social-reproduction/.

Moos, Katherine A. 2021. 'Coronavirus Fiscal Policy in the United States: Lessons from Feminist Political Economy.' *Feminist Economics* 27 (1–2): 419–35.

Moraitis, Alexis B., and Jack Copley. 2017. 'Productive and Unproductive Labour and Social Form: Putting Class Struggle in Its Place.' *Capital & Class* 41 (1): 91–114.

Munro, Kirstin. 2019. '"Social Reproduction Theory", Social Reproduction, and Household Production.' *Science & Society* 83 (4): 451–468.

Munro, Kirstin. 2021. 'The Welfare State and the Bourgeois Family-Household.' *Science & Society* 85 (2): 199–206.

Munro, Kirstin. 2023. *The Production of Everyday Life in Eco-Conscious Households: Compromise, Conflict, Complicity*. Bristol: Bristol University Press.

Neocleous, Mark. 2000. *The Fabrication of Social Order: A Critical Theory of Police Power*. London: Pluto Press.

Netting, Robert McC., Richard R. Wilk, and Eric J. Arnould. 1984. "Introduction." In *Households: Comparative and Historical Studies of the Domestic Group*, edited by Robert Netting, Richard R. Wilk, & Eric J. Arnould. Berkeley, CA: University of California Press.

O'Kane, Chris. 2018. 'Moishe Postone's New Reading of Marx: The Critique of Political Economy as a Critical Theory of the Historically Specific Social Form of Labour.' *Consecutio Rerum* 3 (5): 485–501.

O'Kane, Chris and Kirstin Munro. 2022. 'Marxian Economics and the Critique of Political Economy.' In Werner Bonefeld and Chris O'Kane, eds. *Adorno and Marx: Negative Dialectics and the Critique of Political Economy*, 77–95. London: Bloomsbury Academic.

Postone, Moishe. 1993. *Time, Labour, and Social Domination: A Reinterpretation of Marx's Critical Theory*. Cambridge: Cambridge University Press.

Quick, Paddy. 2018. 'Labor Power: A "Peculiar" Commodity'. *Science & Society* 82 (3): 386–412.

Rancière, Jacques. [1987] 1991. *The Ignorant Schoolmaster: Five Lessons in Intellectual Emancipation.* Translated by Kristin Ross. Palo Alto: Stanford University Press.

Rao, Smriti, Smita Ramnarain, Sirisha Naidu, Anupama Uppal, and Avanti Mukherjee. 2021. 'Work and Social Reproduction in Rural India: Lessons from Time-Use Data.' University of Massachusetts Amherst Political Economy Research Institute Working Paper #535.

Schmidt, Jeff. 2001. *Disciplined Minds: A Critical Look at Salaried Professionals and the Soul-battering System that Shapes their Lives.* Lanham: Rowman & Littlefield.

Sears, A. 2016. 'Situating Sexuality in Social Reproduction.' *Historical Materialism* 24 (2): 138–163.

Sears, A. 2017. 'Body Politics: The Social Reproduction of Sexualities.' In *Social Reproduction Theory: Remapping Class, Recentering Oppression,* edited by Tithi Bhattacharya, 171–191. London: Pluto Press.

Shange, Savannah. 2019. *Progressive Dystopia: Abolition, Antiblackness, and Schooling in San Francisco.* Durham: Duke University Press.

Statistics Canada. 2021. 'Table 14–10–0288–02: Employment by Class of Worker, Monthly, Seasonally Adjusted (x 1,000).' Accessed March 1, 2021. https://doi.org/10.25318/1410028801-eng.

Taylor, Emmeline. 2013. *Surveillance Schools: Security Discipline and Control in Contemporary Education.* New York: Palgrave Macmillan.

Thompson, M. 2020. 'Sounding the Arcane: Contemporary Music, Gender and Reproduction.' *Contemporary Music Review.* 39 (2): 273–292.

Trotsky, Leon. [1938] 1981. *The Death Agony of Capitalism and the Tasks of the Fourth International: The Mobilization of the Masses around Transitional Demands to Prepare for the Conquest of Power: The Transitional Program.* Royal Oak, Michigan: Labor Publications.

UK Office for National Statistics. 2019. 'Who works in the public sector?.' Accessed March 1, 2021. https://www.ons.gov.uk/economy/governmentpublicsectorandtaxes/publicspending/articles/whoworksinthepublicsector/2019-06-04#workers-in-the-public-sector-are-more-likely-to-be-women.

US Bureau of Labour Statistics. 2021. 'Table B-5b. Employment of Women on Nonfarm Payrolls by Industry Sector, Not Seasonally Adjusted.' Accessed March 1, 2021. https://www.bls.gov/web/empsit/ceseeb5b.htm.

Vishmidt, Marina and Sutherland, Zoë. 2020. 'Social Reproduction: New Questions for the Gender, Affect, and Substance of Value'. In: Jennifer Cooke, ed. *The New Feminist Literary Studies.* Cambridge: Cambridge University Press, 143–154.

Vaught, Sabina E., and Angelina E. Castagno. 2008. '"I don't think I'm a Racist": Critical Race Theory, Teacher Attitudes, and Structural Racism.' *Race Ethnicity and Education* 11 (2): 95–113.

Vogel, Lise. [1983] 2013. *Marxism and the Oppression of Women: Toward a Unitary Theory*. Leiden: Brill.

Wilson, Elizabeth. 1977. *Women and the Welfare State*. London: Tavistock Publications Limited.

Social Murder: Capitalism's Systematic and State-Organized Killing

Nate Holdren

Capitalism kills, continually, in its normal operations, by subjecting working-class people to harmful conditions which vary in their specifics over time and place. Friedrich Engels made this argument in his 1845 book *The Condition of the Working Class in England*, naming this ongoing killing 'social murder' (Engels [1845] 2009, 36.). The term reflected his opposition both to capitalism as a death-dealing social system and to capitalism's apologists' portrayal of mass death as an unavoidable and thus apolitical fact of social life. In this chapter I draw on Engels' insights and on Marx's further development of them in order to present a theory of both the necessary lethality of capitalist social relations and the capitalist state's necessary implication in this ongoing death-dealing.

My account of social murder participates in a renewal of interest in both the concept and the social phenomena it serves to explicate. In a pair of articles, health policy scholars Piara Govender, Stella Medvedyuk, and Dennis Raphael provide a comprehensive account of uses of the concept of social murder in recent journalism (Govender et al. 2022),

N. Holdren (✉)
Drake University, Des Moines, IA, USA
e-mail: nate.holdren@drake.edu

and in academic uses going back over a hundred years, especially related to the social determinants of health (Medvedyuk et al. 2021). They document a recent increase in use of the concept—especially in the United Kingdom—which they attribute to concern over three factors: 'the Grenfell Tower Fire (GTF), the effects of austerity imposed by successive Conservative UK governments, and governmental mishandling of the COVID-19 pandemic' (Govender et al. 2022).[1] My aim in this chapter is to contribute to this renewal by theorizing social murder as a tendency inherent to capitalist social relations. I further argue that understanding this tendency is both enriched by and further enriches analysis of the capitalist state.

In what follows, I give an account of Engels' analysis and Marx's further development of that analysis in the first and third volumes of *Capital* as providing a theory of social murder, a theory with two facets. The first facet involves a claim that all versions of capitalism will tend to generate depoliticised mass killing of working-class people, as part of capitalism's ordinary operations.[2] The second facet is a theory of the capitalist state and social contestation, insofar as mass killing tends to generate patterns of conflict and of state management thereof. Specific forms of

---

[1] What Govender, Medvedyuk, and Raphael describe characterises much of my own route to the concept of social murder. In writing my book on workplace injury, I found commentary in UK media describing the Grenfell Tower Fire as social murder apposite to my claims about occupational safety and health (Holdren 2020, 180 n 15). In late 2019, after finishing my book, I began in earnest my own effort to theorize social murder, an effort I soon found all the more compelling with the advent of the pandemic. As part of this research I finally read Engels' 1845 book, a work I unfortunately had not previously taken seriously despite having been a Marxist for twenty-plus years. One of my hopes for this chapter is to encourage readers to take Engels' book far more seriously than I did for so long. Finally, Beatrice Adler-Bolton and Artie Vierkant's *Health Communism* (2022) is especially notable among recent works for giving explicit attention to social murder. They argue for a communist politics of health against both social murder and capitalism's tendency to define health in its own terms.

[2] My aim here is not to identify all of the ways capitalism kills. I do not address capitalism's tendency to generate war, for example, though I do believe capitalism has such a tendency (cf. Jasmine Chorley-Schulz's contribution to the present volume). Rather, my aim is to clearly identify social murder as one specific tendency for capitalism to cause mass death, a tendency that has a relatively coherent social logic. In my view this deadly tendency has been a significant influence on the histories of occupational injury and illness, famine, poverty, addiction, harms resulting from ecological devastation, and related social ills in the century and a half since Marx and Engels.

social murder sometimes become contested in part through state institutional channels. These conflicts can, if intense enough, force the state into action in a variety of ways, including reorganizing parts of itself and mitigating specific forms of social murder. These reactive state actions simultaneously exert a shaping influence on social movements. Hence, while struggles over social murder tend to shape the state, at the same time the state tends to shape how social conflicts play out—generally in ways that make them more compatible with capitalism. The theory of social murder, then, helps explain the systematic generation of both widespread harm and social conflict in capitalist society, conflict-driven processes of change in the organization of the capitalist state over time, and, finally, how state action in response to social movements is itself a method of governing over, and thus shaping the character of, social movements.

1   Capitalism in General

All capitalist societies share some general qualities which make them identifiable as capitalist, including market dependency and the subordination of social relations to the imperatives of valorization. At the same time, capitalist social relations are subject to widespread variation in the specific ways in which they are organized or institutionalized. These differences help us distinguish different capitalist societies from each other and identify patterns in types of capitalism across time and space. All specific ways of institutionalizing capitalist social relations are, in Simon Clarke's words, 'institutional forms of capitalist class domination' (Clarke 1988, 84). The specific forms of institutionalized class domination at any time and place are shaped by general patterns present in all capitalist societies.

1.1   *Market Dependence and the Valorization Imperative*

Market dependence is especially key to capitalist societies. By market dependence I mean that an important proportion of what people want and need in order to live a good life can only be had by buying it. Since purchasing requires money, having money is a social requirement in capitalist societies. As the philosopher Tony Smith (2017, 121) has demonstrated, the requirement to have money in capitalist society limits human flourishing, because in capitalism to lack money is to lack a good life, and many people lack money. Market dependence afflicts both the capitalist class and the working class, and in important respects the state as well. Market dependence generates general patterns over time within capitalist societies. These patterns include competitive pressures on enterprises, the compulsion to profit maximization and to capital accumulation, and the extension of commodification into new arenas (Meiksins-Wood 1994, 1998; Clegg 2020).

In capitalist societies human needs are likely to be neglected for some persons because, as Simon Clarke (1994, 281) has put it, capitalism is a 'system of production in which the production of things is subordinated to the production, appropriation and accumulation of surplus value'. This means that capitalism 'detaches the production of things from the need for the product'. Human well-being is thus only ever at best a secondary priority. The relationship between wages and the working class's subsistence illustrates this point. Capitalists do not pay wages at a level necessary to sustain the working class, let alone at a level that promotes human flourishing. Instead they pay wages at whatever rate is required to keep employees showing up the next day. As Marx details in his discussion of so-called relative surplus populations: there are often large numbers of impoverished workers—the working poor or under-employed in contemporary parlance—as well as the unemployed, all of whom capitalists often seek to use against the employed (Marx [1867] 1990, 793). Absent collective action to raise wages, workers are generally left to subsist at whatever level currently facilitates their employers' profits, a level relatively indifferent to the creation of shortages, injuries, illness, and death. Overall, the subordination of society to surplus value production means that institutions in capitalist societies tend to exhibit inhumanity and indifference to members of those societies. This too generates patterns over time, as the imperative to accumulate intensifies the tendency for people to instrumentalize each other and generates new forms of organizing that instrumentalization.[3]

---

[3] In referring to instrumentalization, I mean not only the exploitation of workers by capitalists, but more broadly to people using other people as means to their own ends. Marx discusses working-class parents forcing their children into work in order to take their wages—behaviour which is exploitative in a common-sensical meaning of the term but not in Marx's technical sense of the term (Marx [1867] 1990, 326 n 7). Other forms of instrumentalization are too numerous to mention, as the tendency to treat other people as stepping-stones on the path to one's own goals is nearly everywhere in capitalist society.

In addition to market dependence, capitalism is characterized by subordination of society to the valorization imperative. In the second volume of *Capital* Marx depicts capital as a social process in motion, which he terms a circuit, and which he abbreviates as M–C...P...C'–M' (Marx [1885] 1992, 109). The capitalist buys commodities including labour power and means of production, sets that labour power to work producing new commodities, which are then sold for more money than the initial outlay. This circuit can never stop repeating, a condition Tony Smith calls 'the valorization imperative', which he summarizes as 'M must become M'!'. Each time one circuit concludes in a new sum of money, M', the capitalist must repeat the circuit again, treating that money as the initial outlay for that circuit (Smith, 2017, 108). If the circuit is not repeated, businesses close and workers lose their jobs. While capitalists certainly receive a larger share of social wealth than workers, they too are subject capitalism's drives, being in important ways controlled by the money they own. They cannot rest content but must constantly put their money in motion under the pressure of the valorization imperative.

Thus while capitalism is characterized by ongoing market dependency and class domination, these are not static conditions. Rather they are patterns of motion over time. As Marx puts it, 'the total process' of capital 'can only be grasped as a movement, and not as a static thing' (Marx [1885] 1992, 185). Marx terms that movement 'self-valorizing value' (Marx [1885] 1992, 185). All actors in capitalist society are subordinated to the compulsory repetition of capital's circuits. In capitalist society, capital accumulation is 'an end in itself. The ceaseless reproduction and expansion of capital is the driving force, the inner telos, of each individual capital circuit and the ultimate end of a capitalist social order as a whole' (Smith 2017, 116). Other priorities, such as human flourishing, are forced to be secondary to making M into M'.

1.2   The Capitalist State and the Concrete Institutionalization of Capitalist Social Relations

Market dependence and the valorization imperative are general qualities of capitalist social relations, qualities which only exist in the world as time- and place-specific forms of institutionalized class domination (Clarke 1988, 84). A society's capitalist character creates a set of problems and challenges, including social murder, which I elaborate on below; conflicts between classes; conflicts between members of the same class in the form of competition; and between members of society (of whatever class) and state personnel over how to deal with the above problems. These conflicts occur in time- and place-specific ways, influenced by and also generative of institutional variations within specific capitalist societies. At the same time, the variation in the particular institutional forms of capitalist social relations has limits because institutional variations must be kept compatible with capitalism's imperatives (Smith 2017, 190).

Marxists understandably emphasize class and class struggle but it is worth noting that intra-class struggle in the form of competitive conflicts among capitalists is significant in capitalism as well. As Clarke (1989, 6) puts it, 'capital-in-general only exists in the form of particular capitals, and the relationships between these particular capitals are essentially contradictory' because 'each individual capitalist seeks to realise his interests at the expense of other capitalists'. This competition among capitalists plays out across sectors of the economy as well as among capitalists in the same sector. Capitalists thus do not share a common interest that disciplines their behaviour. No capitalist takes the role of capital-in-general. That role must be played by the state.

The state governs over capitalists as the representative of a capitalism-specific form of general interest, in that it maintains the order which makes surplus value production possible. As Michael Heinrich (2012, 206) has put it, there are 'material conditions for the accumulation of capital' which 'cannot be established by individual capitals in a capitalist way, since doing so would not yield a sufficient profit'. Those general conditions can only be secured by the state. To secure those conditions, the state must at times impose real restraint upon individual capitalists. In Clarke's words, 'the general interest of capital appears to each individual capitalist as a barrier to the realisation of his individual capital' (Clarke 1989, 6). Hence it is no surprise that individual capitalists tend to oppose action by the state even when that action serves the reproduction of capitalist social relations.

Actually existing capitalist societies thus face problems that they generate for themselves, which are dealt with in historically specific ways through those societies' institutions. The pattern over time historically seems to be that institutions tend to see a decline in their capacity to answer the challenges posed by the capitalist character of society and that new problems are generated to which existing institutions are inadequate. That decline and inadequacy fosters both inter- and intra-class conflicts, which tend to generate new institutions, both via relatively sudden crises and via relatively slower processes as well (Holdren 2021, 249–50). Scholars have tended to use the different sets of institutions and patterns of institutional change that exist in capitalism to periodize capitalist societies in a variety of ways, and to identify different versions of capitalism that co-exist in a specific time period (Holdren 2021, 250). Generally speaking, the analysis of particular forms of capitalism, including capitalism's tendency towards social murder, must be conducted at a fairly granular level of analysis, less abstract that I have articulated thus far; yet this analysis is informed by more abstract theorizing. Marx and Engels' analyses of social murder, as discussed in more detail below, are exemplary of the relationship between different degrees of abstraction within inquiry into capitalism.

Capitalism thus has a general set of social patterns including market dependency, class domination, the imperative for capital to stay in motion, and a tendency to generate conflict among systemic actors including workers, capitalists, and the state. These conflicts tend to transform each of those systemic elements: the capitalist social totality is always in motion and metamorphosing, as are all of its constitutive moments. Capitalist social relations and the conflicts composing those social relations are always expressed in specific institutional forms. These forms tend to be relatively temporary, partly as a result of capitalism's tendency to generate conflicts. This general picture can help us see the importance of Engels' and Marx's understanding of social murder, and likewise the theory of social murder enriches this general picture of capitalist social relations.

It is important to also stress that institutions are not only externally related to social problems, such that a problem arises and then is solved by an institution. Institutions are expressions of capitalism's tendencies, tendencies that exist in historically specific institutional forms. These tendencies generate change in a society's institutions while at the same time the specific institutions that exist shape the specific manner in which capitalism's tendencies manifest, and shape struggles over those tendencies as well. I now turn to Engels and Marx's analyses of social murder, which will concretize this point.

2   Engels and Marx on Social Murder and Its Transformation

Engels and Marx emphasized that the particular ways in which a capitalist society kills are historically specific, mediated by the concrete manner in which capitalist social relations are institutionalized in a given time and place. They provided a broad account of some general areas of social life where capitalism would inflict social murder, including areas such as dangers in waged workplaces and unsafe means of subsistence such as tainted foods. This identification of general areas of danger can help inform investigation of specific instances of social murder. In addition, they took the concrete phenomena they examined in mid-nineteenth century England as representative of patterns in capitalist social relations, treating specific forms of social murder as exemplary of capitalism's general tendency to systematically generate killing. From this perspective, reorganizing capitalism to mitigate specific forms of social murder is a humanitarian good but one that ultimately does as much to redistribute as to end social murder, for all versions of capitalism will in some fashion commit social murder—hence Marx and Engels' enduring commitment to socialist revolution.

2.1   Engels on Social Murder

Engels drew heavily on government commission hearings and factory inspectors' reports to examine the particulars of social murder in the England of his day. He identified harms that arose both in waged workplaces and in working-class life off the clock. In workplaces, he argued, workers faced serious dangers from accidents, environmental hazards, and occupational illnesses (Engels [1845] 2009, 172–74). Outside of workplaces, Engels emphasized that workers were exposed to harms related to substandard housing and food. His discussion of housing included what we would today call issues of sanitation, public health, and pollution, such as vermin, garbage, and ash and smoke from fires burnt for cooking and heating (Engels [1845] 2009, 39–40). He had said that 'many have died of starvation' and suffered malnutrition and illness due to 'long continued want of proper nourishment' (Engels [1845] 2009, 38). These conditions left workers vulnerable to disease, while their misery and lack of free time fostered addiction (Engels [1845] 2009, 109–110, 113).

For Engels, unhealthy food and housing resulted directly from capitalism's prioritizing profit over meeting human needs. The working class 'is so ill-provided with the most necessary means of subsistence' that working-class people 'cannot be healthy and can reach no advanced age' (Engels [1845] 2009, 107). This was because the 'production and distribution of the means of subsistence' in capitalism 'is carried on not directly for the sake of supplying needs, but for profit' (Engels [1845] 2009, 93–94.) As a result, the unemployed and low waged workers lacked access to sufficient amounts of means of subsistence, and what they could access was often substandard and unhealthy.

For Engels, then, capitalism was a society which 'deprives thousands of the necessaries of life, places them under conditions in which they cannot live—forces them, through the strong arm of the law, to remain in such conditions until that death ensures which is the inevitable consequence' (Engels [1845] 2009, 106). The capitalist regarded the worker 'simply as a piece of capital for the use of which the manufacturer pays', so employers' treatment of workers was no surprise: workers were instrumentalized, made use of to create profits, and discarded when not profitably usable (Engels [1845] 2009, 33). Because 'the worker is less than a human being' to the capitalist class, 'brutal and brutalizing treatment' was the inevitable result (Engels [1845] 2009, 136, 140).

2.2   Marx on Social Murder's Specificity to Approaches to Accumulation

Marx's grasp of social murder can perhaps be summarized in his remark that 'capitalist production is in general thoroughly wasteful of human material' (Marx [1865] 2015, 155). Capitalism reduces the working class to objects to be used or discarded (or used up and then discarded), and both processes greatly harm working-class people. Marx made related inquiries into capitalism's wasting of working-class lives in the tenth and fifteenth chapters of the first volume of *Capital*. In these chapters Marx went over similar ground multiple times in historical analyses that gradually and mutually enrich each other, making them difficult to summarize. I stress, with Søren Mau (2023, 14), that the 'empirical and historical parts of Capital and related manuscripts are not simply illustrations of concepts. Not only do they often contain substantial historical and empirical analyses in their own right', they also contribute to Marx's process of developing concepts for understanding capitalist society. In these chapters,

Marx repeatedly cited Engels' book as a work he saw himself as building on. He stressed that Engels had written a key work for understanding the capitalist mode of production, praising 'how well Engels understood the spirit of the capitalist mode of production', adding that 'the official reports of the Children's Employment Commission, published 18 to 20 years later (1863–7)' showed that little had changed in the conditions Engels examined (Marx [1867] 1990, 349 n 15). Given Marx's praise for Engels' book and how he drew on the book in chapters ten and fifteen, it makes sense to say as well that Engels' historical analysis too contributed, via his empirical analysis of social murder, to the conceptual development of the critique of political economy.

Like Engels, Marx emphasized working-class food and working conditions as sources of danger. He detailed how working-class food was often unhealthy, with bread having been found to contain alum, sand, cobwebs, and dead cockroaches. Marx noted that bakery employees were particularly short-lived, usually dying by age 42—yet it was the consumer side of conditions in the baking industry that created more public scandal (Marx [1867] 1990, 361). In a premonition of what happened in the United States about forty years later with the publication of Upton Sinclair's muckraking novel *The Jungle*, Marx argued that attention to adulteration of food products occluded attention to the working conditions to which food workers were subjected (Sinclair 1906). The public, Marx wrote, was moved 'not in its heart' over workers' lives but 'in its stomach' over their own worries about tainted food (Marx [1867] 1990, 359). Marx's anticipation of Sinclair supports Marx and Engels' claims that the England of their day offered a premonition of the terrible future in store for so many around the world and speaks to how social murder is a pattern in capitalist society.

Occupational dangers loomed particularly large in Marx's account. Among Marx's many examples is that of Mary Anne Walkley, killed by exhaustion. Walkley, a twenty-year-old dressmaker, typically worked sixteen and a half hour days with no breaks. After working twenty-six and a half hours straight, Walkley took ill, dying two days later from overwork (Marx [1867] 1990, 364–65). Marx examined railway accidents as another source of killing for workers off the clock. Increasing hours of work for railway workers lead to exhaustion and thus train accidents, harming employees, passengers, and people nearby (Marx [1867] 1990, 363).

Like Engels, Marx took his examples not as exceptional but as instances that illustrated systemic patterns. Walkley, for example, illustrated what Marx saw as a tendency for English capitalism to kill through inflicting overwork, because capitalists excessively expanded the time they required employees to spend in employment, thus not allowing enough of the time necessary for workers to rest and recover (to say nothing of having an actually fulfilling human life). Like Engels, Marx noted other harms that overly long work hours had on workers' lives outside their workplaces, including social dislocation and the reduction of working-class families to repositories of labour power for capitalist use. On Marx's account, work-time was so long that it was shortening workers' life-spans, eroding their ability to work in the future, and making it harder for working-class families to produce future workers. Marx also saw a tendency at work for capitalism to render many people un- or under-employed and thus subject to deprivation because unable to afford the necessities of life.

Marx depicted a transformation of the organization of social murder, resulting from a shift in mid-nineteenth century capitalism from accumulation centring heavily on what he called absolute surplus value to accumulation centring heavily on what he called relative surplus value. He argued that workers generally produce an amount of goods equivalent to the employer's cost in wages. He referred to the labour time required to produce that equivalent as necessary working time and referred to production above that amount as surplus labour time. Capitalists pursue absolute surplus value by extending the total duration worked in order to increase surplus labour time. In addition, capitalists pursue relative surplus value by reducing the amount of labour time necessary to produce the equivalent to wages, with all work-time afterward being surplus.

Capitalists earlier in the nineteenth century, the period Engels wrote about, had primarily emphasized extending the workday, i.e. absolute surplus value, and so Engels' treatment of social murder followed suit. In the chapter on the working day in *Capital*'s first volume, Marx similarly focused on absolute surplus value and emphasized the kinds of harms it generated, above all harms due to overwork. As he detailed in the chapter on machinery, however, by the mid-nineteenth century English capitalism had begun to shift towards greater emphasis on relative surplus value. For Marx this transformation was the result of the labour movement's struggles to mitigate the harms of overwork by limiting work hours, struggles Marx referred to as 'a civil war lasting half a century' (Marx [1867] 1990, 409). Those conflicts eventually led to the creation of legislation limiting work hours. Marx stressed that these laws were 'the result of a long class struggle' rather than state beneficence or an independent employer response to social murder (Marx [1867] 1990, 395).

At first, individual capitalists began to look for ways to get around these laws, such as requiring workers to put in a total of ten daily hours spread out over a period of fifteen hours, costing the worker more time without breaking the law (Marx [1867] 1990, 403). Eventually, however, as a result of further struggle, these laws became adequately enforced such that work hours really were limited, with some resulting degree of improvements in workers' well-being (Marx [1867] 1990, 408–409). These limits on working time are an example of the dynamic I discussed above, where the state acts to discipline individual capitalists in service of a specifically capitalist form of the general interest, a role social struggle often forces the state to play.

Once limitations on work hours became effective, capitalists sought new ways to accrue greater profits under the new limits on their pursuit of absolute surplus value, and so turned to greater pursuit of relative surplus value. Marx especially emphasized employers' introduction of new machinery as a mechanism for this pursuit. Growing industry and a new emphasis on relative surplus value brought about new forms of social murder, different from death by overwork in their specifics manner of killing, but no less deadly, as Marx showed in Chapter fifteen of the first volume of *Capital* and in parts of the manuscripts later published as the third volume.

Growing use of machinery led to more and cheaper products being sold, causing prices to fall. Because machinery was unevenly distributed, enterprises with older, less machine-intensive production techniques were put out of business. Marx argued that there had been a 'fearful increase in death from starvation' since people producing by hand had become forced to compete with machine-based production, and so could no longer earn enough to live (Marx [1867] 1990, 601, 559). Machinery also generated unemployment, as machines replaced some employed workers, leaving the unemployed subject to the deprivations entailed by poverty.

Machine-based relative surplus value production brought new dangers into the labour process as well. Rather than working at speeds they controlled, workers had to keep up with the speed at which employers ran machinery, a rapid pace set by the demands of profits. As Marx put it, this meant the 'subordination of the worker to the uniform motion of the instruments of labour' (Marx [1867] 1990, 549). Work's physical intensity increased, becoming exhausting and unhealthy in new ways. Furthermore, capitalists increasingly forced 'workers to huddle together in confined spaces—which amounts to savings on buildings' (Marx [1865] 2015, 154–55.) Within crowded, polluted, poorly ventilated workplaces, workers were subject to extremes of temperature and exposed to powerful mechanical forces and chemical processes that could break their bodies. Thus, with the shift to relative surplus value, waged workplaces became sites of greater hazard.

While to some degree it was possible to take steps to mitigate workers' exposure to those hazards, such as improving ventilation and covering dangerous parts of machines, capitalists faced competitive pressures not to provide such measures. As Marx put it, 'capitalist production is...most economical of realised labour, labour realized in commodities' because capitalists must pay for machinery and raw material (Marx [1865], 2015, 157). At the same time, capitalism 'is a greater spendthrift than any other mode of production, of men, of living labour, a spendthrift not only of flesh and blood, but of brains and nerves' (Marx [1865] 2015, 157). This gave capitalism a repeated 'tendency to sacrifice human lives', a tendency towards the 'squandering of the worker's life and health', unless there were counteracting measures put in place (Marx [1865] 2015, 173).

The rise of relative surplus value and machine-based production meant that new populations became exposed to danger as well. Machinery made work require less physical strength, making child labour more feasible (Marx [1867] 1990, 517). An eight-year-old child might not be able to lift or carry what an adult could, but that child could tend machinery. The new employability of children combined with financial constraints on working-class families in effect pushed working-class children into employment, leading to what Marx called their 'physical deterioration' and 'enormous mortality' (Marx [1867] 1990, 520–21). The growth of child labour expanded the supply of labour power on the labour market as well, so that capitalists could lower wages and better resist workers' demands for wage stabilization or wage increases. This led to even further working-class poverty and disruption of workers' families, communities, and social support systems, fostering more of the harms Engels had written about.

The transformation in capitalism that resulted from hours limitations brought about mitigation of specific forms of social murder, those resulting from the pursuit of absolute surplus value; simultaneously, the new ways of institutionalizing capitalist social relations that resulted from this transformation generated new forms of social murder, resulting specifically from the pursuit of relative surplus value. While hours limits did accomplish some good, workers continued to breathe polluted air and starve due to poverty, while facing new dangers such as being forced into waged work at a younger age and of being pulled into the gears of machinery. Thus social murder had been as much redistributed as it had been mitigated.

2.3   Engels and Marx on the Systemic Necessity of Social Murder

Engels and Marx believed that capitalism had a systemic logic to it, so that imperatives generated by capitalist social relations played out in similar ways in different capitalist societies. This meant that investigating the concrete versions of capitalism existing before them in England, including the tendency to commit social murder, could help make clear patterns that would occur in other capitalist societies. In Engels' view, in the England of his day there appeared 'proletarian conditions in their classical form, in their perfection' (Engels [1845] 2009, 12–13, 15). He argued that socialists in other countries should thus expect to see social murder occur in generally similar forms as those in which it occurred in England. Marx similarly argued that England was 'the classic representative of capitalist production' (Marx [1867] 1990, 349 n 15). He stressed that 'nothing characterizes the spirit of capital better than the history' of work and its regulation in England from 1833 to 1864 (Marx [1867] 1990, 390).

The reason why all capitalist societies would commit social murder like capitalism did in England, Marx and Engels argued, was that social murder was systematically generated by capitalist social relations. Wherever the same social 'root causes' existed—market dependency and the subordination of society to the valorization imperative—'in the long run [they] must engender the same results' (Engels [1845] 2009, 13). This was not something capitalists chose, but rather something that was compelled: 'the immanent laws of capitalist production confront the individual capitalist as a coercive force external to him' (Marx [1867] 1990, 381). As Marx put it elsewhere, individual capitalists were just character-masks: 'the personifications of economic categories, the bearers of particular class-relations and interests' (Marx [1867] 1990, 92). Social murder, then, is not the result of individual capitalists' moral character, but rather the result of systemic pressures. One important implication of this point is that moral suasion of capitalists is of very limited political use. 'Forced to act in such ways, managers look for rationales and slowly re-make their moral character to fit. Capitalism produces both mass death and people in positions of institutional authority who are able to live with mass death' (Holdren 2022).

Marx argued that capitalism was possessed of a 'boundless' 'vampire thirst for the blood of living labour', a 'werewolf-like hunger for surplus labour' (Marx [1867] 1990, 345, 353)—metaphors for what he saw as a systemic 'drive towards a limitless draining away of labour power' (Marx [1867] 1990, 348). Working-class people were treated as a 'mass of cheap human material' for satisfying capitalism's drives (Marx [1867] 1990, 600). The result was 'sheer brutality' and 'robbery of every normal condition requisite for working and living' (Marx [1867] 1990, 599). In general, Marx wrote, capitalism 'only develops the techniques and the degree of combination of the social process of production by simultaneously undermining' working-class health (Marx [1867] 1990, 638). For Marx and Engels, the 'ceaseless reproduction and expansion of capital'— the unfolding of the imperative that value continue to self-valorize—are also ceaselessly murderous. The 'accumulation of misery' for the working class is 'a necessary condition, corresponding to the accumulation of wealth' for the capitalist class (Marx [1867] 1990, 799).

Marx called the accumulation of wealth and misery two poles of capitalist production (Marx [1867] 1990, 799). Different historically specific forms of institutionalized class domination generate historically specific forms of killing. Capital's circuits of money in motion, on its way to becoming more money, are simultaneously circuits of ongoing social murder: the repetition of the circuit M–C...P...C'–M' is not an external cause of working-class death but rather should be understood as inherently an ongoing process of killing.

2.4   Patterns in Where and How Social Murder Occurs

Marx and Engels not only argued that capitalism would kill, they presented in broad strokes some ways to investigate the social production and distribution of that killing, by analysing social murder as occurring throughout the circuit from M to M'. Specifically: (1) harms within the capitalist consumption of labour power; (2) workers enduring neglect and deprivation due to the need to have money to access the means of subsistence, which are generally available only as commodities; (3) harms within the means of subsistence introduced as a result of their having been produced in a capitalist manner, i.e. for profit rather than need; and (4) the presence of capitalist production's by-products within the working class's living environment.[4]

By capitalist consumption of labour power I mean hours and conditions in employment, as with Marx and Engels' discussions of occupational accidents and illnesses. As I discussed above, Marx especially emphasized how these forms of social murder varied with the particulars of how class domination was institutionalized in relation to different approaches to accumulation. Examples of neglect and deprivation due to commodification being the form of regulating access to means of subsistence include starvation (Marx [1867] 1990, 601) due to unemployment, rising food prices, and falling wages, as well as the harms resulting from substandard housing provided by for-profit housing markets, harms including periodic epidemics of cholera and other diseases due to lack of sufficient sanitation (Engels [1845] 2009, 71–77). There are threats of deprivation built in to market dependency per se, in that a market-dependent society is one where access to subsistence is contingent on possessing money, and possessing money is not guaranteed.

In attrition to deprivation, a related problem arises from the commodification of means of subsistence—specifically harmful qualities of the means of subsistence that result from their having been produced in a capitalist manner. The adulteration of bread as Marx described is a paradigmatic example. This kind of harm arises because the point of commodified means of subsistence is not to facilitate working-class well-being but rather the profits of these commodities' sellers, like any other commodity. That often leads to pressures to reduce the quality of the goods, which can harm those goods' consumers.

By the presence of capitalist production's by-products I mean phenomena such as pollution, the ways in which transportation of goods crosses through spaces where working-class people live, and the effects of working conditions on workers' lives outside the workplace. Marx's

---

[4] The identification of these general areas of death-dealing also helps distinguish social murder from other tendencies for capitalism to kill, such as in the systematic generation of imperialist warfare, colonialism, and white supremacist violence. In my view these forms of violence are systematically generated as well, but they are differently organized. There are, so to speak, multiple species of systemic death-dealing in capitalism, with social murder being one such species with its own distinct logic rooted in what Marx called 'the silent compulsion of economic relations' (Marx [1867] 1990, 899); see also Mau (2023).

discussion of railroad accidents and his and Engels' discussions of addiction fall under this heading. The COVID-19 pandemic and the effects of capitalism-generated climate catastrophe that are currently playing out are contemporary and especially lethal forms of capitalist production's by-products as well.

In sum, capitalism kills working-class people in ways which are unpredictable in their particulars, in that we might not always know in the short term who will die and how, but which are generally predictable, in the sense of being recurrent and unsurprising as general social patterns. All versions of capitalism institutionalize the tendency to social murder in a manner particular to that society's historically specific forms of institutionalizing class domination. The particulars vary but every form of capitalism kills. That the particulars vary can sometimes obscure the general tendency and thus protect the social death machine.

3   Social Murder and the State

In his account of social murder in the 1840s, Engels depicts the state as a relatively static presence in society, carrying out roles like organizing urban and productive space in ways that sweep social murder under the rug for the better off, and that quietly document social murder via practices like factory inspection. In Marx's account of the two decades after the publication of Engels' book, the state appears as far more dynamic. Marx depicted the state as capable—especially when pushed by social struggle—of intervening in social relations to actively discipline capitalists, as in the example of the Factory Acts. At the same time, the state is itself disciplined by capitalist social relations, since social crises create political consequences. The pressure of capitalist social relations on the state in turn presses the state to discipline capitalists to those social relations, though state action is often not so much proactive as reactive to crises and workers' collective action. The difference between Engels' and Marx's accounts is historical: Marx wrote about processes that were not as pronounced in the 1840s, and he wrote after serious social conflicts had compelled the state into action.

3.1   The Capitalist State

The shift from accumulation centred on absolute surplus value to accumulation centred on relative surplus value resulted in large part from the

Factory Acts, passed to limit killing due to excessive work hours. State intervention to mitigate specific forms of social murder helped cause the reorganization of forms of institutionalized class domination. These reorganizations redistributed social murder rather than ending capitalism's general tendency to kill. Social murder, then, is part of a pattern of institutional dynamism in capitalist society. Capitalism kills, and people respond with collective action which sometimes forces the state to help facilitate institutional reorganization. We can see this general pattern in the history of conflict and legislation over occupational safety and health (Holdren 2020) and housing (Clarke 1991, 31–34).

It is important not to conceptualize the state as outside of class or capitalist social relations. Rather the state is a moment of the totality of these social relations, all of which consist in processes of struggle (see Hunter, this volume; Clarke 1991; Smith 2017). The state is both constituted by and constitutive of capitalist social relations. Conflicts in capitalism always become struggles over the state, at least if they reach a high enough pitch or intensity. As Simon Clarke (1988, 84) puts it, under any given set of 'existing institutional forms of capitalist class domination' there develop struggles which occur 'in and against' those forms. The conflicts that Marx analysed which led to the Factory Acts, and eventually to the shift to greater emphasis on relative surplus value, are important cases in point. These struggles arose in response to specific expressions of capitalism's built-in tendency to kill, and resulted in a reorganization of the institutionalization of that tendency.

Conflict not only occurs within and shaped by institutions, 'but is at the same time a struggle to reproduce or transform them' (Clarke 1988, 84). These struggles 'necessarily take on a political form and so impose themselves on the state. The state does not stand above these struggles' because 'the state is an aspect of the institutional forms of capitalist class relations, and so is itself the object of struggle' (Clarke 1988, 84). That means 'struggle over the forms of capitalist domination necessarily becomes a struggle over the form of the state' (Clarke 1988, 85). While struggles in capitalism shape the state, the state too shapes how struggles occur, and often far sooner and at a much lower intensity of conflict than when struggles have reshaped the state. As Werner Bonefeld has put it, the capitalist state 'imposes law on the basis of order; it is the concentrated force of social order' (2014, 184). Within capitalist society, social order is synonymous with capitalist social relations. The state is 'the political form of the capitalist social relations' (Bonefeld 2014,

165). Hence the capitalist state compels people to seek to resolve social conflicts in a manner compatible with capitalism. This resolution often includes some measure of discipline being imposed on both workers and capitalists (Clarke 1989, 7). Again, the struggles over social murder and the resulting mitigating legislation that Marx examined are cases in point. The Factory Acts limited specific kinds of social murder, pushed capitalists in England to become more productive, and the newly reorganized capitalist social relations killed in new ways.

Fundamentally, the state serves to 'confine social reproduction within the alienated forms of the wage relation and the monetary relation, by enforcing the laws of capitalist property and contract, [and] by regulating the reproduction of the working class through the system of social administration' (Clarke 1988, 85). While that confinement is contested and those contestations shape the state itself, this means that the state tends to shape the forms and practices of struggle. The confinement of struggle within the forms of capitalist social relations in part occurs through the ways in which conflicts and the state relate to one another. While the state is shot through with struggle, it does not necessarily appear as such, nor do struggles within, against, and over the state necessarily appear as class struggles. Acting within state institutional channels tends to encourage social struggles to express themselves in ways that do not disrupt the operation of the valorization imperative, let alone threaten to end capitalism. We can see these patterns in Marx's sources for his analysis, the reports of factory inspectors and testimony before parliamentary commissions.

Struggles that break out in society may be militantly opposed to specific forms of institutionalized class domination, but that is not the same as anticapitalism (Holdren 2021). State influence on social conflicts occurs in part due to the ways the state is predicated on and reproduces what Tony Smith calls the 'bifurcation of the political'. As Smith puts it, 'the political dimension of social life has a far greater scope than has been recognised' but 'the structures and practices of capitalist market societies' including the capitalist state 'systematically generate an impoverished form of "the political"' (2017, 187). As Jack Copley (2021, 16–17) has analysed, state personnel themselves face pressures to render the state's disciplinary actions as specifically depoliticized. Social movements seeking to get the state to regulate areas of social life tend to face corresponding pressures to make their actions and demands legible within—or, simply to inhabit—the impoverished forms of politics that Smith and Copley analyse. These pressures to enact an impoverished form of politics are part of how the state serves 'to confine the aspirations of the working class within the limits of capital' (Clarke 1988, 86). This is what occurred in what Marx called the 'civil war' that led to the Factory Acts (Marx [1867] 1990, 409). Those conflicts were terribly important on humanitarian grounds and Marx clearly wished them success, but they conceptually presumed and practically did not challenge the bifurcation of the political and the confinement of society within capitalism's alienated forms.

3.2   Stability Through Instability; Reproduction by Transformation

While social murder does not always become a matter of political conflict, it often does so, when politicized by mass movements. This means that any particular form of capitalism may eventually become friction-laden or conflict-prone, and thus unstable. This is not a cause for optimism on the part of anticapitalists, because the instability of any specific set of forms of institutionalized class domination is not at all the same thing as instability of class domination as such. If anything, class domination seems to persist through—capitalism's reproduction over time is a process of—the ongoing breakdown of one set of forms of institutionalized class domination and the rise of another set of such forms, with all such forms facilitating the circuit from M to M'. That these historical processes involve significant conflict is not evidence that these processes are fragile. Indeed, conflict over specific ways to institutionalize class domination and specific forms of social murder tends to be a source of dynamism, generating revisions to existing forms of institutionalized class domination or the creation of new forms, without challenging class domination or capitalism as such.

Left to their own devices, conflicts over social murder are generally likely to be either compatible with the existing set of forms of institutionalized class domination or to become struggles for a reorganization of the current forms of institutionalized class domination. This is in part due to the effects of the state on social movements. When struggles against specific forms of social murder are successful, the result will be the reorganization or redistribution of capitalism's tendency to social murder rather than an end to that tendency.

The capitalist state is shaped by struggles over the social murder that capitalism systematically generates. Simultaneously, the state shapes those struggles, pressing them to remain compatible with capitalism, however intensely they might contest specific forms of institutionalized class domination. Capitalism kills. The state is a force for capitalism's reproduction. The capitalist state is thus a force for the organization, reorganization, and persistence of social murder. When it mitigates one specific manner of killing, it does not do so in order to end social murder per se but rather to keep society capitalist and thus murderous.

4   Conclusion: Capitalism is Always Death-Dealing

Capitalism should be understood as having a tendency to generate widespread killing. Whatever particulars may change in capitalism, the general dealing of death will continue until capitalism ends. The tendency to generate killing will always be expressed in concrete ways shaped by the specific forms of institutionalized class domination that characterize an actually existing capitalist society. Because the general pattern always takes specific forms, it can be hard to perceive the general tendency. In Simon Clarke's (2001, 67) words, 'it is not immediately apparent to workers who or what is their ultimate enemy and how they can most effectively channel their opposition to capital'. Making these realities apparent and effectively channelling opposition to capital is a difficult set of tasks, tasks that require theorizing (whether or not such theorizing is specifically academic is another matter). These tasks include 'supplement[ing] the intellectual resources of the labour movement' (Clarke 2001, 68). Engels and Marx wrote about social murder as one part of their multifaceted and life-long efforts to provide some of this intellectual supplementation to the labour and socialists movements of their day. Their goal was to help these movements to expand their understanding 'and [their] horizons, to analyse the movements of capital, to contribute to the critique of the modern forms of vulgar economy, [and] to find and learn from new ways of organising and new forms of struggle' against specific forms of institutionalized class domination and against capitalism as such (Clarke 2001, 68).

As long as it exists, capitalism will continue to kill. In order to understand that killing, and, ultimately, to end it, social movements need specifically Marxist critical theory. The theory of social murder helps us to understand that social murder is not accidental and that expressions of capitalism's lethality are not isolated occurrences, but rooted in capitalism's fundamental architecture. Furthermore, the capitalist state tends to redistribute rather than to end mass killing. In doing so, the state tends to encourage opposition to social murder to become fragmented and to deal only with immediate forms of social murder, leaving its root causes unaddressed and dissipating movements' anger and organization. Marxists and socialists today should draw on Marx and Engels' concepts intellectually and follow in their footsteps politically, seeking to help the movements of our day with these same kinds of tasks. Until these tasks are accomplished through struggle, social murder will continue—many more will die—because capitalism is fundamentally a death machine.

Acknowledgements I thank Kirstin Munro for first encouraging me to write what would eventually become this chapter and Tony Smith for telling me this was a subject worth pursuing at a time I wasn't sure. I also thank Matt Dimick for helpful comments on a draft. I received similarly helpful comments from several other authors in this volume in a workshop setting where the ideas were hard to individualize—the best sorts of intellectual spaces!—so I thank all the authors collectively.

References

Adler-Bolton, Beatrice, and Artie Vierkant. 2022. *Health Communism: A Surplus Manifesto*. London: Verso.

Bonefeld, Werner. 2014. *Critical Theory and the Critique of Political Economy: On Subversion and Negative Reason*. London: Bloomsbury.

Clarke, Simon. 1988. 'Overaccumulation, Class Struggle and the Regulation Approach.' *Capital & Class* 12 (3): 59–92. https://doi.org/10.1177/030981688803600104.

———. 1989. 'Configurations of Dissent: Fractions of Capital, Class Struggle and the Decline of Britain.' http://homepages.warwick.ac.uk/~syrbe/Publications.html. Accessed May 25, 2022.

———. 1991. 'The State Debate.' In *The State Debate*, edited by Simon Clarke, 1–69. London: Macmillan.

———. 1993. *Marx's Theory of Crisis*. London: Macmillan.

———. 2001. 'Class Struggle and the Working Class: The Problem of Commodity Fetishism.' In *The Labour Debate: An Investigation Into the Theory and Reality of Capitalist Work*, edited by Ana Dinerstein and Mike Neary, 41–60. Aldershot: Ashgate.

Clegg, John. 2020. 'The Theory of Capitalist Slavery.' *Journal of Historical Sociology* 33 (1): 74–98. https://doi.org/10.1111/johs.12259.

Copley, Jack. 2021. *Governing Financialization: The Tangled Politics of Financial Liberalisation in Britain*. Oxford: Oxford University Press.

Engels, Friedrich. [1845] 2009. *The Condition of the Working Class in England.* Oxford: Oxford University Press.

Govender, Piara, Medvedyuk, Stella, and Dennis Raphael. 2022. 'Mainstream News Media's Engagement with Friedrich Engels's Concept of Social Murder.' *TripleC: Communication, Capitalism, & Critique* 20 (1): 62–81. https://doi.org/10.31269/triplec.v20i1.1323.

Heinrich, Michael. 2012. *An Introduction to the Three Volumes of Karl Marx's Capital.* Translated by Alexander Locascio. New York: Monthly Review Press.

Holdren, Nate. 2020. *Injury Impoverished: Workplace Accidents, Capitalism, and Law in The Progressive Era.* Cambridge: Cambridge University Press.

———. 2021. 'The Reproduction of Moral Economies in Capitalism: Reading Thompson Structurally.' In *Research Handbook on Law and Marxism*, edited by Paul O'Connell and Umut Özsu, 242260. Cheltenham: Edward Elgar. https://doi.org/10.4337/9781788119863.00020.

———. 2022. 'Depoliticizing Social Murder in the COVID-19 Pandemic,' March 21, 2022. At *Bill of Health*, https://blog.petrieflom.law.harvard.edu/2022/03/21/depoliticizing-social-murder-covid-pandemic/ Accessed May 25, 2022.

Marx, Karl. [1867] 1990. *Capital: A Critique of Political Economy.* Translated by Ben Fowkes. Volume I. London: Penguin Books.

———. [1885] 1992. *Capital: A Critique of Political Economy.* Translated by David Fernbach. Volume II. London: Penguin.

———. 2015. *Marx's Economic Manuscript of 1864–1865*, edited by Fred Moseley. Leiden: Brill.

Mau, Søren. 2023. *Mute Compulsion: A Marxist Theory of the Economic Power of Capital* London: Verso.

Medvedyuk, Stella, Piara Govender, and Dennis Raphael. 2021. 'The reemergence of Engels' Concept of Social Murder in Response to Growing Social and Health Inequalities'. *Social Science & Medicine* 289 (November). Science Direct. https://doi.org/10.1016/j.socscimed.2021.114377.

Meiksins-Wood, Ellen. 1994. 'From Opportunity to Imperative: The History of the Market'. *Monthly Review* 46(3): 14–40.

———. 'The Agrarian Origins of Capitalism'. *Monthly Review* 50(3): 14–31.

Sinclair, Upton. 1906. *The Jungle.* New York: Doubleday.

Smith, Tony. 2017. *Beyond Liberal Egalitarianism: Marx and Normative Social Theory in the Twenty-First Century.* Leiden: Brill

Beyond Abstractionism: Notes on Conjunctural State Theory

Michael A. McCarthy

1 CONTINGENCY AND CONSTRAINTS

André Gorz wrote of one of his key concepts, 'non-reformist reforms', that they principally concern the 'modification of the relations of power' (Gorz 1968, 8). Gorz noted that to 'fight for alternative solutions and for structural reforms (that is to say, for intermediate objectives) is not to fight for improvements in the capitalist system; it is rather to break it up, to restrict it, to create counter-powers which, instead of creating a new equilibrium, undermine its very foundations' (1968, 181). But he only specified how that may happen at a very abstract and conceptual level, concluding that non-reformist reforms develop the *autonomous* power of workers and their organizations instead of power *subordinate* to corporate organizations and political actors.

Gorz's non-reformist reforms seek an alternative path to two stylized views of emancipatory politics. On the one hand, the popular view of the state treats it as a neutral institution. Were it occupied and captured

M. A. McCarthy (✉)
Department of Social and Cultural Sciences, Marquette University, Milwaukee, WI, USA
e-mail: Michael.mccarthy@marquette.edu

© The Author(s), under exclusive license to Springer Nature Switzerland AG 2023
R. Hunter et al. (eds.), *Marxism and the Capitalist State*,
Political Philosophy and Public Purpose,
https://doi.org/10.1007/978-3-031-36167-8_10

by politicians with the right ideas, the progressive view suggests, our society could be made more just. Yet this has led to cycles of progressive governance that have failed to overcome the private power of capitalists which have forced governments into market-oriented reversals. On the other hand, a revolutionary Leninist conception of the state as an instrument of class rule argues that it must be 'smashed' to overcome the private power of capitalists and capitalism. Yet such a view has failed to find widespread support of the working classes in the advanced capitalist countries. In the less developed countries where it has mobilized revolutionary struggles of vanguard groups, top-down, authoritarian forms of political power have often been the long-run result. The progressive path of emancipatory change rests on a theory that presumes contingency in the dynamics of the state, while the revolutionary path rests on an alternative view of pure functional necessity in the state's internal dynamics. In the former, institutional and structural constraints are largely elided. In the latter, those constraints overdetermine the behaviour of the role of state institutions and the actions of the people that occupy its positions. In other words, contingency suggests the absence of significant structural constraints that impose limits on what can be done by state institutions and political actors; whereas functional necessity suggests that political institutions and actors are overwhelmed by the structural need to govern *for* capitalism.

State, Power, Socialism by the Greek sociologist and political theorist Nicos Poulantzas offers us a useful entry point for developing a theory of political strategy that carves a middle—and I suggest Gorzian—path between contingency and functional necessity.[1] Indeed, this is precisely

---

[1] The book is more a gesture towards certain insights than a comprehensive and internally coherent theory. Stuart Hall commented that, 'The book opens up a series of Pandora's boxes. Often, there is a too-swift attempt to secure their lids again, before their untameable genies escape. This produces a real theoretical unevenness in the book. Yet this unevenness also constitutes, by its reverse side, the stimulus of the book, its generative openness...He leaves us with a book which is, in many ways, clearly coming apart at the seams; where no single consistent theoretical framework is wide enough to embrace its internal diversity. It is *strikingly unfinished*...This is Poulantzas adventuring' (1980, 68–69). And as Bob Jessop noted, *State, Power, Socialism* is 'a provisional and transitional work' (1985, 115). In other words, it is a text beset by contradictions and inconsistencies. But even if the adventurer falls into the occasional pit trap, *State, Power, Socialism* does offer up an exploratory advance into the theoretical space between contingency and necessity in the institutions of liberal, capitalist democracy.

what Poulantzas himself takes as his own theoretical project.[2] Between his first major work on the state, *Political Power and Social Classes* (1973), and his final one, *State, Power, Socialism*, Poulantzas shifted from a regional view of the state largely inspired by Gramsci and Althusser to a relational view, in part through a dialogue with and critique of Foucault. Among many things, this shift moved Poulantzas' analysis away from an abstract one that treated the state as playing a functional role within capitalist reproduction towards a more differentiated one, which treated the state as a contradictory terrain and an expression of social struggles and conflicts. Nevertheless, this chapter argues that while Poulantzas did make important inroads, *State, Power, Socialism* fails to escape from his earlier abstract and functionalist account of the state. Through a critical engagement with the limitations of his final book, it offers some ideas for building on its advances. In particular, this chapter lays out some of the key ways that state institutions vary with respect to the distribution of social power, providing a brief sketch of a theory of emancipatory politics, which I term 'democratic ruptures'. Though Poulantzas directly considers the place of the rupture for his political theory, pointing to the intensity of class struggle, the internal divisiveness of state institutions, and the disunity of the 'power bloc', he does not provide the conceptual tools necessary to elaborate how one occurs at the level of state structures and with respect to a redistribution of power. Developing them not only extends Poulantzas' conjunctural analysis beyond the abstract impasse it finds itself in; it also provides us with a more concrete and conjunctural basis for understanding Gorz's non-reformist reforms.

2   WHITHER POULANTZAS?

Poulantzas understands the capitalist state as a *contradictory* social relation—as an alternative to both the view of the state as merely a neutral ensemble of institutions and the revolutionary view that it is a monolithic instrument of capitalist class domination. In the somewhat vague phrase he repeats often in the text, it is the 'material condensation of a relationship of forces among classes and class fractions' (Poulantzas 1978, 129).

---

[2] The theory of the state that it begins to articulate is of an entirely different sort than the one more coherently developed in Poulantzas' first major work on the state, *Political Power and Social Classes* (1973), which decisively comes to more Leninist strategic conclusions because of its more structuralist orientation.

For Poulantzas, the capitalist state is not a thing or instrument acting at the behest of the capitalist class (Sweezy 1942; Miliband 1969, 22). Nor is it a unitary bureaucratic subject with its own predefined organizational interests dominated by bureaucrats and experts (Weber 1978). Neither is it an alienated socio-political form that is superimposed upon humanity's democratic essence, to be smashed wholesale in a great final battle once working-class power has been sufficiently built up outside of it (Lenin [1917] 2014). Lastly, it is not a political form that can be thought of as derivative of the logic of capital itself (Barker 1978). In *State, Power, Socialism*, Poulantzas instead treats the state as a strategic field composed of apparatuses that are themselves expressions and results of class struggles. This means, importantly, that it is not simply a thing that can be taken by a left government in a single election or even progressively won through a series of elections. As Poulantzas says, '[t]he centralized unity of the State does not rest on a pyramid whose summit need only be occupied for effective control to be ensured' (Poulantzas 1978, 138).

Instead, in Poulantzas' view, the capitalist democratic state is a social relation in much the same sense that the Marxist conception of capital itself is a social relation. It is the political expression of active material forces—in particular, class struggles—whose power is in part both produced and reproduced through its formal institutions. This conception of the state in capitalist democracies, where the relations of class struggle are both constituted by the state and traverse its terrain to produce and resolve internal contradictions, is a useful starting point. State institutions in capitalist democracies contain and articulate the contradictions among and between social classes that persist in society. The upshot of this view is that while—as we will see below—there are deep biases in the institutions of the capitalist democratic state to govern in favour of the reproduction of capitalism, those biases coexist with opportunities for democratic forces to counter-organize on that same terrain precisely because they are *historically contingent*.

To develop Poulantzas' incomplete later shift in analytically useful directions, our analysis of liberal capitalist politics should not be articulated at the very high level of abstraction of the mode of production. This is the preferred level in Poulantzas' early work, which he never quite frees himself from. This study of 'abstract-formal objects', i.e. invariable concepts, as opposed to concrete historical facts (Barrow 2002, 13) continues to ossify political and social theory in the Marxist tradition more generally.

In *Political Power and Social Classes*, Poulantzas articulates a theory that begins from the highest level of abstraction, the capitalist mode of production, and treats the capitalist state as a specific region within it. And to the extent that the concrete facts are engaged, it is to illustrate that abstract theory. Yet such abstract theorizations only flatten and render invisible the institutional variability, both internal and external, of capitalist democracies. Yet that variability is the core object of conjunctural ruptures. As I will show, such theorizations thus inevitably slide into a monolithic view of the state as a seamlessly functional reproducer of capitalist power, free of internal contradictions. Therefore, our analysis of the state needs to be articulated at a level of abstraction that can explain variation across both the forms of capitalist states (i.e. fascist, military dictatorial, or liberal) as Poulantzas himself does in *Fascism & Dictatorship* (1974) and *The Crisis of Dictatorships* (1976a), but also variation within those state forms as well. In this chapter, I concern myself with capitalist politics in liberal democracies—such as those that obtain in a good part of the contemporary capitalist world—to argue that concepts need to be developed at a more *conjunctural* level of abstraction in order to explain their variability across time. Poulantzas moves from the highly abstract mode of production down to the social formation but rarely extends the analysis further. Such a move might enliven state theory. As Poulantzas notes, on the one hand, structuralism/necessity is 'a theoretical conception that neglects the weight of class struggle in history' (Poulantzas 1976b, 72). On the other hand, pure agency/contingency leaves everything up to the fight, wholly neglecting the constraints of capitalist social relations. A conjunctural theorization might offer insights at the intersection.

Poulantzas unfortunately leaves incomplete the task he sets out for himself (see Jessop 1985, 128–35). He ends *State, Power, Socialism* with a sharp defence of a democratic socialism, which aims 'to transform the State in such a manner that the extension and deepening of political freedoms and the institutions of representative democracy (which were also the conquest of the popular masses)...[are] combined with the unfurling of forms of direct democracy and the mushrooming of self-management bodies' (Poulantzas 1978, 256). Yet his own political theory, contradictory as it is, snuffs out the contingent effects of struggle on state institutions, leading us back into the impasse that capitalist democracy must, in the end, seamlessly reproduce the capitalist mode of production. Poulantzas is ever aware of class struggle—as expressed in divisions in

actual state institutions and parties, in the ruling 'power bloc', and contradictions within classes. Yet for all his sophistication, he largely elides a
discussion of how transformations in state structures through class struggles also transform state functions. On this particular point, his theory
remains abstract and undynamic. This is the functionalist trap that the
state theorists so often found themselves in when they relied on a highly
abstract understanding of capitalist politics. Like Gramsci, Poulantzas
wanted to get beyond ahistorical proclamations about the capitalist state
and socialist strategy, but could not move beyond his own arguments
in *Political Power and Social Classes* that the state must, in the end,
necessarily function to reproduce capitalism.

Though Poulantzas' late work offers a starting point for theorizing the
state conjuncturally to include both structural and contingent processes,
we must avoid the pitfalls that Poulantzas himself stumbles into in his
own unfinished exploration which force him back into this impasse. Here
I identify three crucial problems that an alternative formulation must
avoid: (1) mechanism-free functionalism, (2) abstract formalism, and (3)
a failure to identify the conditions under which state ruptures occur in
capitalist politics. As this chapter progresses, I will address each of these
pitfalls, and in doing so offer some gestures towards an alternative.

3   Varieties of Liberal Democracy

The first pitfall which Poulantzas repeatedly falls into, particularly in
Political Power and Social Classes, is what I term mechanism-free functionalism.[3] Though he begins with the definitional claim that the capitalist
state is the material condensation of class struggles and a strategic field
of struggle itself, he fails to take this claim to its necessary conclusion
for thinking about how to understand the state conjuncturally. Instead,
when articulating what the state itself does, he considers it from the level
of abstraction of a mode of production in which the balance of class forces
bend invariably in favour of capital. Occasionally, in books like *Fascism &
Dictatorship* and *The Crisis of Dictatorships*, he descends down to the level
of a social formation to understand exceptional state forms. But in his

---

[3] In simple terms, a mechanism in the social sciences and philosophy of science is an
account of a cause. Mechanisms are not always the visible social relations we see, but are
often hidden. But they are nonetheless real and as a result are considered the object of
social science (Bhaskar 1975, 47).

theorizations of capitalist politics the lens of the mode of production is prioritized over the conjuncture. In both *Political Power and Social Classes* and *State, Power, Socialism*, even though Poulantzas aims to show how class struggle practices transform state structures, the state's structures themselves remain determined by their functional role in the reproduction of capitalist social relations.

Three examples illustrate this, though more could be cited: (1) Poulantzas' own reductionist conception of relative autonomy, (2) his functionalist theory of how power blocs are formed, and finally, (3) his theory of how power moves in the state's strategic field. I will return to the third one later, when I consider his theory of ruptures. Let us first turn to (1) to clear up some large misconceptions that seem to beset radical theories of politics.

3.1   What is Relative About Relative Autonomy?

Relative autonomy is the notion that the state in capitalist society needs, and therefore has, a degree of autonomy from particular capitalist class fractions and individuals within the capitalist class so that it can govern on their behalf. When explaining relative autonomy in *State, Power, Socialism*, Poulantzas reverts back to his earlier structuralism, arguing that the state maintains its relative autonomy 'so that it may ensure the organization of the general interests of the bourgeoisie' (Poulantzas 1978, 128). In much the same way that birds have hollow bones so that they can fly, the state has relative autonomy so that it can organize the power bloc and disorganize the working classes. Functionalism worked for Darwin's evolutionary theory because he identified the mechanisms: mutation and natural selection. But Poulantzas provides us no such mechanisms for the state's functionality.

Writing two years before the publication of *State, Power, Socialism* in response to Ralph Miliband's provocation of *how relative* is relative autonomy, Poulantzas writes that 'the degree, the extent, the forms, etc. (*how* relative and *how* is it relative) of the relative autonomy of the State can only be examined...with reference to a given capitalist State, and to the precise conjuncture or the corresponding class struggle' (Poulantzas 1976b, 72). Yet because he does not identify the elements that account for the variability of relative autonomy itself his analysis slides back into the impasse of structuralism that he had hoped to move beyond. When push comes to shove, the state's basic role is the reproduction of capitalism, which it happily fills in the last instance. While *State, Power, Socialism* argues that 'the establishment of the State's policy must be seen as the result of the class contradictions inscribed on the very structure of the State' it does not show us why (Poulantzas 1978, 132).[4]

Mechanism-free functionalism is a non-starter when it comes to understanding the Gorzian emancipatory potential of transformations of the state because it results in a view of the state as a monolithic bloc, rendering invisible the internal contradictions in the state that Poulantzas appears concerned about from the outset. In such a view, state theorists read functions into the state based on what they see capitalism needing in general, making those very functions eternal truths and evacuating any *real contradiction* from the state itself. This again, leads us back down the slippery slope to theorizing the state at the level of a mode of production, which for all intents and purposes is not very useful for understanding emancipatory politics. The level of abstraction of the mode of production renders the variability of the form of the state itself invisible, and the form the state takes at a given conjuncture is the crucial factor for emancipatory strategy.

Instead, capitalist democracies are relatively autonomous for entirely historical and developmental reasons. Those early capitalist states that were captured by their incipient capitalist classes, acted at the behest of capitalists rather than on their behalf. As a direct result they governed in ways that ran counter to capitalist growth. Democratic institutions, such as universal suffrage, were not functional adaptations aimed to cement bourgeois power, but rather, hard-won conquests by working classes, which permanently and positively imprinted their voice on the dynamic process of state institution making (Rueschemeyer et al. 1992). This gives concrete substance to Poulantzas' abstract idea of political action as concerning 'the present moment...the nodal point where the contradictions of the various levels of a formation are condensed in the complex relations governed by overdetermination and by their dislocation and uneven development' (Poulantzas 1973, 41).

---

[4] This basic critique of relative autonomy is made powerfully by Bob Jessop (1985) in his intellectual biography of Poulantzas.

If relative autonomy does serve some function, that political autonomy is contingently realized rather than a determination at the outset.[5] This leads to a critical contradiction present in any capitalist democracy, a contingent contradiction that might be termed 'the Frankenstein problem' that is at heart for understanding the space of conjunctural ruptures.[6] If the capitalist state needs autonomy to help reproduce capitalist property relations, like Frankenstein's monster, it also then has the capacity to wield its power against those capitalist relations.

By way of a functionalist starting point, Claus Offe identifies this problem in his pivotal essay on 'the crisis of crisis management' (Offe 1984). There he shows that if we grant that the logic of capitalism contains a self-destructive tendency towards crisis, then it becomes clear that there is a functional necessity for systems that intervene to ensure that capitalism does not destroy itself economically. The state has historically played this role of external stabilizer; take, for instance, the large bank and auto bailouts after the 2008 downturn and extraordinary central bank interventions during the pandemic. Yet, the deeper these crises run, the greater the need for the autonomy of state institutions from direct control of sectors of capitalists, so they might support capitalist accumulation in general by rescuing it when it self-destructs. As Offe writes, key

[5] Even so, that the most developed capitalist countries are also capitalist democracies—at least in that they nominally have competitive elections and near universal suffrage—must be reckoned with. Without this distance from particular capitalists, the capitalist democratic state would not be able to govern as effectively for capitalist growth. A state simply captured by capitalists faces two basic constraints on their capacity to foster competitiveness and growth. First, capitalists are too short-sighted and concerned with profit making to engage in the kind of social investments that make capitalism thrive. If either capital or capitalists wielded the state like an instrument, capitalist democracies would be unlikely to engage in spending on infrastructure, research and development, and education that help commerce and increase profits. Second, capitalism itself is too self-destructive to thrive without active state intervention. Competition, falling profits, crises of demand, and social crises are all more effectively managed by a political authority that can act independently for the long-term interest of capitalism, even if at the cost of the immediate short-term interests of particular capitalist class fractions. In many cases democracy offers up the mechanism necessary for the generation of this governing distance. But as the herculean rise of China shows so well, relative autonomy can also be secured by other means than formal democracy.

[6] Terming it the 'Frankenstein problem' was the idea of Erik Olin Wright and can be found in his unpublished lectures on Claus Offe and the contradictory functionality of the state.

is 'the problem of whether the political administrative [system] can politically regulate the economic system without politicizing its substance and thus negating its identity as a capitalist economic system' (Offe 1984, 52).

This paradox leads to a critical upshot for Offe: once state capacity for intervention against capitalism is created, it can also be manipulated. The boundary between what is considered an object of regulation versus something left to the free market might be pushed back and forth through this manipulation in a Polanyian double-movement, and normative expectations about what is legitimately public versus private will in turn change as well. Through several mechanisms, Offe argues that state expansion will also increase the degree of contradictions and dysfunctions within the state itself (Offe 1984).[7] Far from playing a static, functionalist role, the state instead features internal contradictions that are developmentally tied to capitalist dynamism itself (see McCarthy and Desan 2023).

While the capitalist democratic state *does* tend to govern for capital because of a combination of structural constraints and historical contingencies that I will turn to below, metaphorically speaking, like Frankenstein's monster, it can—and indeed has—become a force against capital itself. This lays at the core of its emancipatory potential.

3.2   Class Capacity in Politics as Variable

The very apparatuses and institutional bodies of liberal democracy are not just the creation of class struggles but strategic sites for them. But class capacities for struggle on this terrain are widely different. Capitalists do not sit idly by for direction from state personnel, but instead use their resources to directly shape and imprint their interests on internal processes and the policy outcomes of formal politics. Working classes, though profoundly out-resourced and beset by collective action problems, do so as well. To explore variation in class capacities, it is necessary to come down to the more conjunctural level. Note the high level of abstraction at which Poulantzas first developed the idea of relative autonomy. In *Political Power and Social Classes*, relative autonomy is principally defined at the level of the mode of production. It pertains specifically to the separation of the economic and the political levels in such a system, and offers

---

[7] Offe points to fiscal crises of the state, the undermining of administrative rationality and the onset of legitimation crises when the state does not further decommodify as core sources of internal state contradiction.

insight into the way that the political level plays an organizing role in the economy that reproduces the capitalist mode of production. This analytical move is traceable to Althusser's general and quite static theory of the capitalist mode of production where it helped account for a 'structure in dominance' (Jessop 1985, 125).

But as I argued in the previous section, relative autonomy does not mean that state institutions and actors are shielded from external influence. As the later Poulantzas notes, the state is a strategic field 'traversed by tactics which are highly explicit at the restricted level of their inscription in the State: they intersect and conflict with one another, finding their targets in some apparatuses or being short-circuited by others, and eventually map out that general line of force, the state's policy, which traverses confrontations within the state' (Poulantzas 1978, 136). It is through these battles that state institutions are constituted and its policies formed and enacted. Concretely, this is what it means to say that the state is the specific material condensation of class forces. Not only do the class struggles *outside* of the state shape those institutions, but the ones *inside* the state's formal institutions do as well. Those institutions are subject to possible capture. Capitalists and the organized working classes know this, thereby expending huge amounts of resources to achieve greater leverage in them. Yet at such a high level of abstraction, Poulantzas fails to identify clear mechanisms that explain how this struggle plays out conjuncturally. What are the conditions under which it varies in a capitalist democracy?

Offe and Wiesenthal's pivotal essay, 'The Two Logics of Collective Action' (1980), helps to bridge this gap in the theory. Though Poulantzas often speaks of the way that the state organizes a hegemonic bloc of the capitalist class and disorganizes workers, classes are organized and unorganized in historically specific ways with specific inter-relationships with other classes, where much depends on their own organization as political actors. To this issue, Offe and Wiesenthal demonstrate that capitalists and workers have very different logics of collective political action.

Political organization of capitalists: For their part, capitalists have control of key resources in society, namely wealth. In capitalist societies, as Marx urged us to grasp with the general law of capitalist accumulation, this control tends to concentrate. Rising levels of inequality in income and in particular wealth, unless mitigated by countervailing forces of wartime devastation or growing labour-power, have borne out in capitalism's historical record. In short, resource inequality gives capitalists greater *capacity* to influence the policymaking process. They are better able to use concentrated resources to both control and influence politics by hiring legal talent, contributing to campaigns, developing coordinated lobbying efforts, hiring technical consultants, enhancing social prestige, and reshaping information available to the electorate.

These resources also afford the fractions of the capitalist class a networked status that other classes simply do not have. In most capitalist democracies they are a fixture of the policymaking process, using their involvement in think tanks and research institutes to help write policy papers for policymakers. They also share a similar cultural background with politicians. That their children go to the same elite schools and they have vacation homes in the same places affords them additional political capacities. This combination of material and social resources simply makes the capitalist democratic state more easily traversable for capitalists than ordinary workers (power elite theorists have most thoroughly explored these mechanisms; see, for example, Mills 1956 and Domhoff 1967).

Taking a conjunctural view, today the financial sector occupies a hegemonic role in the advanced capitalist world, sitting in the driver's seat of the global accumulation model. Let us very briefly consider finance's conjunctural capacity through, first the character of its assets and second its political networks for lobbying. First, because its asset power is rooted in financial assets that are more mobilizable (relative to, say, manufacturing or agricultural equipment), not only is there a capacity imbalance but additionally the *form* of wealth that the hegemonic sector holds affords it better ability to utilize that capacity through investment reallocation. Further, finance capital's networked status has taken on a distinct character today. Shadow banking is now intertwined with the monetary policy that has been pursued by the Federal Reserve and the European Central Bank (Braun and Gabor 2020). And finance increasingly maintains and manages the commercial activities of non-financial firms. Because real estate, banks, and private equity have become increasingly vital for flows of credit in an era of debt-dependent zombie firms, other sectors have become indirectly reliant on it. As evidence of this intertwined network, no sector of business is defended by other sectors of business against regulations through lobbying more than finance (Pagliari and Young 2020).

Political organization of workers: How do the working classes fare in their struggles within the state? Prior to even beginning to wage their battle inside or outside of the state, workers first have to discover their own political aims and then their shared political commitments. The political interests of capitalists are largely transparent to them: generating profits. This objective is largely defined by the very structure of the firm which compels them to seek rents and innovate or go out of business. On the other hand, workers have a heterogenous set of goals made complex by their skill level, their geography, their race, their gender, their citizenship, their sexuality, and so on. They therefore have to engage in a dialogic process of communication with each other to discover their common interests—and hence common purpose to act collectively. This is necessary for workers, because their power is associational and dependent on forming collective organizations (such as movements, unions, or parties), whereas the power of capitalists is structural and not entirely dependent on collective organization (Wright 2000).

But collective action does not simply follow once workers come to recognize their shared goals. They must then forge strong solidarities to overcome free-rider problems. Crucially, capitalists are able to get what they want in politics because of their willingness to pay via lobbying, campaign financing, and associational interaction. Workers, on the other hand, derive their political power from their willingness to act collectively through strikes, protests, and voting. Yet these forms of collective action are much more prone to collective action problems, especially if they come with significant personal costs. In the absence of solidarity, there is a strong risk of ordinary people opting out of the struggle itself by free riding and ultimately undermining it entirely. These contradictions in capacities for struggle between capitalists and workers are the raw material of the struggles that unfold on the terrain of the state. Conjunctural ruptures in state structures will weaken capitalists' advantage in policy-making and institute processes that help to overcome the collective action problems that undermine the capacities of ordinary people.

Though popular sentiment has decidedly shifted against finance capital in the last two decades around the world, it is also hard to imagine a moment when the working classes, especially in the advanced capitalist countries, were more atomized and differentiated, compounding the problems of collective organization even abstractly conceived. Because it is only through specific historical analyses of actual societies and places that we can explain how class formations might emerge, problems of worker organization are always historical (Wright 1985, 129; 1989, 278). Today, spider-webbed supply chains, a shift towards a gig economy, and remote work spurred on by the pandemic have all resulted in a working class that is increasingly disconnected both spatially and communicationally. And the global working class is increasingl1y fragmented and differentiated, by skill, authority, and other circumstances (Botwinick 1993). This renders myriad other structural locations salient in politics, such as citizenship, gender, sexuality, race, and place—further raising challenges to collective action.

3.3   Role of State Personnel as Variable

We do not need mechanism-free functionalism or abstract formalism to account for why class struggle on the terrain of the state tends towards governance for accumulation and growth at the expense of workers. The key, however, is theorizing the location of state personnel. Poulantzas understands this well when he notes that, 'the personnel constitutes a social category' with a distinct position in 'the social division of labour' (Poulantzas 1978, 154). Yet again he does not interrogate the basic conditions of that category to understand its historical variability, and instead functionally argues that divisions in the state personnel reflect divisions in the power bloc. He writes, 'Contradictions between the dominant and dominated classes reverberate as gaps between these sections of the state personnel and the strictly bourgeois summit, thus manifesting themselves in the shape of cracks, splits and divisions within the personnel apparatuses of the State' (Poulantzas 1978, 154). But the view of the personnel as simply a reflection of class struggle falls far short, as it fails to give proper attention to their actual distinctiveness as a social category, which has two broad constraints that can sometimes run directly counter to one another: accumulation and legitimation.

3.3.1   Compelled Towards Accumulation

Even in the event that money, connections, and influence were eliminated from politics wholesale, politicians and personnel in liberal democracies would still be dependent on the investment of capitalists into the economy *qua* their role in the position of state personnel (Block 1977). Though capitalist work is undemocratic, exploitative, and a source of frustration and misery for workers, in a capitalist society it is necessary for workers to sell their labour-power in order to survive. Recall that in capitalism, workers must be free in the double sense. Without that freedom from subsistence workers could exit and opt out of work entirely. Historically, capitalists have fought tooth and nail against this exit option, or anything that makes life easier without work. Without a viable exit option, the welfare of most workers then depends directly on the welfare of firms. Consider a firm that moves its factory because of new emission regulations, resulting in the loss of the main source of income in a given town. On a larger scale, if the business environment sours enough, capitalists can withdraw their investment, causing a recession. The result is that everyone suffers right alongside capital.

The ability to redirect investment is not just the chief way that business exercises its economic power; it is also a key source of businesses' political power as well (Block 1977). Politicians both anticipate and react to disinvestment to govern in ways that not only avoid it, but actively boost the confidence of capitalists that theirs is a good place to invest and make profits. This is not because politicians are ideologically committed to capitalism, even though they often are. More fundamentally, it is because they know what will happen if they do not and instead put forward policies that are do not run counter to the profit interests of firms. In such an event, businesses will disinvest, the state will lose tax revenue, people will lose their jobs, and come the next election cycle those same politicians will likely be voted out of office—if their government doesn't first collapse or get toppled by a coup.

This crucial aspect of the capitalist democratic state generates a built-in structural compulsion for the state personnel to govern for capitalist profitability, which cannot be avoided by simply replacing the personnel in the state with socialists. Capitalists have this investment power because of their structural prominence in the economy more generally, relative to non-capitalist sources of work and revenue (such as the public sector). In having such an elevated position, when firms simply allocate investment in ways that follow market signals it is often enough to shape politics. They might do this intentionally, as in a coordinated investment strike, but even if it is unintentional the political consequence can be much the same. As we saw above, conjuncturally in the era of finance capital, this power is simply deepened by capital's increased exit capacity.

We have now identified several mechanisms to help explain some of the core functions of Poulantzas' capitalist state. Because of *both* the dependence politicians and state managers have on capitalist investment and the pronounced role of corporate influence in politics, capitalist democratic states *tend to be* strategic sites for the organization of the political hegemony of the capitalist classes and *tend to* disrupt and disorganize the working classes. But a tendency is no certainty, and to conclude this—as it appears Poulantzas does at times in *State, Power, Socialism*—is to evacuate the state of real contradictions and the grounds to offer fruitful insight into how those contradictions bear on future ruptures and openings for emancipatory politics.

This limitation is evident in the now famous Poulantzas-Miliband debate. In response to Miliband's question, how relative is relative autonomy, Poulantzas replied in part,

> The (capitalist) state, in the long run, can only correspond to the political interests of the dominant class or classes. But I do not think that this can be the reply which Miliband expects of me. For since he is not some incorrigible Fabian, he of course knows this already. Yet, within these limits, the degree, the extent, the forms, etc. (how relative, and how is it relative) of the relative autonomy of the state can only be examined (as I constantly underline throughout my book) with reference to a given capitalist state, and to the precise conjuncture of the corresponding class struggle (the specific configuration of the power bloc, the degree of hegemony within this bloc, the relations between the bourgeoisie and its different fractions on the one hand and the working classes and supporting classes on the other, etc.). I cannot, therefore, answer this question in its general form precisely on account of the conjuncture of the class struggle. (1976b, 72)

Yet as the state theorist Bob Jessop (1985, 100–102) has demonstrated, it is a logical contradiction to insist on the one hand that the state must reproduce capitalism 'in the long run' while arguing that conjuncturally class struggle can alter the relative autonomy of the state on the other. This amounts to an abstraction problem at the level of theorization, with the conclusion eliding the insights articulated at the conjunctural level.

3.3.2   Compelled Towards Legitimation

Though violence is a critical part of the state's governance techniques over populations both domestic and foreign, capitalist democracies also rely on a social peace between the classes that only the consent or resignation of the exploited, expropriated, and dispossessed can generate. Here, the second key constraint that the state personnel face potentially runs counter to the first. In the event that confidence breaks down, the state could face what Habermas (1975) has termed a legitimation crisis. We can consider this consent or resignation, or some combination of the two as the case might be, the main source of the state's legitimacy. Politically, it is primarily generated through public acquiescence and electoral stability. In other words, the population in any given capitalist democracy has one of two ways to de-legitimize a government in a capitalist democracy: either through disruption (protests, marches, strikes, and riots) or elections (politicians can be voted out of office). The so-called free and fair election and the party system are key means for governments to claim mandates from 'the people' and, in Poulantzas' view, to interpellate workers as 'the people' and 'the nation'.

Yet governing for accumulation sometimes comes into contradiction with the imperative to secure legitimacy, and often the latter is sacrificed for the former. A legitimacy crisis takes hold when the old hegemonic order breaks down and what was once common sense and taken for granted by politicians is viewed with public scorn. Historically this tends to go one of two ways. The legitimacy of the old order is restored—either by its bruised champions or by boosters fresh on the historical scene—or another set of ruling principles is foisted into its place. In the context of such a crisis, expectations are in flux and new spaces open for ideas and practices that were once at the margins, either left, right, or both. The accumulation model of finance capitalism in the advanced capitalist democracies of the world today is now deeply embroiled in such a legitimacy crisis (Fraser 2015). Therefore, while the state personnel remain constrained by the drive for capitalist growth, they are nonetheless also subject to growing public outrage—and therefore more inclined towards policy experimentation than they might be otherwise.

4   Democratic Ruptures

I have laid out some of the core areas of class power variability on the terrain of liberal democracies. More of course could be added when thinking about social structures beyond the state itself, and there we might spend significant time highlighting the centrality of worker organizations, unions, and political parties. But for now, let's remain at the level of formal state structures. In this final section, I lay out what I mean by democratic ruptures as a means to transform the state against capitalism. Poulantzas is again a useful entry point. In contrast to Lenin and Gramsci, Poulantzas argues that state ruptures need not be singular and decisive or between the state *en bloc* and an externally mobilized working class. Instead, ruptures can take place *within* the state apparatus itself. He makes this argument principally about the conjuncture he was living in, in the late 1970s. As he commented in an interview with the French militant Henri Weber at the time,

> There will be a rupture, there will be a moment of decisive confrontation, but it will pass through the state. The organs of popular power at the base, the structures of direct democracy, will be the elements which bring about a differentiation inside the state apparatuses, a polarization of the popular movement of a large fraction of these apparatuses. This fraction, in alliance with the movement, will confront the reactionary, counter-revolutionary sectors of the state apparatus backed up by the ruling classes. (Poulantzas 2008, 341)

Poulantzas maintains that there can be no *general* strategy against capitalism. Instead, he readily concedes that his view of ruptures might be inadequate in other historical contexts. But based on his assessment of the Western European arena of the time, it is fair to say that he would evaluate the current context in much the same way. He notes that in contemporary capitalist societies, it is both extremely unlikely and undesirable to 'smash' the state, precisely because of the extent to which the state has become integrated into people's lives and, moreover, it has, imprinted upon its very institutions, working-class gains that we would not want to do away with, even despite historic rollbacks in public goods such as welfare provisioning (McCarthy 2017, 2019). Again, however, Poulantzas fails to identify the conditions under which a rupture would or would not occur (Poulantzas 2008, 356).[8]

Democratic ruptures at the level of the state, I argue, principally concern changes in the institutions of the state and *restructure power relations in society*. As I showed in the prior section, the particular forms that liberal democracies take are constituted and vary in a multitude of ways. Principally for our purpose we can identify four axes of variation which are important sources of social power against the power of business:

---

[8] In the same interview with Weber, Poulantzas suggested that he based his perspective on internal crises in the army, judiciary, and police (2008, 356). More important is his 'second element' about introducing changes in the 'structures of the state'. He does not specify the precise conditions under which 'structures of the state' are changed so as to produce a rupture, but he suggests in 1977, again without elaboration, that the Common Programme being developed in France, which was adopted but then subjected to a hard reversal under the Socialist Mitterrand government, was precisely one such ruptural possibility.

1. *Formal democratic rights*: the degree to which working-class people can formally participate and influence the outcomes of constitutional politics. A crucial way in which working classes have influenced politics is through extra-institutional and contentious politics such as strikes, protests, and riots. Yet the formal extension of democratic rights and capacities of the working classes is also a source of power. Formal rights are here not limited to political representation in politics, but also include various forms of economic rights, both in the workplace and with respect to investment allocation, that are ensured by the state.

2. *Class consolidation of the body-politic:* the degree to which state structures reorganize the experiential level of politics for workers as the terrain of class struggle (Riley 2022, 30). As Poulantzas himself has deftly shown liberal capitalist democracy atomizes working-class political forces into legally equivalent monads called the individual (1978, 63). Thus the relevant subject of politics as individual becomes the 'institutional materiality' of the state that generates an ideology obscuring class relations at the political level (1978, 66).

3. *Decommodification of labour*: the degree to which states either subject their citizens to the market or decommodify labour by making certain means of survival formal rights (i.e. private health care versus universal health care, temporary assistance versus universal basic income, etc.). Decommodification of work disentangles workers from the private sector, thereby reducing their dependence on the private activity of firms and reducing the power of those firms.

4. *Composition of the economy*: variation in the relative size of the private sector versus the democratic public sector. Capitalist democracies with very small public sectors, such as the United States and Ireland, will be more vulnerable to private investment moves and capital strikes. As the public sector crowds out the private sector as a jobs provider, the relative autonomy of the state to govern is strengthened as well. Miliband's question, 'How relatively autonomous is the capitalist state?' is largely answered by the composition of the economy.

From a bird's eye view, the balance of power between business and workers in democracies reflects the history of class struggle and political organization imprinted on the formal institutional terrain of politics. As with the length of the working day, for example, when workers achieve political victories, they are able to change the conditions of their own survival and sometimes expand their capacities—political and otherwise. These gains have to be continually defended against encroachments by capital and the erosion of state enforcement, again much like the length of the working day or other benefits or gains won at the workplace. But even so, gains can still be durable; they need not be erased 'in the long run', to return to Poulantzas. This points to yet another contradiction about the capitalist democratic state itself that helps us understand the rupture. It is *simultaneously* true that the capitalist democratic state confronts constraints in capitalism that can lead it to crush working-class movements and that laws, policies, and rights organized through it can help enhance working-class power. Conjunctural ruptures, then, occur through policies of the state that enhance working-class political capacity while at the same time weakening capitalist class capacity.[9]

The degree of relative autonomy of the state is variable over time and between existing capitalist states. I have argued that ahistorical theoretical pronouncements from an abstract theoretical level about the nature of

---

[9] If the state *only* demobilised and weakened working-class capacities, as a highly structural reading of Poulantzas might lead one to believe, it would run counter to worker interests to aim for any kind of reforms upon its terrain. Such reforms, in this simplistic—and, dare I say, undialectical—view of the state, would be co-opted and twisted for the purposes of capital the moment they were tainted by capitalist democracy. Yet this has not been the case, historically, across a wide range of working-class initiated state transformations.

Capitalist democracy does vary substantially across place. It would be foolish to equate the Norwegian state, for instance, with the American one. That some capitalist states have robust welfare provisioning and worker representation, albeit in limited and constrained ways, suggests that reform does not simply lead to reversal—even if it is indeed possible as we have seen with respect to liberalization since the 1970s. Working-class struggles during the nineteenth and twentieth centuries played a significant role in the emergence of modern welfare states, as well as the bolstering of liberal rights and the installation of democratic practices. Among these were universal suffrage, free speech and association, and, in the United States, abolition. That some of these conjunctural ruptures have been durable underscores the point that the capitalist democratic state is not solely an object of repression and that when it comes to transformation, we need to take a long view. The state is then Janus-faced, with another side offering possibility for relative empowerment.

the capitalist state are no substitute for understanding actually-existing capitalist states. Conjunctural analysis is therefore necessary to understand the actual configurations of power in capitalist society and the possible pathways to democratic ruptures.

REFERENCES

Barker, Colin. 1978. https://www.marxists.org/history/etol/writers/barker-c/1978/07/stateascap.htm

Barrow, Clyde W. 2002. 'The Miliband-Poulantzas Debate: An Intellectual History.' In *Paradigm Lost: State Theory Reconsidered*, edited by Stanley Aronowitz and Peter Bratsis, 3–52. Minneapolis: University of Minnesota Press.

Bhaskar, Roy. 1975. *A Realist Theory of Science*. London: Verso.

Block, Fred. 1977. 'The Ruling Class Does Not Rule: Notes on the Marxist Theory of the State.' *Socialist Revolution* 33 (May/June): 6–28.

Botwinick, Howard. 1993. *Persistent Inequalities: Wage Disparities Under Capitalism*. Princeton: Princeton University Press.

Braun, Benjamin, and Daniela Gabor. 2020. 'Central Banking, Shadow Banking, and Infrastructural Power.' In *The Routledge International Handbook of Financialization*, edited by Philip Mader, Daniel Mertens, and Natascha van der Zwan, 241–52. London: Routledge.

Domhoff, William G. 1967. *Who Rules America?* New York: Prentice-Hall.

Fraser, Nancy. 2015. 'Legitimation Crisis? On the Political Contradictions of Financialized Capitalism.' *Critical Historical Studies* 2 (2): 157–89.

Gorz, Andre. 1968. *Strategy for Labor: A Radical Proposal*. Boston: Beacon Press.

Habermas, Jürgen. 1975. *Legitimation Crisis*. Boston: Beacon Press.

Hall, Stuart. 1980. 'Nicos Poulantzas: "State, Power, Socialism."' *New Left Review* I/119 (January/February): 60–69.

Jessop, Bob. 1985. *Nicos Poulantzas: Marxist Theory and Political Strategy*. Basingstoke: Macmillan.

Lenin, V. I. [1917] 2014. *The State and Revolution*. Chicago: Haymarket.

McCarthy, Michael A. 2017. *Dismantling Solidarity: Capitalist Politics and American Pensions Since the New Deal*. Ithaca: Cornell University Press.

———. 2019. 'Structural Contingencies: Capitalist Constraints and Historical Contingency in the Rise and Fall of Pensions.' *Critical Historical Studies* 6 (1): 63–92.

McCarthy, Michael A., and Mathieu Hikaru Desan. 2023. 'The Problem of Class Abstractionism.' *Sociological Theory* 41 (1) (March): 3–26.

Miliband, Ralph. 1969. *The State in Capitalist Society*. London: Weidenfeld & Nicolson.

Mills, C. Wright. 1956. *The Power Elite*. Oxford: Oxford University Press.

Offe, Claus. 1984. *Contradictions of the Welfare State*. Boston: MIT Press.

Offe, Claus, and Helmut Wiesenthal. 1980. 'Two Logics of Collective Action: Theoretical Notes on Social Class and Organizational Form.' *Political Power and Social Theory* 1: 67–115.

Pagliari, Stefano, and Kevin Young. 2020. 'Capital United? Business Unity in Regulatory Politics and the Special Place of Finance.' *Regulation & Governance* 11 (1): 3–23.

Poulantzas, Nicos. 1973. *Political Power and Social Classes*. London: New Left Books.

———. 1974. *Fascism and Dictatorship*. London: New Left Books.

———. 1976a. *The Crisis of the Dictatorships*. London: New Left Books.

———. 1976b. 'The Capitalist State: A Reply to Miliband and Laclau.' *New Left Review* I/95 (January/February): 63–83.

———. 1978. *State, Power, Socialism*. London: New Left Books.

———. 2008. 'The State and the Transition to Socialism.' In *The Poulantzas Reader: Marxism, Law, and the State*, edited by James Martin, 334–360. London: Verso.

Riley, Dylan. 2022. *Microverses*. London: Verso.

Rueschemeyer, Dietrich, Evelyne Huber Stephens, and John David Stephens. 1992. *Capitalist Development and Democracy*. Cambridge: Polity Press.

Sweezy, Paul. 1942. *The Theory of Capitalist Development*. New York: Monthly Review Press.

Weber, Max. 1978. *Economy & Society*. Edited by Guenther Roth and Claus Wittich. Berkeley: University of California Press.

Wright, Erik Olin. 1985. *Classes*. London: Verso.

———. 1989. *The Debate on Classes*. London: Verso.

———. 2000. 'Working-Class Power, Capitalist-Class Interests, and Class Compromise.' *American Journal of Sociology* 105 (4): 957–1002.

The Marx Revival and State Theory: Towards a Negative-Dialectical Critical Social Theory of the State

Chris O'Kane

1 Introduction

The 2007 financial crisis led to the revival of Marxist theory, leading to the development of two broad approaches to Marxism, the state, and socialist strategy. In the years immediately following the financial crisis a number of Marxist theorists—notably Aaron Benanav and Endnotes (2010), and Paul Mattick, Jr (2011)—focused on developing revolutionary theories of the unfolding crisis. However, the predominant role that the crisis played in these theories meant that the state was primarily criticized for its inability to counteract the ongoing secular crisis of capitalism. Several years later, the rise to prominence of democratic socialism led to the proliferation of state theories premised on theorizing democratic socialist strategy (see Tarnoff 2018; Day 2018; McCarthy 2019; Maher and Khachaturian 2021). In these theories, the state is conceived of as a 'terrain' of struggle; a means for counteracting crisis and building democratic socialism. Given these two trajectories, and despite the important

C. O'Kane (✉)
Saint John's University, Queens, NY, USA
e-mail: theresonlyonechrisokane@gmail.com

© The Author(s), under exclusive license to Springer Nature Switzerland AG 2023
R. Hunter et al. (eds.), *Marxism and the Capitalist State*, Political Philosophy and Public Purpose, https://doi.org/10.1007/978-3-031-36167-8_11

231

developments in value-form theory and critical theory during this time, including Bonefeld (2014, 2021), Smith (2017), and Reuten (2019)'s work on the state, there has not yet been a critique of the state that both draws on critical theory and engages with these predominant approaches to the state in the Marx revival.

This chapter brings critical state theory into the Marx revival by developing a negative-dialectical critique of the state's role in the reproduction of the negative totality of capitalist society. It draws together Horkheimer and Adorno's Marxian critical theory and its subterranean lineage: the new readings of the critique of political economy as a critical social theory (see Bonefeld and O'Kane 2022). This negative-dialectical critique of the state also points to a number of antitheses and shared assumptions between the revolutionary crisis theory and democratic socialist theories of the state in the Marx revival that prevents both approaches from fully grasping the relationship between the state, the reproduction of capitalist society, and its emancipatory abolition.

The focus on developing a critical state theory that critiques the state by virtue of its role in the reproduction of the negative totality of capitalist society is tied to my larger research project on critical theory. This project is concerned with two related areas of research in critical theory: (1) Reconstructing the development of a heterodox Marxist critical theory of social domination in the negative totality of capitalist society by Horkheimer, Adorno, Schmidt, Backhaus, Reichelt, Postone, and Bonefeld; and (2) developing my own critical theory of the social domination of negative totality that draws on these and other figures to criticize contemporary political economy and critical theory and critique capitalist society (see O'Kane 2018a, 2018b, 2020, 2021a, 2021b, 2021c; O'Kane and Munro 2022). By engaging with the two predominant contemporary approaches to state theory in the Marx revival from the perspective of my newly developed idea of the negative-dialectical critique of the state, this contribution draws on and further develops this larger research project on critical theory, while also bringing these areas of research to bear on contemporary Marxist state theory.

However, I want to highlight that what follows is not intended as an authoritative critique of either the revolutionary crisis or democratic socialist theories of the state. Nor do I claim to provide the definitive negative-dialectical critical theory of the state. Space not only prevents me from pulling off these theoretical feats, but I am also at the initial stages of thinking them through. This chapter is thus intended to parallel and complement Rob Hunter's and Kirstin Munro's chapters in this book in hopes of reviving and developing a critical social theory of the state. This chapter's provisional discussion of the revolutionary crisis and democratic socialist theories of the state also aims to engage with the other perspectives provided in this book (and elsewhere) with the aim of starting a comradely debate on the questions of the state, capitalist society, and its emancipatory transformation.

Section 2 provides an overview of the two predominant approaches to the state in the Marx revival—the revolutionary crisis and democratic socialist theories of the state—outlining how their antithetical theories of the state and socialist strategy are premised on foreshortened accounts of the relationship between the state and the reproduction of capitalist society. Section 3 discusses the development of criticisms of crisis theory and social democracy, the state, and capitalist society in Horkheimer and Adorno's critical theory, and the new readings of the critique of political economy as a critical social theory. Section 4 develops a negative-dialectical critique that grasps the state's roles in the reproduction of the negative totality of capitalist society. The conclusion contrasts the negative-dialectical critical social theory of the state with both the revolutionary crisis theory of the state and the democratic socialist theory of the state, drawing out their respective shortcomings with regard to grasping the role of the state in the reproduction of capitalist society. On this basis, the chapter concludes by gesturing towards a negative-dialectical notion of strategy and emancipation.

2   State Theory in the Marx Revival

The revolutionary crisis theory of the state was developed in the early years of the Marx revival following the 2007 crisis. As the name suggests, this theoretical approach to the state was articulated in the context of revolutionary crisis theories. Thinkers such as Benanav and Endnotes (2010), Paul Mattick, Jr (2011), Joshua Clover and Aaron Benanav (2014), among others, drew on the Marxian crisis theory developed by figures such as Robert Brenner (2006) and Paul Mattick, Sr (1969) to argue that the 2007 crisis was an expression of the long-term secular crisis of capitalism. So too were the spontaneous global uprisings of the 'Arab Spring' and the Occupy Movement in response to the crisis. While the state was an object of revolutionary abolition, the revolutionary crisis theory of the state did not provide a complex account of the role that it played in the perpetuation of capitalist society. This was because, understandably, such a theory focused instead on the inability of states, due to declining revenue, to effectively counteract crises and stagnation by restoring profitability, which was itself an expression of the secular crisis tendency of capitalism. Therefore, since short-term or long-term reforms were not possible, revolution was necessary.

What I term the democratic socialist theory of the state responded to and supplanted the prominence of the revolutionary crisis theory of the state on the basis of markedly different conceptions of crises, the state, socialism, and socialist strategy. According to this perspective, the formation of neoliberal hegemony following the conjunctural crisis of 1970s led to several decades of 'class warfare from above': corporate and state social and economic policies that revived profits at the expense of workers' wages. The bank bailouts and uneven recovery that characterized the 2007 financial crisis and its aftermath culminated in a crisis of neoliberal hegemony (see La Botz 2018). This trajectory has led to 'rising militancy and mobilization' so that 'for the first time in decades, socialism is something more than a subculture'. However, while 'socialism is now more than a subculture…it still lacks a mass base' (Tarnoff 2018). This is because social democratic parties have supported neoliberalism while 'vanguardist strategies that prioritize extra-parliamentary struggles have been unable to build a substantial following among the working class or advance a credible strategy for socialist transition today' (Maher and Khachaturian 2021, 192). Consequently, the democratic socialist theory of the state is coupled with a 'credible' strategy of building such a 'mass base' as part of the democratic road to socialism.

Drawing on Luxemburg, Gramsci, Offe, Wright, and especially Poulantzas, this approach to democratic socialist strategy (see Tarnoff 2018; Day 2018; McCarthy 2019; Maher and Khachaturian 2021) grasps the state within a dialectical theory of dual power. Capitalism and socialism are conceived in terms of which class controls the means of production and the state. On this basis the state and 'wider society' (Tarnoff 2018) are both seen as concurrent terrains of struggle to build working class power. Hence the election of democratic socialist representatives is intended to pass 'non-reformist reforms', such as Medicare For All or the Green New Deal, that build political power and empower the working class. At the same time, mass movements and democratic socialist institutions build 'popular power' outside of the state. Taken together this reciprocal process of the 'democratic road to socialism' aspires to build collective power and tip the balance of class forces from the capitalist class to the working class, culminating in the collective democratic socialist rule of the state.

As this brief sketch indicates, democratic socialist state theory and the revolutionary crisis theory of the state are antithetical to one another. The revolutionary economic criticism of the state's inability to counteract capitalism's secular crisis is opposed to a political theory of using the state to overcome the conjunctural crisis of neoliberalism and build democratic socialism. Hence a theory of the immediate revolutionary self-abolition of the proletariat and the communization of society is opposed by a theory of building class power and the long march through institutions.

Both of these approaches certainly have merit. Many of the thinkers who have developed these ideas have also made the foremost contributions to the Marx revival.[1] Yet their shared purpose for theorizing the state—emancipatory strategy in a time of crisis—means that both of these theories are unsatisfying when it comes to critically understanding the role the state plays in the reproduction of capitalist society. For despite their antithetical precepts, these two prevalent approaches to state theory are both premised on an approach to the state from the perspective of an emancipatory dynamic coupled with an unexamined theory of needs that abstracts the state from the reproduction of capitalist society.

For the revolutionary crisis theory of the state, the secular economic crisis not only serves as the basis of its criticisms of the inability of the state to counteract the crisis. The historical trajectory of the secular crisis also increasingly displaces labourers from the wage relation, leading to the necessity of revolutionary uprisings that communize reproduction for people to meet their material needs. Conversely, in the democratic socialist state theory's conception of the democratic road to socialism, the shifting balance of class forces will use the state to implement redistributive programmes that will minimize exploitation and build public power. This will meet people's needs, strengthening the political will of the masses for socialism, which will be realized in a progressive historical

---

[1] Some have also made later contributions to state theory that have been overlooked and do much to redress the gaps in their earlier work (see, for example, Jasper and Clover 2014; Benanav and Clegg 2018). Since this contribution is more concerned with criticizing what I take to be the prevalent revolutionary crisis theories of the state within the Marx revival that have drawn on the particular aforementioned works by these thinkers, I do not address their later overlooked work here.

trajectory that further shifts the balance of class forces, public power, and redistribution. Such a conjunctural historical trajectory will be realized in democratic socialism.

Consequently, neither of these approaches to state theory in the Marx revival considers how the economy, the state, classes, or needs are created by the historically specific form of capitalist society or how the state's expansive powers are an integral moment in the reproduction of this historically specific form of society. Therefore, in what follows, I bring heterodox Marxist critical theory and the critique of the state into the Marx revival by developing a negative-dialectical critique of the state that grasps the state as a moment in the perpetuation of the negative totality of capitalist society. In so doing, I draw out the aforementioned shortcomings of the revolutionary crisis and democratic socialist theories of the state, while gesturing towards a negative-dialectical notion of emancipation.

I do so by first outlining the critiques of crisis, the state, and society developed by Horkheimer and Adorno and the New Readings of the critique of political economy as a critical social theory. I then develop a negative-dialectical critique of the state that draws together and builds on these works in critical theory to critique the state as a moment in the perpetuation of capitalist society as a negative totality. On this basis, by way of conclusion, I contrast the negative-dialectical critique of the state as a moment in the reproduction of the negative totality of capitalist society with the revolutionary crisis and democratic socialist theories of the state, in order to indicate their respective shortcomings and point towards a negative-dialectical notion of emancipation.

3   Critical Theories and Critiques

Karl Marx's work is full of ambiguities and inconsistencies. The revolutionary and reformist currents of classical Marxism crystallized around two inconsistencies. The ambivalences of the first volume of *Capital* were integral to the revolutionary current of classical Marxist collapse theory. Their logico-historical reading of Volume 1 held that Marx had deciphered the laws of historical development, from prehistory (in Chapter 1) to the inevitable collapse of capitalism and the revolutionary seizure of the means of production in Chapter 32 (see O'Kane 2022). The reformist current of classical Marxism rejected Marx's secular crisis theory and drew on other writings by Marx and Engels to argue that socialism should be built by workers' parties being elected into government and passing legislation to build socialism.

In distinguishing themselves from both of these strands of classical, pre-World War I Marxism, Horkheimer and Adorno developed a heterodox Marxist critical theory of society. In distinction to the collapse theory of crisis and the social democratic theory of the state, Horkheimer and Adorno's critical theory drew on and expanded Marx's account of the social constitution and reproduction of the capitalist *mode of production* into an account of the social constitution and reproduction of *capitalist society*.

Following from an interpretation of Marx's critique of political economy as a critical social theory, Horkheimer's critical theory of society 'held on to the realization that the free development of individuals depends on the rational constitution of society. In radically analysing present social conditions it became a critique of the economy' (Horkheimer 2002, 243). Moreover, in contrast to classical Marxism, Horkheimer held that 'economism, to which the critical theory is often reduced, does not consist in giving too much importance to the economy, but in giving it too narrow a scope' (Horkheimer 2002, 249). The critical theory of society developed by Horkheimer thus focused on how the antagonistic organization of capitalist society was realized in the 'reified authority' of capital accumulation, which as a social process, comprised the economy, state, and family. Hence, in contrast to social democracy's theory of the state as the means of emancipation, for Horkheimer the state was an object of critical theory. Moreover, in contrast to collapse theory, while crises issued from the antagonistic organization of capitalist society, they were realized in the persistence of suffering and the emergence of new types of barbarism (see O'Kane 2021b).

Adorno's later writings developed a negative-dialectical critique of the negative totality of capitalist society. In Adorno's account of late capitalism, the secular crisis of capitalism had been counteracted by the development of the productive forces, the state management of the economy, and people's reproductive and psychic reliance on capitalist society. Capitalist society was thus a negative totality comprising these objective and subjective moments. Adorno's negative dialectic illuminated how these objective and subjective dimensions of negative totality relied on each other to break 'the spell' of identification and awaken a global subject that would negate negative totality (see O'Kane 2018a, 2022).

The new readings of the critique of political economy as a critical social theory further developed Horkheimer and Adorno's criticisms of classical Marxism into critiques of traditional Marxism. The new readings also developed components of their critical theory of society. Hans-Georg Backhaus (1997) and Helmut Reichelt (1972) criticized the logico-historical and neo-Ricardian interpretations of *Capital* first developed by classical Marxism. Their interpretations of Marx attempted to ground Adorno's notion of exchange on Marx's monetary theory of value. Back-haus and Reichelt also conceived of Marx's critique of political economy as a negative-dialectical social theory: The sensible organization of capitalism necessarily appears in the supersensible form of value, which as a type of social rationality, compels the dynamic of accumulation and reproduction (see Bellofiore and Redolfi Riva 2015, 2018).

Moishe Postone (1993) distinguished between traditional Marxism and his interpretation of the critique of political economy as a critique of the historically specific form of private and social, and concrete and abstract, labour. According to Postone, traditional Marxism's criticism of capitalism from the standpoint of labour amounts to a criticism of capitalism as a mode of distribution. Classical Marxism, in all of its currents, proposed a type of socialism that would perpetuate the capitalist organization of labour at the behest of the state. Postone's interpretation of Marx grasped the concrete and abstract, private and social, aspects of labour as historically specific and self-mediating (see O'Kane 2018b).

Open Marxism, particularly the work of Simon Clarke and Werner Bonefeld, criticized the modern adherents of both the revolutionary and social democratic theory of the state. Clarke (1999) and Bonefeld (1999) criticized Brenner's account of the long downturn for neglecting the social form of capitalism. Clarke (1994) likewise criticized the adherents of Marx's secular theory of crisis for neglecting relative surplus value and argued that Marx's theory of crisis amounted to a theory of the crisis-ridden development of capitalism. Clarke (1991) and Bonefeld (1993) also criticized Poulantzas, Hirsch, and Jessop's state theories for their reliance on structural functionalism and bourgeois sociology. Moreover, Clarke and Bonefeld criticized the widespread practice of conjunctural analysis for focusing on epiphenomenal changes that did not grasp the persistence of the capitalist organization of production and distribution (see Clarke 1991, 1992; Bonefeld and Holloway 1991). Finally, Clarke (1994) and Bonefeld (1992) developed their own critiques of the state as essential to the perpetuation of the capitalist social form and permanent class struggle (see Memos 2018).

As can be seen, this tradition of heterodox Marxist critical theory developed criticisms of crisis theory and social democracy, the state, and capitalist society that have been missing from the Marx revival.[2] In what follows, I draw them together and expand upon them to develop a negative-dialectical critique of the state as an essential moment in the reproduction of the negative totality of capitalist society.

4   Towards a Negative Dialectical Critique of the State

In contrast to both the revolutionary crisis and democratic socialist theories of the state, the negative-dialectical critical social theory of the state is not premised on the long-run secular crisis of capitalist profits, nor the balance of class forces. Nor is it premised on the predominance of the economy over the state or the state over the economy. Finally, it is not premised on an emancipatory strategy that follows from these premises. Rather, the negative-dialectical critique of the state is grounded on the persistence of suffering and misery incurred by the organization and perpetuation of capitalist society in all its linked dimensions.[3]

Such a notion of capitalist society is grounded on Marx's insight that the capitalist production process 'proceed[s] from specific economic and historical relations of production, that produces and reproduces these relations of production themselves, and with them the bearers of this process, their material conditions of existence, and their mutual relationships, i.e. the specific economic form of their society' (Marx 1981, 957).

---

[2] Why this perspective has been missing is not clear or straightforward. Given the context in which the current Marx revival has occurred, the criticisms of crisis theory and periodization developed by this Marxian critical theoretical approach may have been untimely. The preoccupation of what passes for contemporary Frankfurt School critical theory with justice and discourse ethics may have also contributed to this perspective being overlooked.

[3] Such an approach has certainly been interpreted as moralist and humanist, or criticized for its incomplete normative standpoint. However, the crucial difference between such a conception of critical theory and moral or humanist criticisms of capitalism has to do with the fact that suffering and misery are not premised on human essence or abstract notions of the good, but instead pertain to the socially mediated experiences of suffering and misery incurred by the organization of capitalist society.

For 'the totality of these relationships which the bearers of this production have towards nature and one another, the relationships in which they produce, is precisely society, viewed according to its economic structure' (Marx 1981, 957). Those conditions, like these social relations, are on the one hand the presuppositions of the capitalist production process, on the other its results 'and creations; they are both produced by it and reproduced by it' (Marx 1981, 957). Consequently, 'every pre-condition of the social reproduction process is at the same time its result, and every one of its results appears simultaneously as its pre-condition. All the production relations within which the process moves are therefore just as much its product as they are its conditions. The more one examines its nature as it really is, [the more one sees] that...in the capitalist process, every element...is already an inversion and causes relations between people to appear as the attributes of things and as relations of people to the social attribute of things' (Marx 1972, 507–8).

In the negative-dialectical critique of the state, accumulation and reproduction *do not* consist in production for need which is misallocated by the capitalist mode of exploitation and distribution, due to the rising organic composition of capital or the balance of class forces. Instead, the negative-dialectical critique of the state draws on the aspects of Marx's critique of political economy that demonstrate how domination, class antagonism, and misery are inherent to the historically specific social organization of the capitalist mode of production. Along these lines Marx states that 'the mode of production produces, both objectively and subjectively, not only the object consumed but also the manner of its consumption' (Marx 1973, 92). Production, needs, the balance of class forces, accumulation, and reproduction are thus all indelibly shaped by the organization of capitalist society as a historically specific type of 'all-around dependency', in which 'the social character of activity, as well as the social form of the product, and the share of individuals in production appear as something alien and objective, confronting the individuals, not as their relation to one another, but as their subordination to relations which subsists independently of them and which arise out of collisions between mutually indifferent individuals'. Consequently, individuals are now ruled by 'abstractions which are nothing more than the theoretical expression of those material relations which are their lord and master' (Marx 1973, 166).

On this basis, following Horkheimer and Adorno, the negative totality of capitalist society is conceived of as a sort of linking structure between human beings in which everything and everyone depend on everyone and everything; the whole is only sustained by the unity of the functions fulfilled by all its members, and each single one of these members is in principle assigned such a function, while at the same time each individual is determined to a great degree by his membership in this total structure. (Institute for Social Research 1972, 16)

Consequently,

... Sociology becomes a critique of society as soon as it does not merely describe and weigh institutions and processes of society, but confronts them with what underlies these, with the life of those upon whom these institutions have been imposed, and those of whom the institutions themselves are to such a great extent composed. (Institute for Social Research 1972, 23)

Backhaus's contribution to the development of the critique of political economy as a critical social theory provides a way of uniting Marx's notion of value and Adorno's negative totality. As Backhaus writes, '[v]alue for Marx is thus not an unmoving substance in undifferentiated rigidity but something which unfolds itself in differentiations ... It is self-evident that the doubling of the commodity into commodity and money is first deciphered when it can be shown that this antagonistic relation between things expresses a relation between people which is similarly structured in an antagonistic way' (1980, 112). Conversely, these 'social relations of people' must be so defined that from their structure the antagonistic 'relation of things' becomes comprehensible (Backhaus 1980, 112).

The negative-dialectical critique of the state that I will now outline proceeds from these theoretical bases by contextualizing the state in the reproduction of the negative totality of capitalist society. Such a negative totality is constituted by historically specific and antagonistic social relations that result in the moments of the negative totality of capitalist society: the economy, the state, and the household. Each of these moments socializes and compels individuals to act in certain ways that reinforce the other spheres and reproduce capitalist society, resulting in the persistence of suffering and misery. On this basis, the negative-dialectical critique of the state proceeds by identifying how the state contributes to the reproduction of these other spheres, which taken together ultimately perpetuate the constitutive premises of capitalist society.

Drawing on and extending Bonefeld (2014), the constitutive premises of capitalist society were created by primitive accumulation. In that process, the state separated people from their means of reproduction and expropriated land and wealth for the ruling class. This created the capital relation and the historically specific forms of property, labour, and wealth. A class of workers who were 'doubly free' were compelled to compete with each other to sell their labour power in exchange for wages to a class of capitalists who were compelled to purchase their labour power to compete with each other to valorize value. Private households emerged as the domain of domestic labour which sustained the sellers of labour power. The state transformed into the capitalist state, an entity which sustained these moments and such a society. Hence, these constitutive premises appear in the result: the negative totality of capitalist society. Moreover, as I now indicate, each of these spheres compels individuals to act in certain ways that reinforce the other spheres and reproduce capitalist society, and thus its constitutive premises of separation.[4]

In contrast to traditional Marxism, the capitalist economy is not criticized on the basis of how the distribution of the proceeds of labour do not meet the needs of labourers. Rather, following Postone, such a critical theory demonstrates how the historically specific social form of labour creates the abstractions of value that compel individuals to organize labour in a way that perpetuates capitalist society. Following Backhaus and Reichelt, the categories of political economy are not just forms of thought but real abstractions that grasp the necessary appearance of such a historically specific antagonistic social reality. Although a fully fledged recapitulation of these categories exceeds the confines of this chapter (see Hunter in this collection), they consist in the historically specific dual character of labour, the forms of value and their subsidiaries, which mediate the process of production, accumulation, and reproduction via the 'personification of things and the reification of persons' (Marx, 1976, 209).

---

[4] As this implies, my extension of Bonefeld's reading of primitive accumulation differs from other contemporary readings developed by Wood (1999) and Harvey (2004) by grasping primitive accumulation as a historical and ongoing process that is the premise and the result of capital accumulation and reproduction.

From this it follows that capitalists are 'personifications of economic categories' (Marx, 1976, 92) compelled by the historically specific natural laws of accumulation to compete to acquire profit in the form of money. As 'character masks', workers are compelled by the 'silent compulsion of economic relations' (Marx 1976, 899) to compete with each other to sell their labour power as a commodity in exchange for a wage determined by the labour market in order to survive. Capitalists purchase the commodity labour power on the labour market because it is a peculiar commodity that can produce more value than it costs. Since profit is dependent upon selling commodities on the market while maximizing surplus value, capitalists are compelled to maximize working hours, to reduce wages, and to increase productivity. This leads to the revolutionizing of production via supervision, and an increasing division of labour and reliance on machinery, resulting in the deskilling, maiming, displacement, and fragmentation of workers. This dynamic is replicated across the social division of labour as a whole. The accumulation of capital is therefore not the production of an expanding basket of goods that would serve as the basis of socialism if it was not pilfered by capitalists; nor is it an inevitable process in which wage labour is replaced by the rising organic composition of capital. Rather, the 'productive' worker is an 'appendage of a machine' and a 'fragment of a human' Marx 1976, 799) who cares as 'much about the crappy shit he has to make as does the capitalist himself who employs him, and who also couldn't give a damn for the junk' (Marx 1973, 273). Moreover, the result of this form of production is a blind, crisis-ridden process of 'accumulation of wealth at one pole' and the accumulation of misery, the torment of labour, slavery, ignorance, brutalization and moral degradation at the opposite pole' (Marx 1976, 799), through the 'multiplication of the proletariat' (Marx 1976, 764) and the reproduction of separation on an 'extending scale' (see O'Kane, forthcoming).

The household is not a private sphere separate from the economy or state, nor is domestic labour separate from productive labour. Rather, '[p]rivate life, the zone of individuality' is 'absorbed by so-called social activities and thus likewise moulded by ... the schemata of society' (Adorno 2019, 64). The existence of the household is predicated on private property and the state. Possessing a household also requires wages and/or state revenue. Reproducing a household consists in domestic labour performed in accordance with these imperatives. The household is thus inherent to private property, atomization, and competition.

Domestic labourers, moreover, are sustainers of private households and the commodity of labour power, and domestic labour is rationalized in response to different types of revenue (see Munro 2019). In this marty-rology of reproductive labour, the stultifying and maiming activities of domestic labour sustain individuals as bearers of the commodity of labour power. In so doing, the household and domestic labour also sustain private property, competition, exploitation, and the maiming of subjec-tivity, contributing to the reproduction of the negative totality of capitalist society (see O'Kane and Munro 2022).

The negative-dialectical critique of the state focuses on how the state mediates and reinforces the economy and household. Such an approach critiques the form of the state as a supra-individual, autonomous entity that is separate from but related to the economy and household. On this basis the negative-dialectical critique of the state illuminates how the form of the capitalist state and its administrative capacities perpetuate the nega-tive totality of capitalist society. Contra both the revolutionary crisis and democratic socialist theories of the state, the state is not an institution that stands outside the economy and the household that is then rendered ineffectual by the secular dynamic of accumulation. Nor is the state a 'contradictory terrain' whose institutions might be used to build work-ers' power on the road to socialism. Rather, expanding on Bonefeld, the state is the 'political form' of capitalist society: an essential moment in the negative totality of capitalist society that reinforces and facilitates the reproduction of the negative totality of capitalist society via its specific form, which is separate from and reinforces the economy and household.

The capitalist state's form and attendant form of law and constitution formalize and reinforce the separation of producers from the means of production, the possession of wealth and the means of production, in the codification and enforcement of property laws (as mentioned above, these laws also establish and preserve the private household). The form of law as a real abstraction treats individuals as equal citizens by abstracting from this historically specific form of separation and class antagonism.

This process of abstraction is supplemented in the public sphere and electoral politics which, as Johannes Agnoli argues, are presupposed by the separation of the economic and political spheres and codified in a constitution. According to Agnoli, a constitution 'guarantees the predom-inance of the capitalist mode of production and, at the same time, satisfies the demand for mass political participation by the population'. This is because a constitution establishes a democratic 'framework' that 'guarantees' and 'safeguards' the capitalistic 'organization of social reproduction' (Agnoli 2000, 201). The constitutive premises of capitalist society are preserved in electoral political contests that replace class antagonism and anti-capitalist struggles with juridically equal citizens and ensure that 'all opportunities, beyond the democratic virtue of "voting", of active meddling in politics are excluded from the "liberal democratic" principles of government' (Agnoli 2000, 199).

As a consequence, anti-capitalist political movements that enter the political sphere are absorbed and depoliticized by what Agnoli calls the process of 'statification'. Citizens' active participation in progressive and democratic socialist social movements that embrace electoralism are replaced by electoral platforms developed by parties and extolled by elected representatives. The policies in these party platforms are limited by the form of law and the constitution so that even if progressive policies are passed into law, progressive or democratic socialist demands are transformed 'into bureaucratic apparatuses of integration' (Agnoli 2014; also see O'Kane 2021c).

Consequently, whether Keynesian or monetarist, redistributive or de-distributive, reformist or non-reformist reforms, these policies do not empower or disempower, advance, or set the class struggle back. This is because 'each parliamentary reform that is realized within states ... serves not to expand the possibility for the masses to take part in decision-making processes, but rather to contain that possibility by intensifying parliament's function of domination' (Agnoli 2014). Indeed, whether funded by demand or supply side economics, progressive taxation or mounting debt, regressive and progressive, social democratic and democratic socialist reforms aid accumulation and reproduction, which as history has shown, is compatible with this variety of approaches. Moreover, as history has further shown, the implementation of these economic and social policies via bureaucratic administration likewise depoliticizes class struggle, preserving the atomization of individuals while subjecting them to a dominating and coercive bureaucratic rationality that undermines autonomy. Finally, These economic and social policies also contribute to the sustenance of the economy and households (see Clarke 1994; Bonefeld 2014; Munro 2021; O'Kane and Munro 2022).

Such a process of bureaucratic depoliticization and atomization is mirrored in the predominant approach to public and private education, which Adorno aptly described as 'house training'. The purpose of this approach to education is not to develop autonomous individuals who can grasp the suffering society inflicts upon them and act collectively to emancipatorily negate society. Rather, education trains and disciplines people into using their skills and competing with their peers to sell, reproduce, or purchase labour power in order to survive.

Finally, there is policing. As Mark Neocleous (2000) notes, not only do policing and legislation possess the same etymology, but the activity of law enforcement as law-making violence unveils the violent truth of the state's purpose. The electoral sphere of the state reproduces capitalist society by depoliticizing class struggle and the organization of capitalist society. The policy arms of the state reproduce capitalist society through the violence of administration, depoliticization, and the sustenance of the economy and household. Policing reproduces capitalist society through the mechanisms of law enforcement as counterinsurgency; criminalizing acts that attempt to undermine the organization of capitalist society; and demonizing, brutalizing, and incarcerating those who perform these acts.

The objective aspects of these moments of the negative totality of capitalist society are mirrored in the constitution of subjectivity and needs. People's subjectivities and needs are shaped by the economy, the household, and the state, which as a whole, compels people to act in the myriad of aforementioned antagonistic ways that reproduce capitalist society. This process of socialization maims people's ability to think critically and act autonomously; the objective reliance of people upon the negative totality of capitalist society is mirrored in a tendency to become subjectively reliant upon it. Hence, as Horkheimer indicates, '[t]here is not only the general, systematically engineered brainwashing but the threat of economic ruin, social ostracism, the penitentiary and death to deter reason from attacking the key conceptual techniques of domination' (Horkheimer 1978, 17).

The negative-dialectical critique of the state does not then merely take aim at the institution of the state by virtue of its inability to counteract economic crises, nor does it conceive of the state as an 'arena' or a 'terrain' of class struggle. Rather, the negative-dialectical critique of the state critiques the form and capacities of the capitalist state by virtue of its place in the negative totality of capitalist society, and illuminates how the form and capacities of the capitalist state mediates the economy and household as a moment in the 'negative unity of society in its overall unfreedom' (Adorno 2019, 70). Such a negative-dialectical critique further demonstrates how the state form and its capacities are inherent to the negative totality of capitalist society and its objective subject process of reproduction via its reliance on and reinforcement of the economy and household. All three are the results of the constitutive premise of separation inherent to capitalist society that is perpetuated by its reproduction, culminating in the persistence of unfreedom, misery, and suffering.

5   Conclusion

The contemporary revival of Marxist theory has led to the development of two predominant approaches to state theory. The crisis theory of the state focuses on criticizing the state's inability to counteract the unfolding secular crisis of capitalism. The democratic socialist theory of the state conceives of the state as an object of socialist strategy. On this basis, the crisis theory of the state criticizes reformism as an impossibility and advocates for revolutionary immediacy, while democratic socialist state theory advocates non-reformist reforms as part of the process of building class power on the revolutionary road to socialism. Despite their merits, these mutually antithetical approaches offer foreshortened notions of the role of the state in the reproduction of capitalist society.

This chapter has attempted to clarify these shortcomings by developing a negative-dialectical critique of the form and capacities and role of the state in the reproduction of capitalist society as a negative totality. In contrast to the revolutionary crisis and democratic socialist theories, according to the negative-dialectical critical social theory of the state, it is not a question of conceiving of what role the state plays in relation to the economy, nor of secular crisis, nor the balance of class forces. Rather it is a question of conceiving of the economy, class, and the state as moments in the reproduction of the historically specific negative totality of capitalist society in order to demonstrate the 'negative unity of society in its overall unfreedom' (Adorno 2019, 70) and the suffering and misery that results from this historically specific, antagonistic organization of society.

Contra the revolutionary crisis theory of the state, the negative-dialectical critique of the state does not underestimate the state on the basis of the reified dynamic of secular crisis; nor does it assume that once people's needs are not being met, they will rise up. Instead the negative-dialectical critique of the state holds that even if there is a secular crisis that cannot be counteracted by state's fiscal and monetary policy, leading to spontaneous revolutionary uprisings, that such a revolutionary crisis theory passes over the other elements of the state and subjectivity—notably policing, law, the military, and education—integral to reproducing the historically specific social form of capitalist society. At the same time, in distinction to the democratic socialist theory of the state, even if the conjunctural analyses of democratic socialist state theory were to prove right and a wave of elections resulted in a shift of the balance of class forces in the terrain of the state and redistributive policies, the negative-dialectical social critique of the state holds that democratic socialist state theory does not address the form of state, nor its role in depoliticization. Following Agnoli, the negative-dialectical critique of the state holds that 'state institutions do not allow themselves to be used in any manner whatsoever, for their logic is not their own, but is determined by the reality whose functioning they serve. State institutions are not there to realize either freedom or human rights, not to mention social emancipation; rather they have solely the responsibility of organizing and securing the social reproduction of a capitalist society' (Agnoli 2014, 190).

Consequently, following Clarke, redistributive state policies do not then build either public power or the political will for class struggle; instead, they create bureaucratic agencies that undermine workers' autonomy and depoliticize class struggle. Hence following and adapting Horkheimer, '[n]umerous unsavory activities are required if society is to be held together, including the maintenance of prisons and the production of murderous weapons' (Horkheimer 2013, 145). Moreover, as Horkheimer further notes 'The way the police occasionally treat the workers during an uprising or beat the imprisoned unemployed with the butts of their rifles, the tone the factory porter uses with the man looking for work, the workhouse and the penitentiary, all these function as the limits that disclose the space in which we live' (Horkheimer 1978, 76).

Socialist strategies and theories of emancipation should not then rest on theories of crisis or the state that divorce crises and the state from the reproduction of capitalist society. Rather, emancipatory movements must grasp crises and the state, class, and needs as integral to the historically specific organization of capitalist society, and conceive of the perpetuation of that society, in any guise, as permanent catastrophe perpetuating suffering, misery, and domination. Hence the negative-dialectical critique of the state amounts to a critique of the perpetuation of capitalist society as permanent class struggle and a notion of revolutionary negativity that abolishes its historically specific form.

This approach to emancipatory politics will no doubt be unsatisfactory to those who want to identify the new subjects or agents of transformation, or to those who believe a programme should be developed that will create them. Yet developing such a negative-dialectical critique of the state, as outlined here, aims to break the spell of state theory and of the identification of emancipatory politics with the secular crisis or the state, illuminating how the historically specific premises and the objective and subjective domains of capitalist society reinforce each other, perpetuating domination, pain and misery, in order to develop the critical insight and desire to overcome them. Such a negative emancipatory approach is already mirrored in constellations of movements and moments that reject the reified authority of capitalist society and move to immediately negate the negative totality of capitalist society by overcoming the historically specific forms of separation, antagonism, and domination it is premised on. This chapter hopes to accompany these movements by intervening in the Marx revival to raise these urgent questions and contribute to the awakening of a global subject that abolishes the historically specific negative totality of capitalist society.

Acknowledgements I would like to thank the reviewers for their helpful comments and the editors for their patience and support.

References

———. 2019. *Philosophical Elements of a Theory of Society.* Cambridge, MA: Polity.

Agnoli, Johannes, 2000. 'The Market, the State and the End of History.' In *The Politics of Change: Globalization, Ideology and Critique,* edited by Werner Bonefeld and Kosmas Psychopedis, 196–206. London: Palgrave.

———. 2014. 'Theses on the Transformation of Democracy and on the Extra-Parliamentary Opposition.' *Viewpoint Magazine.* https://viewpoint mag.com/2014/10/12/theses-on-the-transformation-of-democracy-and-on-the-extra-parliamentary-opposition/.

Backhaus, Hans-Georg. 1980. 'On the Dialectics of the Value-Form.' *Thesis Eleven* 1 (1): 99–120.

———. 1997. *Dialektik der Wertform.* Freiburg: Ça Ira.

Benanav, Aaron, and Endnotes. 2010. 'Misery and Debt.' *Endnotes* 2.

Benanav, Aaron, and John Clegg. 2018. 'Crisis and Immiseration: Critical Theory Today.' In *The Sage Handbook of Frankfurt School Critical Theory,* edited by Beverly Best, Werner Bonefeld, and Chris O'Kane, 1629–1648. London: Sage.

Bellofiore, Riccardo, and Tommaso Redolfi Riva. 2015. 'The *Neue Marx-Lektüre*: Putting the Critique of Political Economy Back into the Critique of Society.' *Radical Philosophy* 189 (January/February): 24–36.

———. 2018. 'Hans-Georg Backhaus: The Critique of Premonetary Theories of Value and the Perverted Forms of Economic Reality.' In *The Sage Handbook of Frankfurt School Critical Theory*, edited by Beverly Best, Werner Bonefeld, and Chris O'Kane, 386–401. London: Sage.

Bonefeld, Werner. 1992. 'Social Constitution and the Form of the Capitalist State.' In *Open Marxism Volume 1*, edited by Werner Bonefeld, Richard Gunn, and Kosmas Psychopedis, London: Pluto.

———. 1993. 'Crisis of Theory: Bob Jessop's Theory of Capitalist Reproduction.' *Capital & Class* 17 (2): 25–47.

———. 1999. 'Notes on competition, capitalist crises, and class.' *Historical Materialism* 5 (1): 5–28.

———. 2014. *Critical Theory and the Critique of Society: On Subversion and Negative Reason*. London: Bloomsbury.

———. 2021. 'On the State as Political Form of Society.' *Science & Society* 85 (2): 177–84.

Bonefeld, Werner, and Chris O'Kane, eds. 2022. *Adorno and Marx: Negative Dialectics and the Critique of Political Economy*. London: Bloomsbury.

Bonefeld, Werner, and John Holloway, eds. 1991. *Post-Fordism and Social Form: A Marxist Debate on the Post-Fordist State*. London: Palgrave.

Brenner, Robert. 2006. *The Economics of Global Turbulence: The Advanced Capitalist Economies from Long Boom to Long Downturn, 1945–2005*. London: Verso.

Clarke, Simon, ed. 1991. *The State Debate*. London: Palgrave.

———. 1992. 'The Global Accumulation of Capital and the Periodisation of the Capitalist State Form.' In *Open Marxism 1: Dialectics and History*, edited by Werner Bonefeld, Richard Gunn, and Kosmas Psychopedis, 133–50. London: Pluto Press.

———. 1994. *Marx's Theory of Crisis*. London: Palgrave Macmillan.

———. 1999. 'Capitalist Competition and the Tendency to Overproduction: Comments on Brenner's *Uneven Development and the Long Downturn*.' *Historical Materialism* 4 (1): 57–72.

Clover, Joshua, and Aaron Benanav. 2014. 'Can Dialectics Break BRICS?' *South Atlantic Quarterly* 113 (4): 743–59.

Day, Meagan. 2018. 'Why Socialists Should Fight for Structural Reforms.' *Socialist Forum* (Fall 2018). https://socialistforum.dsausa.org/issues/fall-2018/why-socialists-should-fight-for-structural-reforms/.

Frankfurt Institute for Social Research. 1972. *Aspects of Sociology*. Translated by John Viertel. Boston: Beacon Press.

Harvey, David. 2004. 'The "New" Imperialism: Accumulation by Dispossession.' *Socialist Register* 58: 63–87.

Horkheimer, Marx. 1978. *Dawn and Decline: Notes 1926–1931 and 1950–1969*. New York: The Seabury Press.

———. 2002. *Critical Theory: Selected Essays*. London: Continuum.

———. 2013. *Critique of Instrumental Reason*. London: Verso.

Jasper, Bernes, and Joshua Clover. 2014. 'The Ends of the State.' *Viewpoint* 4.

La Botz, Dan. 2018. 'The New Deal Is Not Enough.' *Socialist Forum* (Fall 2018). https://socialistforum.dsausa.org/issues/fall-2018/the-new-deal-is-not-enough/.

Maher, Stephen, and Rafael Khachaturian. 2021. 'Socialist Strategy and the Capitalist Democratic State.' *Science & Society* 85 (2): 191–99.

Marx, Karl. 1972. *Theories of Surplus Value Part III*. London: Lawrence & Wishart.

———. 1973 *Grundrisse: Foundations of the Critique of Political Economy*. Translated by Martin Nicolaus. London: Penguin Books.

———. 1976. *Capital: A Critique of Political Economy*. Translated by Ben Fowkes. Vol. I. London: Penguin Books.

———. [1894] 1981. *Capital: A Critique of Political Economy*. Translated by David Fernbach. Vol. III. London: Penguin Books.

Mattick, Paul. 1969. *Marx and Keynes*. Boston: Extending Horizon Books/ Porter Sargent Publisher.

Mattick, Paul, Jr. 2011. *Business as Usual*. London: Reaktion.

McCarthy, Michael A. 2019. 'Seven Theses on the Capitalist Democratic State.' Verso Blog. https://www.versobooks.com/blogs/4308-seven-theses-on-the-capitalist-democratic-state.

Memos, Christos. 2018. 'Open Marxism and Critical Theory: Negative Critique and Class as a Critical Concept.' In *The Sage Handbook of Frankfurt School Critical Theory*, edited by Beverly Best, Werner Bonefeld, and Chris O'Kane, 1314–31. London: Sage.

Munro, Kirstin. 2019. '"Social Reproduction Theory", Social Reproduction, and Household Production.' *Science & Society* 83 (4): 451–68.

———. 2021. 'The Welfare State and the Bourgeois Family-Household.' *Science & Society* 85 (2): 199–206.

Neocleous, Mark. 2000. *The Fabrication of Social Order: A Critical Theory of Police Power*. London: Pluto.

O'Kane, Chris. 2018a. '"Society Maintains Itself Despite All the Catastrophes That May Eventuate": Critical Theory, Negative Totality and Crisis.' *Constellations* 25 (2): 287–301.

———. 2018b. 'Moishe Postone's New Reading of Marx: The Critique of Political Economy as a Critical Theory of the Historically Specific Form of Labor.' *Consecutio Rerum* 3 (5): 485–501.

———. 2020. 'Capital, the State, and Economic Policy: Bringing Open Marxist Critical Political Economy Back into Contemporary Heterodox Economics.' *Review of Radical Political Economics* 52 (4): 684–92.

———. 2021a. 'Critical Theory and the Critique of Capitalism: An Immanent Critique of Nancy Fraser's "Systematic" "Crisis-Critique" of Capitalism as an "Institutionalized Social Order".' *Science & Society* 85 (2): 207–35.

———. 2021b. 'Reification and the Critical Theory of Contemporary Society.' *Critical Historical Studies* 8 (1): 57–86.

———. 2021c. 'Law and the State in Frankfurt School Critical Theory.' In *Research Handbook on Law and Marxism*, edited by Umut Özsu and Paul O'Connell, 261–82. Cheltenham: Edward Elgar.

———. 2022. 'Totality.' In *The SAGE Handbook of Marxism*, edited by Beverley Skeggs, Sara R. Farris, Alberto Toscano, and Svenja Bromberg, 451–73. London: Sage.

O'Kane, Chris, and Kirstin Munro. 2022. 'Marxian Economics and the Critique of Political Economy.' In *Adorno and Marx: Negative Dialectics and the Critique of Political Economy*, edited by Werner Bonefeld and Chris O'Kane, 77–95. London: Bloomsbury.

Postone, Moishe. 1993. *Time, Labor and Social Domination*. New York: Cambridge University Press.

Reichelt, Helmut. 1972. *Zur logischen Struktur des Kaptalbegriffs bei Karl Marx*. Frankfurt: Europäische Verlagsanstalt.

Reuten, Geert. 2019. *The Unity of the Capitalist Economy and State*. Leiden: Brill.

Smith, Tony. 2017. *Beyond Liberal Egalitarianism: Marx and Normative Social Theory in the Twenty-First Century*. Leiden: Brill.

Tarnoff, Ben. 2018. 'Building Socialism from Below: Popular Power and the State.' *Socialist Forum* (Fall 2018). https://socialistforum.dsausa.org/issues/fall-2018/building-socialism-from-below-popular-power-and-the-state/.

Wood, Ellen Meiksins. 1999. *The Origin of Capitalism*. London: Verso.

The Capitalist State as a Historically Specific Social Form

Rob Hunter

1 Introduction

This chapter presents the outline of the social form approach to theorizing the capitalist state. This approach is distinctive for its insistence that the state in capitalist society is the specifically *political* form of appearance of that society. The capitalist state is not self-subsistent, nor is it a trans-historically valid category. It cannot serve as a refuge from, or barrier to, capital's society-pervading and ecology-dismantling compulsion towards endless expansion. The state's fetishistic appearance as being outside or separate from civil society is a socially constituted objective appearance of our social reality, one that must be explained with reference to capitalism as a historically specific social form of production. The capitalist state is historically specific to the society of which it is the political form of appearance; it is essential to the constitution and reproduction of capitalist society. Its fetishistic semblance as being separated from civil society is not an accident; it could not be otherwise and remain the capitalist state. It is the political appearance of 'the anonymous rule of money and

R. Hunter (✉)
Independent Scholar, Washington, DC, USA
e-mail: jrh@rhunter.org

253

R. Hunter et al. (eds.), *Marxism and the Capitalist State*,
Political Philosophy and Public Purpose,
https://doi.org/10.1007/978-3-031-36167-8_12

the law' through which dispossession and expropriation are sustained and the availability of commodity labour-power is reproduced (Clarke 1988, 127). Emancipation requires the negation rather than the affirmation of the capitalist state.

Social form theories of the state feature prominently across the work of multiple thinkers and traditions. Notable examples include Pashukanis (Dimick 2021), Frankfurt School critical theory (Neupert-Doppler 2018), the 'state derivation' debate (Holloway and Picciotto 1978), the Open Marxist school (Bonefeld et al. 1991; Bonefeld 2014, 165–85), and approaches to the critique of political economy focusing on the relationship between Hegel and Marx (Williams 1988; Smith 2017; Reuten 2018). Despite their diversity, all of these contributions have elaborated upon several shared themes. These include claims that (i) the critique of capitalism requires an adequate account of the specificity of the capitalist state as an aspect of a society that is dominated by the real abstractions of the forms of value; and (ii) within capitalist social relations, the state is fetishized either as a trans-historical category, or as anterior to the social constitution of capitalist economic categories.[1] The state is an essential moment of a contradictory totality of historically specific categories—categories that appear to be natural and universal but are actually non-identical with the reality upon which those categories are imposed. They are not self-subsistent; instead, they are constituted through determinate social relations that they also mediate. Such social constitution and mediation occur 'behind the backs' of social individuals in the course of their concrete historical activity, and not as a result of any kind of trans-historical necessity. A social form approach is adequate to the task of theorizing both the capitalist state's historical specificity and its fetishistic semblance as a self-standing entity that is divided from, or anterior to, the class-based civil society of capitalism. It explains why the capitalist state is not a state *in* capitalism but the state *of* capitalism; and it explains why the capitalist state is neither an instrument of direct class domination nor

---

[1] Fetishism is, *inter alia*, a social practice of treating determinate and historically specific categories as natural or trans-historical (that is, anterior to their own social constitution) (Murray 2016, 59). For an overview of the critique of the state as a contribution to the critique of fetishism, see Neupert-Doppler (2018). I explore the fetishism of the apparent separation of the political and the economic in Part 4, below.

a neutral arena of political agonism, but is instead the distinctively political appearance of a society structured by and reproduced through the impersonal domination of the real abstractions of value.

In Part 2, I introduce the idea of the critique of social form, emphasizing that the Marxian critique of political economy is the necessary background for (but not the sufficient elaboration of) a social form account of the capitalist state. In Part 3, I argue for the historical specificity of the capitalist state as just such a form—one that presupposes the other essential determinations of contemporary capitalism *qua* the generalized production and exchange of commodities. Part 4 extends the argument of Part 3 through an examination of the state's fetishization as a neutral, objective mediator of competing interests. I develop the conception of the state as social form and its mutuality with capitalism's other essential social forms—emphasizing the fetishism subtending their social objectivity, and their mediation of the abstract and impersonal domination felt by all members of capitalist society. So understood, the capitalist state cannot be described as dominated or captured by capital—but this does not entail that it is the proper site for contesting capitalist domination and exploitation. Struggles to transform existing social relations and to give form to the institutional mediation of an emancipated society cannot be launched from within, or find their resolution through, the narrow and inverted political form of appearance of capitalist society. Emancipatory struggle does not consist in the struggle to seize, or wield the power of, the capitalist state. Rather, such a state is an appearance of a social reality that must be abolished.

2 THE STATE IN THE CRITIQUE OF POLITICAL ECONOMY

This chapter's argument is premised on contributions to Marxian theory that emphasize Marx's attention to social form.[2] The critique of political economy reveals the domination of our social world by the real abstractions of value, and as such it is necessary to theorize the state with reference to value and its forms. Consequently, the argument proceeds

---

[2] 'A theory of social forms is of central importance to a critical theory' (Postone 1993, 179). An adequate account of value-form theory—and of social form theory more generally—is beyond the scope of this essay. For background see Elson (1979), Smith (1990), Clarke (1991a, 92–143), Postone (1993), Backhaus (1997), Bonefeld (2014, 79–137), and Murray (2016).

from two core assumptions. The first is that Marx's mature critique of political economy is a necessary but insufficient basis for a critique of the capitalist state. The capitalist state 'is a concept that has to be developed on the basis of the analysis already offered in *Capital*', but its infrequent appearances in the text do not add up to a systematic critique (Clarke 1991b, 189). The second assumption is that '[t]here is only one social reality' (Bonefeld 2014, 166). The capitalist state and the capitalist economy are constituent moments of the same social reality (Clarke 1991b; Smith 2017, 183–91).[3] Political relations, together with economic relations, comprise a separation in unity (Reuten 2018, 311). As such, the capitalist state must be apprehended in its relation to the conceptual fulcrum of Marx's critique of capital: value.

Marx begins *Capital* with an account of the forms of value—the most abstract form-determinations of capital. His method of presentation is to begin with capital's essential form-determinations and develop them in successive stages of concretion (Smith 2014). The commodity is the most abstract form-determination of a society characterized by the organization of production for the sake of the valorization of capital rather than the satisfaction of wants and needs. Insofar as they are form-determined as values, commodities are validated as having been produced by abstract labour—affirmed as expressions of socially necessary labour-time—only through the completion of money-mediated exchange. (Private production under conditions of competition is validated as social only through the exchange of commodities for money.) It is in this sense that, for Marx, the commodity is the 'elementary form' of wealth as it appears in capitalist societies (1990, I:125). Without it, capital accumulation— value appearing as 'self-valorizing value' (Marx 1992, II:185)—would be impossible. And commodities themselves may only be produced through the bifurcated (at once concrete and abstract) labour that is distinctive to capitalism.

Value and its forms constitute the ground of all other categories that are developed in *Capital*. Marx's critique of value as social form is an examination of socially constituted and socially objectified categories (cf.

---

[3] 'The analysis of the the capitalist state conceptually presupposes the analysis of capital and the reproduction of capitalist relations of production, despite the fact that in reality, of course, the state is itself a moment of the process of reproduction' (Clarke 1991b, 189). 'While the commodity form is the economic form of society, the state is its political form' (Bonefeld 2014, 179).

Reichelt 2005, 42–44). These categories are objectified social relations appearing simultaneously within the totality of capitalist social relations—a totality that is contradictory and inverted rather than harmonious or well-ordered. They 'mutually presuppose each other in social reality' (Heinrich 2013, 202). Value is an essential moment of a totality that can be apprehended only by focusing on its particular moments (Marx 1992, II:185). Marx's critique of capital starts with the commodity-form of value, but he must navigate layers of abstraction and concretion in order to construct an adequate critique of capital and the form of society that is historically specified by it. Retracing Marx's steps allows us to see that the social constitution of the real abstractions of value—their reproduction through the social objectification of abstract labour validated in exchange for the sake of value's apparent self-valorization—may be discerned as a (contradictory and inverted) totality.[4]

3   Historical Specificity and Social Form

3.1   *The Historical Specificity of Capitalist Social Relations*

The critique of political economy does not examine invariant forms of economic (or political) life. There is no such thing as 'production in general'; production always assumes specific social forms (Marx 1973, 85–88). Capitalist production is no exception; the generalization of the production and exchange of commodities is distinctive only to the current epoch. The abstract form-determinations of capital—commodities that are both use-values and values; exchange-value-positing, commodity-producing labour (labour that is at once abstract and concrete); money as the objectified appearance of labour; capital as self-valorizing value; the reciprocal antagonism of the capital relation—are historically specific forms of appearance of definite social relations (Murray 2016). The challenge for a properly Marxian critique of the state is to grasp its specificity in the light of Marx's critique of capitalism's essential constitutive forms.

The production of commodities with the aim of realising a monetary profit appears earlier in history than do relations of generalized

---

[4] '"[V]alue" is neither a category of production, nor a category of exchange, but a category of mediation between the two, expressing the unity-in-difference of privately undertaken production and the exchange that establishes its social necessity' (Smith 2017, 81).

commodity production and exchange. But prior to the generalization of commodity production and exchange, as well as the growth and consolidation of the world market, such an appearance is not systematic or dominant. Rather, it is merely an 'essentially episodic appearance' (Lukács 1972, 84). Money-mediated exchange comes to dominate economic relations only with the advent of capitalism (Heinrich 2012, 81–82). It is only when particular social relations become generalized—labour-power becomes purchasable as a commodity (the only commodity that most people possess); money becomes world money such that capital subsumes and mediates an expanding array of social relations—that the commodity becomes the elementary form of a society, one in which socially constituted economic categories become real abstractions whose objectivity is a matter of social validity (Reichelt 2005). It is only when the direct producers are continually separated from the means of production and subsistence that the reproduction of the socially constituted real abstractions of value becomes the mode through which society is perpetuated (Bonefeld 2014, 79–95). Capitalism cannot be identified with the existence of money or markets, both of which antedate generalized commodity production. Capital as a totalizing social relation is restricted to a particular epoch. It is possible to speak of wealth and labour in non-capitalist societies, but in such societies they are the forms of appearance of different social relations; under capitalism they have definite and distinct forms of appearance. To imagine that commodity-producing labour is natural or trans-historical is fetishism—the hypostatization or naturalization of social relations that assume determinate forms that are constituted through particular histories of struggle.

The historical specificity of capitalism should not be understood in teleological terms. While it is certainly true that capitalism is historically *contingent* (that is, capitalism need not have obtained in history), this is not the same as saying that capitalism's social form is historically *specific*. The expansion and consolidation of social relations of generalized commodity production and exchange are contingent historical facts. To describe the social form of capitalist production as historically specific, however, is not just a historical claim; it is a conclusion arrived at through critical analysis. Capitalism's constituent determinations are the forms of appearance of determinate social relations, not instantiations of logics of social organization that may or may not obtain in history. Apprehending such forms is a matter of critique, for which it will not suffice simply to elaborate a historical narrative. It is *logically* untenable, and not simply historiographically inadequate, to identify labour per se with the bifurcated labour of capitalism, which is doubled into concrete, use-value-producing labour and abstract, value-positing labour producing commodities for exchange. A critique of capital must be immanent to its object in order to apprehend these distinctions. Simply noting that capitalism is historically contingent will not necessarily clarify that, for example, money, markets, and labour under feudalism are the forms of appearance of a social reality that is radically different from capitalism.

Two objections should be considered here. The first is the claim that discerning historical specificity is a matter of historical inquiry or historiography. According to this objection, the historical specificity of social form can only be determined through empirical inquiry. However, historical specificity is an analytic category, not a natural phenomenon. The discernment of historical specificity is not a positivist or empirical undertaking. It is not a matter of the accumulation of observations of concretions until a summation or considered judgement may be delivered. Theoretical investigation comes first—although it should always be remembered that this 'primacy of the logical [over the historical] is to be understood in a cognitive sense, and not as if the categories are the existential ground of the reality that is mediated through them' (Schmidt 1981, 35). Although a detailed historical understanding is necessary for the articulation of critiques and explanations, it does not suffice as a critique or explanation itself. Merely periodizing the capitalist state in history reproduces the fetishism of the state's form of surface appearance, rather than serving as a critique of it (Clarke 1992). The critical examination of the concepts that mediate our social activity, and are generated through our social activity, is a matter of immanent critique, not of taking an observational view from nowhere. The critique of political economy denies that concepts are self-subsistent, and yet it nevertheless regards them as real. It cannot be a nominalist philosophy that denies the conceptual mediation of social reality.

The second objection is that historical specificity cannot be sketched with sufficient clarity. After all, even now, in globally consolidated capitalist social relations, there are many local examples of people relating to each other and to nature in non-capitalist ways. But this objection is easily met. Part of what is historically distinctive about a society characterized by generalized commodity production is that, although the mass of direct producers is exploited and dominated, what obtains is not the direct exploitation and direct domination of every individual, but class exploitation and class domination. The general availability of commodity labour-power does not entail the impossibility of the sporadic or localized persistence of unfree labour, subsistence agriculture, transhumance, and so on. The formal and real subsumption of production processes by capital can coexist at distinct historical moments; they are not mutually incompatible periods (cf. Banaji 2010; Milios 2018). However, the critique of political economy is concerned primarily with the general tendencies and features of developed capitalist production, in which real subsumption and the pursuit of relative surplus value predominate—as indeed they do in our society, in which value relations have a 'world market validity' that is not restricted to particular regions or sectors (Bonefeld 2014, 147).

3.2   The Historical Specificity of the Capitalist State

States also appear in history before generalized commodity production. Again, however, it is important not to conflate the historical anteriority of states per se with conceptual anteriority. The struggles and processes through which capitalist economic relations emerged were the same ones through which capitalist political relations emerged; such relations are mutually presuppositional (Clarke 1991b, 193). To speak of the state as both historically preceding capitalism and obtaining within, alongside, or coterminously with capitalism is to fetishize the state as self-subsistent with respect to historically definite and determinate social relations. The capitalist state and the capitalist economy are forms of appearance of one and the same historically definite social reality.

Capitalist society is distinguished *politically* by being doubled up into civil society and the state. Such a state does not stand apart from capitalist society and reproduce it from the outside. Instead, it is 'the concentrated and organized force of society' (Marx 1990, I:915)—the institutional form of appearance of the persistent separation of the direct producers from the means of subsistence (Bonefeld 2014, 183–84). 'So-called' primitive accumulation is so-called precisely because it is not an event but an enduring and structuring feature of capitalist society.[5] The political form of appearance of a society characterized by mass dispossession— the condition of possibility for free labour—is a state that expresses 'the

---

[5] For this claim see Bonefeld (2014, 79–95); for additional perspectives see Singh (2016), Roberts (2020), and Gerstenberger (2022).

anonymous rule of money and the law' (Clarke 1988, 127). Such anonymous—impersonal and abstract—rule is the persistence of the domination of social individuals not by other individuals or even by institutions, but by real abstractions mediating and constituted by the activity and relations of those very social individuals. As the expression of 'the anonymous rule of money and the law', the capitalist state also depoliticizes the dispossession of the direct producers; as such, it is a necessarily fetishistic form of appearance of capitalist social relations, inasmuch as dispossession, exploitation, and domination are naturalized.

Capitalist production relations are (most often and for the most part) relations of the *indirect* domination of producers. Sustained and expanding valorization of capital (and, as such, the reproduction of capitalist society) does not require generalized *direct* domination of producers, unmediated by formal legal equality. What is required is the availability of commodity labour-power.[6] The universal availability of labour-power as a commodity is a fundamental premise of capitalist production. Here it may be seen that, far from directly exploiting direct producers, the capitalist state reproduces their double freedom. The direct producers are and remain doubly free, thanks to the formal equality of buyer and seller as well as the separation of the direct producers from the means of production and subsistence—maintained *in extremis* through state violence and coercion. Such dispossession is the condition of possibility of commodity labour-power (which most people must sell in order to acquire the money they need for purchasing commodities to sustain themselves).

Capitalists' existence as a class posits the persistence of a state that cannot be identified with their class. If the *capitalist* state were to become a state of *capitalists*, then the conditions for the production of commodities and the valorization of capital would be negated; labour would no longer be (doubly) free, and labour-power would not universally available as a commodity. The formal separation of capitalists from the capitalist state is an essential feature of capital's social form. Capitalists, as a class, relate to one another through competition (Clarke 1988, 131). For the capitalist state to be a state of capitalists it would be necessary for capitalists to have sublated their own existence as such a class.

---

[6] Cf. Banaji (2010, 131–54) on debates about the extent of the variability in the forms of exploitation that can appear as wage-labour.

The historical emergence of the capitalist state is the appearance of a state that does not directly mobilize and exploit workers in general (Sumida 2018, 56–57).[7] It is true that labour-power is a commodity available for purchase by state personnel. Moreover, the state has employees, and it may own or operate particular enterprises or even sectors. However, capitalist production is globally and preponderantly determined as a multiplicity of competing capitals pursuing surplus value within a system of territorially and jurisdictionally demarcated states. The capitalist state's persistence is predicated on taxation and borrowing, both of which posit continued capital accumulation and hence the reproduction of a social form of production in which direct producers are impersonally compelled to be free to sell their labour-power. As such, the overall conditions for capital accumulation—in particular, the levels of profitability within and across sectors—are urgent considerations for state personnel, even though they grasp them only in fetishized and reified terms. In fact, they matter to state personnel in ways that they do not matter to the owners or managers of private firms, who are concerned with the pursuit of surplus value (which they understand as profit) rather than with the maintenance of the conditions of profitability (which, again, state personnel only apprehend in fetishized terms).

4   The Fetishism of the Political

I have argued that the capitalist state is the historically specific political form of appearance of capitalist society. By apprehending it as a social form, we may grasp its historical specificity and its constitution through concrete, determinate social relations. However, this is not sufficient to establish the particular form-determinations of the capitalist state nor is

---

[7] I am unable to dwell on two issues that are germane to this point. The first is the question of how the account presented here may be related to analytic category of 'state capitalism' as it is applied to development in the global periphery (Alami et al. 2022). The second is the contemporary existence of polities that do not conform to the model presented here. Here it must be emphasized that a theory of the capitalist state, like a theory of capitalist production, seeks to explain the specific and preponderant features of its object in order to apprehend it as a historically determinate social form. As such, the existence of states that do not conform (to lesser or greater degrees) to the contours of the account presented here does not by itself vitiate my overall account; nor does the abstraction necessarily involved in the elaboration of an explanatory model constitute evidence that that model is presumptively invalid. For an introduction to issues of abstraction and model-making in Marxian theory see Mattick (2018, 13–33, 50–71).

it sufficient as an explanation of why the capitalist state appears as separate from the capitalist economy. It is necessary to further elaborate the historical specificity of the capitalist state by exploring the fetishization of its apparent autonomy from the society of which it is a determinate political appearance. The capitalist state's historical specificity prevents us from supposing that the state, as it confronts us in contemporary society, is trans-historical or self-subsistent such that it is prior or anterior to capitalist economic relations. Nevertheless, precisely such a fetishized understanding—to wit, that the state is, as a matter of social ontology, separate from economic relations—is built into the dominant mode of thought in capitalist society (Neupert-Doppler 2018).

Social relations in capitalist society appear in forms that are not only historically specific, but inverted. They are forms that have real social validity, but that efface the processes through which they come to be objectified and assume seemingly law-like appearances. As such, they are inverted forms: they are far from being natural, and yet by virtue of being socially constituted they have an objective, law-like appearance, mediating the relations of social individuals who give rise to them behind their own backs. Being so constituted, these categories 'vanish in their own social world' (Bonefeld 2014, 5). As such, their validity 'is no longer consciously understandable' (Reichelt 2005, 55). They are appearances of essences which are themselves historically specific and socially constituted (Smith 2014, 29–35). The objectivity of the essential categories of capitalist society is not a matter of first-order nature and should not be posited as such; instead, their apparent objectivity is a matter of socially constituted second nature (Schmidt 2014). It is in this sense that the political appearance of capitalist society—that is, doubled up into civil society and the state—may be described both as a 'real appearance' with profound social consequences, but also an 'institutionalised illusion' whose real surface appearance must not be conflated with its own conditions of possibility (Wood 1995, 23; Murray 1988, 32).

The separation of the political and the economic is both real and illusory. It is *real* in that it is a socially constituted category and thereby acquires objectivity. It is *illusory* in that its objectivity is not the objectivity of a self-subsistent, trans-historical concept, but is rather constituted through the antagonistic reproduction of historically specific social relations. This separation is 'an illusion, albeit one *necessarily* generated by the social relations of a capitalist society' (Smith 2017, 189, emphasis added). The doubling up of society into the state and civil society is not a natural feature of rational sociality; it is a historically specific outcome of determinate historical activity, relations, and struggles. As a fetishized form of appearance of bourgeois society, the state/civil society separation is essential to the reproduction of the separation of the direct producers from the means of production. It is through this series of doublings and separations that we can grasp the state form's mediation of the abstract domination that pervades and defines capitalist society. In other words, the separation of the political and the economic is both a fetishized appearance *and* an objective social category—one that is 'socially valid' (Marx 1990, I:169). But understanding the capitalist state requires that we not affirm its necessary appearance—to wit, its apparent autonomy from civil society—as its essence.

It may seem that describing the state as a social form is to invoke an ideal type or a trans-historical category—to impose a ready-made abstraction onto definite social relations. But far from being a procrustean operation of forcing reality into preconceived categories, the critical apprehension of the forms of appearance of social relations involves understanding determinate social relations as they are—that is, as simultaneously concrete and conceptually mediated. There is no such thing as an 'autonomous substance such as could exist independently of its concrete determinations' (Schmidt 2014, 34). The capitalist state is no exception.

4.1   Fetishism and Domination

Specifically *capitalist* states are not anterior (either logically or historically) to capitalist relations of production and exchange. They do not subsist independently of the capitalist economy, and they are not pre-capitalist institutions that have been captured by capital or capitals. If the capitalist state is a historically specific social form, rather than a trans-historically valid category, then it is not possible to speak of the state either as being captured by the capitalist class or as being denatured or deformed through subordination to the imperatives of capital accumulation. Against the first claim, it must be stated emphatically that the state is not the tool, instrument, or possession of any class or class fraction.[8]

---

[8] 'The fact that the rule of economic abstractions benefits the owners of great wealth does not entail that they are in control' (Bonefeld 2020, 161). On the limits of those conceptions of the state, according to which state power is either wielded on behalf of a class, or is the object of struggle between classes, see Clarke (1991b) and Sumida (2018).

The state is not an instrumentality of capitalist class power but the political form of appearance of the antagonism through which capitalist social relations continue to be reproduced. As the mode in which capitalist society exists politically, it is 'merely one moment of the class struggle, complementary to the other moments of that struggle' (Clarke 1991b, 194). As such, while the state is 'subordinated to the reproduction of capital', it must be remembered that 'the subordination of the state is not to be understood in the sense of the subversion of an institution that has some kind of functional existence in abstraction from the class struggle between capital and labour' (Clarke 1991b, 193–94).

The capitalist state's mutual constitution with capitalist production is not a basis for the fetishistic conclusion that either is the unmediated cause of the other. Instead, the historical record belies any claim that capitalist production and exchange emerged independently of the bourgeois state. The consolidation of industrial social relations would itself have been impossible but for the reciprocal and mutually presuppositional activities of workers, capitalists, legislators, and jurists (Steinberg 2010). It could not have been otherwise; '[t]here are no prelegal relations of production' (Banaji 2010, 42). This does not mean that juridical or political relations cause relations of production and exchange. Such a politicist view is simply an inversion of economism, rather than its critique. The various form-determinations of capitalist society present themselves to consciousness as seemingly natural and distinct levels or spheres such as the state or the economy, but they are the forms taken by a totality of social relations that are mutually constitutive.

The seeming naturalness of 'capitalist society is both an actuality and at the same time a necessary illusion' (Adorno 2006, 118). The state's apparent autonomy is necessary insofar as it possesses a real social validity; it is presupposed by the other essential determinations of capitalist society, and it is constituted behind the backs of social individualists in their antagonistic relations with one another. And yet it is an illusion insofar as it is socially objectified rather than self-subsistent. It is in this sense that we may appreciate the state as an appearance of the abstract domination that specifies capitalist society.

Life in capitalism is pervaded by, and experienced as, abstract and impersonal domination. The mass of producers are compelled to work neither by the possessors of the means of production nor by the state; and yet they are exploited by the former and prevented from accessing the means of production and subsistence by the latter. In both cases, impersonal rather than direct domination is fundamental. The mute compulsion of economic relations ensures that the possessors of labour-power continue to sell their only commodity to capitalists, such that they can acquire the money to buy the commodities they need to reproduce themselves. The state's maintenance of the rule of law ensures the on-going dispossession of the direct producers, such that labour-power remains the only commodity they can bring to exchange. Each of these—including the state—must be understood as moments in a totality.

The state's apparent autonomy is directly implicated in the pervasion of impersonal domination in capitalist society. Capitalism is distinguished by impersonal, abstract, or objective domination—it is not simply reducible to direct domination by individual wills. Capitalist domination is the domination of individuals by real abstractions that they make behind their own backs (Bonefeld 2020). Within the critique of political economy, social domination is a matter of abstraction. Abstract domination consists in the fact that capitalist social relations are inverted, such that humans must valorize capital for its sake and not their own. They are dominated by the real abstractions of the value-forms of capital's valorization through the production and realization of value. Value, produced by abstract labour, is validated only in the exchange relation, where it necessarily appears in the form of money. Indeed, abstract labour itself can obtain if and only if production is conditioned by value. In other words, value relations constitute a contradictory unity. Within this unity, seemingly 'self-moving abstractions have the upper hand over human beings' (Bellofiore 2014, 171). The spectral objectivity of capital as an apparently self-moving subject-object is both the intangible (yet socially objective) foundation of unfreedom and the creation of the very subjects whose relations it mediates.

The capitalist state is the political appearance of abstract domination— 'the domination of people by abstract social structures that people themselves constitute', in Postone's influential formulation (Postone 1993, 30). It is manifestly not the case that this or that group of capitalists— let alone *all* capitalists—grasp all the levers of power firmly. The capitalist state's capacity for action is conditioned on revenues obtained through taxation and borrowing; as such, the state continually and continuously posits capital accumulation as absolutely necessary for its own persistence. Capitalist social relations constitute the ground of possibility for the capitalist state, which in turn is the condition of possibility for capitalists' specifically *political* power: '[i]t is the capitalist form of the state that underlies the political influence of capitalists, rather than vice versa' (Clarke 1988, 121 n 2).

There are not competing social ontologies, such that there is one that is proper to the state and another that is proper to the economy. The state is bound up in the abstract domination that is specific to capitalist society; it is not outside of capitalism, and it is not meaningfully separate from capitalist production relations. This means that we should be careful about whether and how we speak of the capitalist state as subordinated to capital. It is not uncommon to hear the capitalist state described as something like 'the armed and servile agent of capital' (Roberts 2020). However, far from critiquing the fetishized separation between the state and civil society, such a view affirms it by positing the specifically capitalist state as historically or conceptually anterior to capital. 'The state is not an *agent* of capital' (Bonefeld 1995, 196, original emphasis). The state and the economy form a contradictory unity. Neither is self-subsistent; the persistence of either is predicated on the persistence of the other.

As the relation through which 'the anonymous rule of money and the law' (Clarke 1988, 127) are expressed, the capitalist state mediates much of the abstract domination saturating capitalist society. Its violence and coercion are among the forms of domination that are most salient in people's everyday lives (cf. O'Kane and Munro 2022).[9] Thanks to the fetishization of the separation of the political from the economic, such domination appears as peculiarly *state* violence rather than as the violence inherent to capitalist society itself. The capitalist state metes out violent coercion in a way that capitalist firms do not because it is the necessary political appearance of a divided and antagonistic society. It appears as a violent intruder into the Eden of liberty, equality, property, and Bentham; but far from being separate from the capitalist economy, it is a determination of one and the same social reality. It is a site of domination, but it neither dominates independently of capitalist production nor on behalf of capitalists. Only capital appears as a 'dominant subject' (Marx 1990, I:255), of which the capitalist state is the political appearance. And yet despite being the dominant subject of a historically specific society, capital is also nothing more than an inverted social form that 'has no capacities on its own' (Smith 2017, 350). It is a real abstraction, but as such it is nothing other than the product of our own (mediated and reified) social

---

[9] On this point see also Kirstin Munro's contribution to the present volume.

activity. Like the critique of political economy, the critique of the capitalist state reveals the horror of a social world in which we are the authors of our own domination.

5   Conclusion

The political form of appearance of capitalist society is one in which society is doubled up, such that the state is apparently distinct from civil society, and apparently exercises political power in a manner that is autonomous from the imperatives or exigencies of the economy. Society is identified with the economic; the scope of the political is restricted to the institutions, practices, and culture of the bourgeois state. Society is simultaneously doubled and diminished. Antagonism is reduced to (parliamentary) politics, while economic categories are both reified and identified with civil society as such. The latter is fetishized as pre-political, unmediated by social antagonism, and beyond the scope of legitimate political contestation. But in fact there is no such entity as 'the economy' with a pre-conceptual existence that is anterior to social reality; nor can this be said of 'the state' (Bonefeld 2014, 182).

Capitalism obtains and persists as a historically specific and contradictory totality. That the state is a moment in such constitution and reproduction may be glimpsed in its depoliticization of the antagonism and violence that constitute the separation of producers and the means of production (such that access to the total social product is mediated by the commodity- and money-forms of value). This separation is constituted and reproduced through the mediation of the state, which necessarily appears as the doubling up of society into civil society and a state whose legitimate power is restricted to the scope of parliamentary politics. Rather than politicizing social relations, the capitalist state reproduces 'the anonymous rule of money and the law' (Clarke 1988, 127) by depoliticizing them. It is not the institutional guarantor of social reproduction per se.[10] Instead its relation to the course of social reproduction is mediated, such that *capitalist* social reproduction is the only mode of social reproduction of which the capitalist state can be a part.

The capitalist state is an essential moment in the reproduction of a society for which value is the most fundamental mediating category.

---

[10] On this point see also Chris O'Kane's contribution to the present volume.

It is the necessary political form of appearance of a society in which labour—taking the doubled form of abstract, value-positing labour and concrete labour—is undertaken under conditions of free exchange, in which the direct producers are continually separated from the means of production and are impersonally compelled to sell their labour-power in order to acquire the universal equivalent that mediates their access to the total social product. It is the political appearance of a necessarily and intractably divided society, one that is constituted through contradictions—between wealth and value, use-value and exchange-value, labour and capital, society and state. The state in its specifically capitalist form can neither serve as a refuge from the society-pervading imperative to valorize capital, nor as the means to overcome it.

Moreover, the capitalist state, being the political form of appearance of capitalist society, cannot be analytically carved away from capitalist social relations *even though it appears as separate from society.* We cannot adequately apprehend social forms by treating them as self-subsistent and trans-historically valid. On the other hand, we cannot apprehend the contradictory totality of capitalist social relations as a whole. The whole can be glimpsed only by apprehending its constituent forms, through attending to the struggles and antagonisms that are constitutive of capitalist social reproduction. The capitalist state is not something prior to—and consequently denatured by or—capital. We should avoid fetishizing the bourgeois state as an embodiment of a timeless category that is simply instantiated in capitalism. The capitalist state is specific to capitalist social relations, and may not be identified with other political forms of appearance of social relations. An adequate critical understanding of the state requires apprehending it as historically specific and rejecting a fetishized conception of the state as a distinct social sphere that was or is unperturbed by the impersonal domination of capital.

The capitalist state is not the object, limit, or horizon of emancipatory struggle. Its determination as being apparently separate from society as such is not evidence for the claim that the state possesses a distinctive social logic; nor does it provide us with reason to think of the state as an ontologically distinctive social sphere with laws of motion unlike those of capitalist society as a whole. The capitalist state cannot abolish the capitalist mode of production, not because it has been denatured or deformed *by* capital, but simply because it is specific *to* and characteristic *of* capitalist society (Smith 2017, 190). The abolition of capitalism does not consist in the affirmation of fetishized conceptions of law or the state. Instead, the abolition of capitalism is the creation of an alternative society—one in which collective decision-making, production validated through planning rather than exchange, and the freedom of each premised on the freedom of all will obtain in social forms wholly unlike those that presently constitute our misery.

Acknowledgements I am grateful to Matt Dimick, Nate Holdren, Rafael Khachaturian, Eva Nanopoulos, Paul Mattick, Chris O'Kane, and Dom Taylor for their feedback, suggestions, and critiques.

REFERENCES

Adorno, Theodor W. 2006. *History and Freedom: Lectures 1964–1965*. Edited by Rolf Tiedemann. Cambridge: Polity.

Alami, Ilias, Milan Babic, Adam D. Dixon, and Imogen T. Liu. 2022. 'Special Issue Introduction: What Is the New State Capitalism?' *Contemporary Politics* 28 (3): 245–63. https://doi.org/10.1080/13569775.2021.2022336.

Backhaus, Hans-Georg. 1997. *Dialektik der Wertform: Untersuchungen zur Marxschen Ökonomiekritik*. Freiburg: Ça Ira.

Banaji, Jairus. 2010. *Theory as History: Essays on Modes of Production and Exploitation*. Leiden: Brill.

Bellofiore, Riccardo. 2014. 'Lost in Translation: Once Again on the Marx–Hegel Connection.' In *Marx's* Capital *and Hegel's* Logic: *A Reexamination*, edited by Fred Moseley and Tony Smith, 164–88. Leiden: Brill. https://doi.org/10.1163/9789004270022_009.

Bonefeld, Werner. 1995. 'Money, Equality and Exploitation: An Interpretation of Marx's Treatment of Money.' In *Global Capital, National State and the Politics of Money*, edited by Werner Bonefeld and John Holloway, 178–209. London: Palgrave Macmillan. https://doi.org/10.1007/978-1-349-14240-8_8.

———. 2014. *Critical Theory and the Critique of Political Economy: On Subversion and Negative Reason*. New York: Bloomsbury Academic.

———. 2020. 'On Capital as Real Abstraction.' In *Marx and Contemporary Critical Theory: The Philosophy of Real Abstraction*, edited by Antonio Oliva, Ángel Oliva, and Iván Novara, 153–70. London: Palgrave Macmillan. https://doi.org/10.1007/978-3-030-39954-2_9.

Bonefeld, Werner, Richard Gunn, and Kosmas Psychopedis, eds. 1991. *Open Marxism 1: Dialectics and History*. London: Pluto Press.

Clarke, Simon. 1988. *Keynesianism, Monetarism and the Crisis of the State*. Cheltenham: Edward Elgar.

————. 1991a. *Marx, Marginalism and Modern Sociology: From Adam Smith to Max Weber*. Houndmills: Macmillan.

————. 1991b. 'State, Class Struggle, and the Reproduction of Capital.' In *The State Debate*, edited by Simon Clarke, 183–203. Houndmills: Macmillan. https://doi.org/10.1007/978-1-349-21464-8_6.

————. 1992. 'The Global Accumulation of Capital and the Periodisation of the Capitalist State Form.' In *Open Marxism 1: Dialectics and History*, edited by Werner Bonefeld, Richard Gunn, and Kosmas Psychopedis, 133–50. London: Pluto Press.

Dimick, Matthew. 2021. 'Pashukanis' Commodity-Form Theory of Law.' In *Research Handbook on Law and Marxism*, edited by Paul O'Connell and Umut Özsu, 115–38. Cheltenham: Edward Elgar. https://doi.org/10.4337/9781788119863.00013.

Elson, Diane, ed. 1979. *Value: The Representation of Labour in Capitalism*. London: CSE Books.

Gerstenberger, Heide. 2022. *Market and Violence: The Functioning of Capitalism in History*. Leiden: Brill. https://doi.org/10.1163/9789004522633.

Heinrich, Michael. 2012. *An Introduction to the Three Volumes of Karl Marx's Capital*. Translated by Alexander Locascio. New York: Monthly Review Press.

————. 2013. 'The "Fragment on Machines": A Marxian Misconception in the *Grundrisse* and Its Overcoming in *Capital*.' In *In Marx's Laboratory: Critical Interpretations of the Grundrisse*, edited by Riccardo Bellofiore, Guido Starosta, and Peter D. Thomas, 195–212. Leiden: Brill. https://doi.org/10.1163/9789004252592_010.

Holloway, John, and Sol Picciotto, eds. 1978. *State and Capital: A Marxist Debate*. London: Edward Arnold.

Lukács, Georg. 1972. *History and Class Consciousness: Studies in Marxist Dialectics*. Translated by Rodney Livingstone. Cambridge, MA: MIT Press.

Marx, Karl. 1973. *Grundrisse: Foundations of the Critique of Political Economy*. Translated by Martin Nicolaus. London: Penguin Books.

————. 1990. *Capital: A Critique of Political Economy*. Translated by Ben Fowkes. Vol. I. London: Penguin Books.

————. 1992. *Capital: A Critique of Political Economy*. Translated by David Fernbach. Vol. II. London: Penguin Books.

Mattick, Paul. 2018. *Theory as Critique: Essays on Capital*. Leiden: Brill.

Milios, John. 2018. *The Origins of Capitalism as a Social System: The Prevalence of an Aleatory Encounter*. Oxford: Routledge.

Murray, Patrick. 1988. *Marx's Theory of Scientific Knowledge*. Atlantic Highlands, NJ: Humanities Press.

————. 2016. *The Mismeasure of Wealth: Essays on Marx and Social Form*. Leiden: Brill.

Neupert-Doppler, Alexander. 2018. 'Society and Political Form.' In *The SAGE Handbook of Frankfurt School Critical Theory*, edited by Beverly Best, Werner Bonefeld, and Chris O'Kane, 3:816–33. London: Sage.

O'Kane, Chris, and Kirstin Munro. 2022. 'Marxian Economics and the Critique of Political Economy.' In *Adorno and Marx: Negative Dialectics and the Critique of Political Economy*, edited by Werner Bonefeld and Chris O'Kane, 77–95. London: Bloomsbury Academic.

Postone, Moishe. 1993. *Time, Labor, and Social Domination: A Reinterpretation of Marx's Critical Theory*. Cambridge: Cambridge University Press.

Reichelt, Helmut. 2005. 'Social Reality as Appearance: Some Notes on Marx's Conception of Reality.' In *Human Dignity: Social Autonomy and the Critique of Capitalism*, edited by Werner Bonefeld and Kosmas Psychopedis, 31–67. Aldershot: Ashgate Publishing.

Reuten, Geert. 2018. *The Unity of the Capitalist Economy and State: A Systematic-Dialectical Exposition of the Capitalist System*. Leiden: Brill.

Roberts, William Clare. 2020. 'What Was Primitive Accumulation? Reconstructing the Origin of a Critical Concept.' *European Journal of Political Theory* 19 (4): 532–52. https://doi.org/https://doi.org/10.1177/147488 5117735961.

Schmidt, Alfred. 1981. *History and Structure: An Essay on Hegelian-Marxist and Structuralist Theories of History*. Translated by Jeffrey Herf. Cambridge, MA: MIT Press.

———. 2014. *The Concept of Nature in Marx*. Translated by Ben Fowkes. London: Verso.

Singh, Nikhil Pal. 2016. 'On Race, Violence, and So-Called Primitive Accumulation.' *Social Text* 34 (3): 27–50. https://doi.org/https://doi.org/10.1215/01642472-3607564.

Smith, Tony. 1990. *The Logic of Marx's* Capital*: Replies to Hegelian Criticisms*. Albany, NY: State University of New York Press.

———. 2014. 'Hegel, Marx and the Comprehension of Capitalism.' In *Marx's Capital and Hegel's Logic: A Reexamination*, edited by Fred Moseley and Tony Smith, 15–40. Leiden: Brill. https://doi.org/10.1163/978900427002 2_003.

———. 2017. *Beyond Liberal Egalitarianism: Marx and Normative Social Theory in the Twenty-First Century*. Leiden: Brill.

Steinberg, Marc W. 2010. 'Marx, Formal Subsumption and the Law.' *Theory and Society* 39 (2): 173–202. https://doi.org/10.1007/s11186-009-9101-9.

Sumida, Soichiro. 2018. 'Die Zusammenfassung der bürgerlichen Gesellschaft in der Staatsform: Zu Marx' Theorie des Staats.' *Marx-Engels Jahrbuch* 2017 (1): 41–60. https://doi.org/https://doi.org/10.1515/mejb-2018-20170103.

Williams, Michael, ed. 1988. *Value, Social Form and the State*. Houndmills: Macmillan.

Wood, Ellen Meiksins. 1995. *Democracy Against Capitalism: Renewing Historical Materialism*. Cambridge: Cambridge University Press.

INDEX